REACHING ALL WRITERS

REACHING ALL WRITERS

A Pedagogical Guide for Evolving College Writing Classrooms

JOANNE BAIRD GIORDANO
HOLLY HASSEL
JENNIFER HEINERT
CASSANDRA PHILLIPS

UTAH STATE UNIVERSITY PRESS
Logan

© 2023 by University Press of Colorado

Published by Utah State University Press
An imprint of University Press of Colorado
1580 North Logan Street, Suite 660
PMB 39883
Denver, Colorado 80203-1942

All rights reserved

 The University Press of Colorado is a proud member of the Association of University Presses.

The University Press of Colorado is a cooperative publishing enterprise supported, in part, by Adams State University, Colorado State University, Fort Lewis College, Metropolitan State University of Denver, University of Alaska Fairbanks, University of Colorado, University of Denver, University of Northern Colorado, University of Wyoming, Utah State University, and Western Colorado University.

∞ This paper meets the requirements of the ANSI/NISO Z39.48-1992 (Permanence of Paper).

ISBN: 978-1-64642-535-8 (hardcover)
ISBN: 978-1-64642-536-5 (paperback)
ISBN: 978-1-64642-537-2 (ebook)
https://doi.org/10.7330/9781646425372

Library of Congress Cataloging-in-Publication Data

Names: Giordano, Joanne Baird, author. | Hassel, Holly, author. | Heinert, Jennifer Lee Jordan, 1977– author. | Phillips, Cassandra, 1971– author.
Title: Reaching all writers : a pedagogical guide for evolving college writing classrooms / Joanne Baird Giordano, Holly Hassel, Jennifer Heinert, Cassandra Phillips.
Description: Logan : Utah State University Press, [2024] | Includes bibliographical references and index.
Identifiers: LCCN 2024002463 (print) | LCCN 2024002464 (ebook) | ISBN 9781646425358 (hardcover) | ISBN 9781646425365 (paperback) | ISBN 9781646425372 (ebook)
Subjects: LCSH: Report writing—Handbooks, manuals, etc. | Report writing—Study and teaching (Higher) | Academic writing—Handbooks, manuals, etc. | Academic writing—Study and teaching (Higher) | English language—Rhetoric—Study and teaching (Higher) | Writing centers.
Classification: LCC PE1404 .G576 2024 (print) | LCC PE1404 (ebook) | DDC 808/.042078—dc23/eng/20220223
LC record available at https://lccn.loc.gov/2024002463
LC ebook record available at https://lccn.loc.gov/2024002464

Cover art: Shutterstock/Arthimedes

CONTENTS

List of Illustrations   vii

Preface   ix

Acknowledgments   xv

PART 1: FOUNDATIONS FOR TEACHING COLLEGE WRITING

1. Introduction: Pedagogical Adaptability   5
2. Practices for Teaching Effective and Equitable Writing Courses   24
3. Thinking Like a Writer: Translating Threshold Concepts in Writing Studies to the Classroom   63

PART 2: THRESHOLD CONCEPTS FOR FIRST-YEAR WRITING

4. Writing Can Be Taught and Learned   83
5. Writers Write for Different Purposes and Audiences, and Often in Genres with Predictable Conventions   108
6. Writing Processes Are Individualized, Require Readers, and Require Revision   142
7. Reading and Writing Are Interconnected Activities   167
8. Writers Make Choices about Language within Cultural and Social Situations   191
9. Conclusion: Continuing to Develop as a College Writing Teacher   221

References   229
Index   247
About the Authors   257

ILLUSTRATIONS

TABLES

2.1. Examples of different types of student learning goals or outcomes   47
2.2. Example of a writing assignment design process   50
2.3. Example of scaffolding and sequencing for a project   55
2.4. Example of building support around learning goals   56
3.1. Threshold concepts for first-year writing courses   77
4.1. Reflect on experiences and assumptions about learning and writing   88
4.2. Reflect on components of your writing course   91
4.3. Student-centered concepts for learning about writing   93
4.4. Developing learning about writing by design   95
4.5. Teaching strategies that support writing development   97
4.6. Strategies for responding to student writing   100
5.1. Key terms for understanding rhetorical choices   115
5.2. Purposes for reading and writing   117
5.3. Learning activities for helping students identify the rhetorical features of a text   129
5.4. Learning activities for teaching rhetorical awareness   130
5.5. Learning activities for reflecting on rhetorical choices   131
6.1. Examples of process activities for a writing project   150
6.2. Examples of quick writing to prepare for workshops (about five minutes)   152
6.3. Examples of short small group workshop activities (about fifteen to twenty minutes)   153
6.4. Examples of longer workshop activities (more than twenty minutes)   153
6.5. Informal feedback strategies for in-person teaching   154
6.6. Informal feedback strategies for online teaching   155
6.7. Examples of reflective writing about process work   159
6.8. Examples of informal activities to assess process work   160
6.9. Examples of process-focused feedback strategies for a draft   162
7.1. Questions for analyzing the features of texts used as sources   175
7.2. Adapting to different reading purposes   177

7.3. Reflective assignments for supporting reading and writing connections   180
7.4. Designing a writing project based on assigned course texts   181
7.5. Designing a writing project that analyzes rhetorical features of a text   182
7.6. Designing a research-based literacy project   183
7.7. Designing an end-of-course reflective assignment   184
7.8. Example of a class session that integrates reading and writing   186
7.9. Example of an online course module that integrates reading and writing   186
8.1. Strategies for designing courses about linguistic diversity   210
8.2. Designing writing courses based on students' goals   212

FIGURES

3.1. Anne Beaufort's conceptual model from *College Writing and Beyond*   72
6.1. Sandy's reflective letter, part 1   163
6.2. Sandy's reflective letter, part 2   163
6.3. Sandy's "paper and pen" revisions   164
8.1. "This Ain't Another Statement! This Is a DEMAND for Black Linguistic Justice"   219

PREFACE

In 2007, we were teaching on campuses of the University of Wisconsin Colleges, a statewide two-year open-access institution within the University of Wisconsin System. Our writing program modeled its assignments, teaching, and assessments on practices used at institutions with selective admissions standards, including the research universities where most department members received their graduate training. Holly and Joanne began to notice gaps between our first-semester writing course (English 101) and our second-semester course (English 102), which fulfilled general education degree requirements across the state. Students had difficulty transitioning from a writing course that had minimal to no reading (depending on the instructor) to a research-based transfer course. Similarly, in developmental (basic) writing, students completed assignments and activities that were disconnected from the reading and writing strategies they needed for first-year writing. Holly and Joanne began a series of research projects to investigate students' transitions to college reading and writing on our campus. We began with a study of English 101 to 102 transfer (Hassel and Giordano 2009), which helped us understand that our students' transitions to college writing can be quite different from what we expect as instructors.

We then expanded our exploration of two-year college students' transitions to postsecondary literacy with subsequent projects that helped us explore placement challenges (Hassel and Giordano 2011), the experiences of multilingual Hmong writers (Hassel and Giordano 2015), and varied experiences of writers across multiple points of placement and access to higher education (Hassel and Giordano 2015). We also studied the writing and experiences of students who were inadmissible at institutions with literacy standards based on their standardized test scores, tracing their academic success outcomes (Giordano and Hassel 2016) and connections between critical reading and source-based writing (Giordano and Hassel 2021). Our goal was to collect data about students' experiences as writers and readers to inform how we designed and taught college writing and to align courses with the needs of students at an open-admissions institution. We began to critically reflect on our own experiences as college instructors and draw from our own research to make adjustments to teaching to reflect what we were learning about students' literacy development in an open-admissions, two-year college teaching context.

Around the same time, Cassie was co-coordinating our statewide department's assessment activities, work that Jen later participated in. Assessment data and institutional research revealed that our students were having significant challenges completing English 102 (the state system transfer course) successfully. A follow-up assessment research project revealed that instructors weren't providing students with consistent reading and writing experiences in English 101 courses across the state. Some students read fiction, some watched movies, some did research projects, and some revised multiple academic essays. Because individual course sections were taught in widely diverse ways, students were differently prepared for English 102 after taking 101. Results from this study, along with the program-level data, allowed us to begin the process of creating department learning outcomes and consistent writing course guides for each level of the writing program.

We came together to redesign a writing program aimed at helping students who start college in non-degree credit developmental or English as a second language (ESL) courses to successfully transition to degree-credit writing and move on to complete their writing requirement for an associate degree (Phillips and Giordano 2016). We also worked through our department's shared governance processes to create a composition committee, other literacy committees, a multiple measures placement process (Hassel and Giordano 2011; Toth, Nastal, Hassel, and Giordano 2019), a redesigned online writing program (Giordano and Phillips 2021), a redesigned developmental education program (Giordano 2020), state-mandated competency-based writing courses (Seas, Heinert, Phillips, and Hassel 2016), an instructor resource and training website, and intensive faculty development activities (Hassel, Giordano, Heinert, and Phillips 2017). We also developed an evidence-based proposal for and subsequently received dedicated program coordinator positions to replace the uncompensated labor happening at the committee level that had previously supported program development work. We also designed and implemented a research, assessment, and faculty development project that examined the experiences of students and instructors across every level of our statewide writing program (Giordano, Hassel, Heinert, and Phillips 2017; Hassel and Phillips 2022; Phillips et al. 2019).

We used a recursive program design process in which our research and assessment activities provided evidence about how and what to change about our program. In turn, our program development work, faculty activities, and our own teaching helped us identify challenges and issues to explore through additional research and assessment. We also began to reach out beyond our own institution to become more fully engaged in the work of advocating for the literacy needs of community college students and the teaching needs of the majority of instructors who work at two-year colleges, open-access institutions, and less selective universities (Giordano and Hassel 2019; Hassel and Giordano 2013; Hassel and Phillips 2022; Kalish et al. 2019). We took a particular interest in the working conditions of full-time contingent and part-time adjunct instructors because they teach most college writing and literacy courses, and their expertise is often ignored (Giordano, Hassel, Klausman, and Sullivan 2021; Hassel and Giordano 2017). We worked toward including them in our program activities, research, conference presentations, and shared governance activities.

Both our writing program and our developmental co-requisite program received recognition awards from the Two-Year College English Association (TYCA) and the Conference on College Composition and Communication (CCCC), and we were able to secure grants for research. The awards and grants helped validate our work within an institution that didn't necessarily value literacy educators run by administrators who did not necessarily welcome our advocacy for change. Our two-year college English department was able to integrate research and assessment with program development, in part because we had access to the robust resources of a state university system, which is not a reality for many community college faculty members. We acknowledge those unique circumstances and the accompanying privilege of course releases, modest summer stipends, and coordinator positions that gave us time to do the work.

After a decade of intensive work and measurable progress for ourselves and our students, the University of Wisconsin System dismantled the University of Wisconsin Colleges and joined our campuses to regional four-year universities (Sullivan 2021). Our program disappeared. Parts of it remained scattered throughout the state in smaller writing programs while some of our former colleagues were required to use new curricula and programs designed by faculty at four-year universities. The elimination of our program forced us to reconsider our professional identities (Hassel and Phillips 2022; Phillips and Giordano 2020) and begin our literacy work again in drastically changed circumstances. Cassie and Jen stayed in Wisconsin and continue to build on the work we did through (re)designing a writing program, institutional assessment, faculty development, and a bridge program at the University of Milwaukee. Joanne left for a position at Salt Lake Community College where she works on placement, integrated reading and writing, and faculty development in a new context. Holly has since taught at North Dakota State University and Michigan Technological University where she prepares graduate students to teach college writing.

Our own experience has taught us that nothing is permanent about any of the work we do as college writing and literacy educators. Our circumstances constantly change, our thinking about teaching and learning evolves every year, and our hard-earned professional work can disappear in an instant. We found ourselves starting over as mid-career professionals less than two years before most members of our profession had to rethink our assumptions about teaching and learning as we adapted to a global pandemic (Griffiths et al. 2021; Tinoco, Suh, Giordano, and Hassel 2022), an increased awareness of social and racial injustices, and a shrinking population of students entering higher education.

In this book, we share learning from our research on student learning and our own teaching experiences. Our coauthor team includes members with first-generation, working-class, low-income, and rural backgrounds. Some of us have experienced contingency and employment instability, but all of us now have tenured positions. We have adequate access to financial resources that support us in doing our professional work. However, our thinking about students and teaching comes in part from the experience of previously having had insufficient resources, low professional status, inadequate knowledge about how higher education works, and unsustainable working conditions at various points in our lives. We acknowledge that our own identities as cisgender, middle-age, white women limit our perspectives on some issues related to inclusive teaching and our profession. In our teaching chapters, we include experiences of students and instructors whose identities and relationships with higher education are different from our own.

This is the book we wish we had had when we started teaching years ago. It's also a book that emerged from radical changes in our own working lives and in the profession of teaching college writing. Our overall message is that college writing instructors and other postsecondary literacy educators need to develop pedagogical skills, strategies, and ways of thinking that will allow them to adapt to new teaching contexts and constantly evolving professional realities. We believe the work of supporting the literacy development of all college students—especially those who have experienced inequities in their prior learning environments—is at the heart of our profession. The teaching practices that support students who struggle to complete writing courses and stay in college are also practices that support every other student in our classes. We believe the work of developing as equitable and inclusive writing instructors happens slowly over time and also depends on access to professional resources, equitable working conditions, and supportive colleagues. Mostly, we believe the future of our profession depends on our collective abilities to develop responsive teaching practices that make it possible for college students to achieve their educational goals and live their best literate lives.

ACKNOWLEDGMENTS

The writing of this book has taken several years. However, that writing would not have been possible without the decades of time we have collectively spent as coauthors together: doing research and collecting data; serving on committees; teaching reading, writing, and learning skills courses; writing grants; presenting at conferences; publishing findings; and working with colleagues on program development.

The experience, research, and reflection that have led to *Reaching All Writers* have taken the measure of our careers to accumulate. We are grateful to the students we worked with at the University of Wisconsin Colleges campuses across many semesters in Waukesha, Wausau, West Bend, Janesville, and through our online program. We spent many hours in classrooms, offices, and writing centers learning about their educational goals and past academic experiences, conversations that informed the questions we asked throughout our research projects. We are especially grateful for the hundreds of students who participated in our studies, sharing both their writing and their college learning experiences.

This book would not have been possible without the generative conversations and collaborative work we engaged in with colleagues on our campuses. We undertook assessment projects with English department colleagues across the state. We served on retention committees and designed online courses. We wrote reports and gave presentations to advisers, faculty across the disciplines, and administrators. We created new positions to do this work: developmental reading and writing coordinator, virtual teaching and learning center coordinator, writing program administrator. Through building these roles, we learned much about how the teaching of college writing is done well and how to make improvements. Throughout this process, we received feedback, support, and encouragement from advisers, campus administrators, writing center directors, academic staff, librarians, and instructors in other disciplines across Wisconsin. We are especially grateful for the contingent faculty who worked in our program, taught the courses we developed, and helped us learn from their teaching experiences.

This work at a variety of stages has likewise been shared in disciplinary venues over the years. We want to acknowledge how vital those conversations were with colleagues in conferences, standing groups, and caucuses for the Conference on College Composition and Communication, the Two-Year College English Association (TYCA) (nationally and regionally), the College Reading and Learning Association, the Council of Writing Program Administrators, and the National Organization for Student Success. We also received invaluable feedback in other professional groups in which we have served—such as the TYCA Workload Issues Committee, the TYCA Research Committee, and other task forces—which enriched our thinking about the needs of diverse students and instructors across the country.

We also found inspiration in relationships with colleagues at our new or newly configured institutions: new writing programs designed or adapted to, new courses taught, new colleges configured, and administrative responsibilities created and taken on. We have each found ourselves in new and evolving writing classrooms, experiences that became part of the fabric of this book.

The University of Wisconsin (UW) System and our respective campuses supported the work that makes up the bones of this book. In the early 2010s, each of us received grants to support systematic investigation into teaching and learning. For many years, the UW System offered "undergraduate teaching and learning grants"—competitive funding that without which, none of the work that has created the foundation of this project would have been able to be carried out, given the very limited resources for research and scholarship at the open-access two-year campuses of the UW Colleges (the institution that was ultimately dissolved in 2018).

We are likewise grateful for the support, feedback, and advice we received throughout the process of pursuing publication of this book. *Reaching all Writers* is a better project for the investment and feedback from our editor, Rachael Levay, at Utah State University Press.

REACHING ALL WRITERS

PART 1

Foundations for Teaching College Writing

1
INTRODUCTION
Pedagogical Adaptability

This introductory chapter defines pedagogical adaptability and outlines reasons why first-year writing instructors and other literacy educators need to develop flexible strategies for adapting their teaching to new and evolving contexts, student communities, educational access, and initiatives aimed at transforming higher education. We explain how pedagogical adaptability helps college literacy educators adapt to different teaching contexts and the learning needs of diverse student populations. We also describe the goals of the book and provide a brief overview of each section.

The work of most postsecondary literacy educators centers on adapting to inevitable and ongoing change (Cole and Hassel 2021). Effective teaching requires instructors to respond to the local learning needs of students in writing programs and in other college literacy courses, including in reading, co-requisite, integrated reading, English as a second language (ESL) and second-language writing, dual credit, and developmental education programs. Instructors also need to develop the flexibility to work within the possibilities and constraints of their programs, institutions, and local communities. Even when writing programs and their courses are able to remain relatively stable, rapidly changing literacies and technologies used for learning require programs and instructors to engage in ongoing change to avoid creating educational opportunity gaps for their students. Engaging in change is difficult and context-specific: there is no single curriculum, reading list, or online resource that prepares instructors for the constant need to adapt their instructional strategies to meet the locally situated learning needs of their students and acknowledge the widely diverse literate lives of first-year college readers and writers. In other words, what and how we teach first-year writing can and should depend on who and where we teach.

At the same time, instructors arrive in the first-year college writing classroom from many disparate training experiences and academic backgrounds in writing studies, rhetoric, literature, creative writing, linguistics and TESOL, education, and/or communications. As coauthors, we share many of these disciplinary backgrounds and experiences. Like others who teach writing, most of us experienced stark differences between the graduate institutions at which we were trained and the places where we ended up teaching. As a result, we weren't initially sure how to negotiate those differences when we came to be department colleagues at an open-access, two-year institution with multiple campuses throughout Wisconsin, where we taught for many years. We had to shift and adapt our thinking for new student populations, policies, practices, resources, professional support, curricula, placement mechanisms, regional norms, state oversight mandates, and local problems. As new instructors we had to adapt to a new department culture and become more independent in developing resources for our own professional and pedagogical development.

As we began to work together, we agreed that to help students transition to college reading and writing, we needed to have clear pathways for them to get from their individual literacy starting points to the end of the first-year writing curriculum and beyond. We realized that we needed to make fundamental changes to our teaching practices to support literacy development for students in an open-access teaching context, but we also needed to build our course redesign work on disciplinary practices and our own research about two-year college student learning. We conducted systematic and intensive research studies and assessment projects to trace diverse students' experiences and literacy development from the point of placement across multiple semesters to their writing program completion (Giordano and Hassel 2016; Hassel and Giordano 2009, 2011, 2015). It took us more than a decade to create, interrogate, assess, and revise our program and curriculum (Giordano and Phillips 2021; Hassel, Giordano, Heinert, and Phillips 2017; Phillips and Giordano 2016). Throughout the process of designing a program and improving our own teaching, we learned how to identify and prioritize the literacy needs of students. The process of learning how to adapt our teaching practices to local learning contexts and evolving circumstances has been invaluable as we have moved on to other writing programs.

Part of the theoretical foundation for our work is the concept of transfer—both material and epistemic.[1] We learned to consider how our students could transfer from our class to the next class (in part,

---

1. Like many teacher-scholars, we are interested in the work of learning transfer and transfer theory (Adler-Kassner, Majewski, and Koshnick 2012; Blaauw-Hara 2014; Hassel and Giordano 2009; Moore and Anson 2017; Tinberg 2015b).

because most open-access institutions have at least two and often three or more courses in a writing sequence). Many of our students had limited experience with academic literacy and often had gaps in their educational experiences; therefore, we had to carefully consider how students' experiences with reading and writing in our courses supported their literacy development in other general education courses and helped create pathways toward an associate degree. We also started to think about how our writing courses prepared our students to transfer to other institutions. It was difficult *not* to think about how our courses and our teaching would impact our students once they left our teaching context because of our institution's transfer mission, but we also had to think about the coursework on our own campuses that they would need to complete before becoming eligible for admission to a university.

We have learned that the concept of transfer is also essential for understanding the work literacy educators do. We've transferred and adapted our teaching strategies to new institutions, different writing programs, and unfamiliar types of literacy courses. Over time, we also realized that writing instructors need intensive support in transferring teaching strategies, professional skills, and disciplinary knowledge to working with students in an open-access institution (Giordano, Hassel, Heinert, and Phillips 2017; Hassel and Giordano 2013). Many of the pedagogical approaches and assumptions about course content instructors bring with them from graduate school at selective research institutions simply do not work for many students, especially at community colleges. Instructors who transition to new teaching contexts need time, ongoing learning, and mentoring to figure out which teaching practices to transfer from their previous experiences, which strategies to draw from but change, and which pedagogical approaches and assumptions about students to leave behind. For example, when we each started teaching at two-year campuses, we learned very quickly that we had to develop new instructional strategies because a majority of our students experienced structural inequities, financial struggles, and complicated educational trajectories in comparison to the students we had previously taught at research universities. We had to adapt our teaching to support students with diverse prior learning and linguistic experiences through their completion of general education writing requirements as well as determine how to align first-year writing and other courses with students' individual goals and literacy needs. We also recognized how gaps between developmental education programs and college writing programs can intensify the challenges of helping students successfully transition to college-level coursework.

We have continued to learn, grow, and change as college literacy educators while adapting to new student communities, colleagues, and institutional realities. Just as we were settling into our new writing programs after our institution was restructured, the Covid-19 pandemic reminded us that our own teaching practices must continue to evolve over the course of our careers to reflect changing learning environments, equity gaps for students, and the unstable nature of higher education. Throughout these constant changes, we relied heavily on evolving disciplinary knowledge and research, but we had to spend a significant amount of time finding sources and doing our own research to synthesize and distill information about teaching and students' literacy development that is relevant to the work of open-access literacy education.

Our own experiences with critically reflecting on and changing our own teaching practices to support students with diverse needs, along with working in constantly changing circumstances, inspired us to write this book. We focus on adapting teaching to meet the literacy needs of all learners so we can share what we learned in a comprehensive way with both new and experienced college writing instructors. Whether it is adjusting to teaching at a new institution, responding to institutional or program change, or managing changing student demographics, an essential part of the work of college writing teachers is adapting teaching practices to meet challenges in an equitable and inclusive way while supporting students' disciplinary learning.

PEDAGOGICAL ADAPTABILITY

The ability to adapt teaching strategies to local student communities and working environments is the most essential part of developing and teaching writing courses that support all learners. Differing institutions, courses, individual class sections, and groups of students bring both constraints and possibilities for how and what a writing teacher teaches. Through our years of working together and with other educators at two-year colleges (as well as instructors teaching developmental English and first-year writing at open-access and less selective comprehensive universities), we learned how important it is to develop *pedagogical adaptability*. Disciplinary conversations about adaptability often focus primarily on students and what they need to know about audience, purpose, and context (see Adler-Kassner and Wardle 2015; Heilker and Vandenberg 2015; Malenczyk, Miller-Cochran, Wardle, and Yancey 2018; Moore 2012; Tinberg 2015a). This same attention is rarely given to instructors and teaching. The field of writing studies does offer many professional disciplinary statements (for example, Conference on College Composition and Communication [CCCC] and National Council of Teachers of English [NCTE] position statements like "Writing Assessment Principles" and "Principles for the Postsecondary Teaching of Writing") that approach teaching writing as static outcomes and guidelines for incorporating principles into classroom teaching. However, first-year writing instructors are rarely given guidance into how pedagogical situations are shaped by their own teaching environments, the missions of their institutions, and the student communities their campuses serve.

To be pedagogically adaptable means to develop and apply the following types of flexible approaches to teaching as a disciplinary expert:

- *Respond to the individual needs of students* in a particular class based on the literacy skills and strategies they bring to college (and not on predetermined ideas about what students should be able to know and do)
- *Change approaches to teaching* based on a student population, mission of an institution and its role in a community, level of a course, and purpose of a course within a sequence of other writing courses
- *Develop an ethical, flexible, and responsive understanding of how to design courses,* use instructional approaches, and apply assessment methods to a particular teaching context
- *Employ a realistic approach to assessing student learning* that responds to students' prior experiences with literacy, their cultural and social backgrounds, and their linguistic strengths
- *Identify and evaluate relevant disciplinary scholarship and resources*; make choices about the appropriateness of applying existing work and new developments in the field based on a student population and teaching context.

The purpose of naming these characteristics of pedagogical adaptability is to help instructors begin to think about ways to bridge the gaps that often exist between their teaching realities compared to their prior learning, experiences in previous but different teaching contexts, and knowledge of disciplinary scholarship. Pedagogical adaptability is fundamental to creating an equitable and inclusive learning environment.

With this book, we hope to distill core knowledge from writing studies and related fields with accompanying teaching strategies in a way that will give new instructors and experienced instructors who are searching for ways to increase equity in their practice the tools for adapting their instructional practices to their own local working environments. Our goal is to help instructors be comfortable with the continuous process of adapting teaching over time as their professional circumstances, working conditions, student populations, institutions, technologies, cultural and social environments, funding, and local community needs change.

Our experiences and research are shaped by the material conditions in two-year colleges and open-access institutions that are often defined by uncertainties, change, and difference, although the strategies we offer in this book are applicable across institutional types. The norms of unpredictability within and across courses that most higher education faculty have faced during the global pandemic are a constant working condition for two-year college writing and developmental English instructors. In other words, our own relatively uncertain working conditions have required us to develop pedagogical adaptability. In contrast, much of the scholarship that informs college writing pedagogy focuses on theory, teaching experiences, and studies based on the work of faculty who teach at institutions where most students have social privilege and are well prepared for college (Hassel and Phillips 2022). While we value and rely heavily on the disciplinary knowledge that has come from this scholarship, the research in this book comes from faculty who regularly teach first-year writing, working with studying the learning of the diverse range of students who enroll at community colleges.

ADAPTING TO SUPPORT EDUCATIONAL EQUITY FOR ALL STUDENTS

Pedagogical adaptability is a central skill that teachers need for supporting equitable educational opportunities to support all students' postsecondary literacy development. In the twenty-first century, a global pandemic (US Surgeon General 2021), economic crises (Bauer, Brody, Edelberg, and O'Donnell 2020; Center on Budget and Policy Priorities 2022), public education austerity measures (Hubler 2020), and calls for social and racial justice (Black Lives Matter 2020) have amplified inequities in communities and in higher education. Addressing inequities requires college English teachers to do more than simply apply social justice theories, change a delivery mode, or express outrage on social media. Equitable higher education requires all instructors to recognize the bias and discrimination their own students experience, critically reflect on ways teaching practices and the work of the discipline can perpetuate inequities, and take action to bring about change in their own classrooms and online learning environments. Today's college students across the board face more material challenges than ever before (e.g., student debt, mental health issues, or caregiver responsibilities), which shapes their ability to learn and succeed in college.

For example, writing instructors can expect to teach students with disabilities in every course, but it's highly unlikely that they will be able to identify all of those students. A National Center for Educational Statistics 2015–2016 study showed that 19 percent of undergraduate college students had a disability, with veterans (26%) and adults over age thirty (23%) reporting disabilities at a higher rate (Institute of Education Sciences n.d.). A later report shows that only about one-third of students who experienced a disability in college notified their institution. Of those who reported a disability to the institution, only 85 percent of four-year college students and 57 percent of two-year college students received accommodations (Institute of Education Sciences 2022). These government reports illustrate the gap between support available at four-year universities compared to community colleges in addition to the reality that instructors must expect that many (and probably most) of their students with disabilities aren't receiving formal accommodations. However, students with disabilities are accessing academic support at higher rates than other students, with more four-year students receiving support compared to two-year college students (Institute of Education Sciences 2022).

A growing number of college students also have mental health challenges, which may or may not give them access to disability accommodations for their courses. Even before the Covid-19 pandemic, an increasing number of students had long-term mental illnesses. The US Surgeon General (2021) reports that anxiety and depression rates among youth globally have doubled during the pandemic, with 20–25 percent of young people experiencing anxiety and depression. Since the Covid-19 pandemic is ongoing, most people—but children and adolescents in particular—continue to face disruptions to their learning, grief or loss related to the disease, and higher levels of distress in everyday life.

Among college students, the rates of mental health issues had been on an upward trajectory even pre-pandemic. For example, the nationwide Healthy Minds Study showed that between 2007 to 2017, the percentage of postsecondary students with a lifetime mental health diagnosis increased from 22 percent to 36 percent (Lipson, Lattie, and Eisenberg 2018). In the 2021 National College Health Assessment survey, almost three-fourths of college students reported moderate to severe "psychological distress," with about 16 percent of cisgender men, 24 percent of cisgender women, and about 46 percent of trans and gender nonconforming students reporting severe psychological distress (American College Health Association 2021, 12). The survey also indicated that most cisgender students (67% of men and 65% of women) experience a sense of belonging in response to the question "I feel that I belong at my college/university"; however, only half of trans/gender nonconforming students reported a similar sense of belonging in college (3). College courses that support equity for all students need to be designed around the reality that many students have disabilities, a majority have mental health challenges, and some can experience additional distress and exclusion based on their gender, social, or racial identities.

Today's students also face an ever accelerating and intensifying demand for more advanced and complex literacy skills in a digital world (Keller 2013; National Council of Teachers of English 2019). A carefully designed college writing course can provide students with the knowledge, skills, and dispositions they need for developing twenty-first-century literacies and achieving their educational goals. However, some students have unequal access to the technology and financial resources required for developing and practicing digital literacy skills. For example, some of our students from rural communities close to our Wisconsin campuses didn't (and still don't) have high-speed internet or reliable cell phone service in their home communities. Some also didn't have access to computers or technology education in school while their peers from urban high schools received take-home iPads or electronic devices from their schools, which they used throughout their secondary education. Inequities in resources can contribute to lower college degree attainment rates in rural communities (Fain 2019). However, a majority of the more than 20 million US residents without broadband internet access in the United States live in urban areas (Federal Communications Commission 2019; Horrigan 2019). Effective writing instruction in the twenty-first century requires instructors to prepare students for a digital world, but educational equity also means recognizing and accounting for the learning needs of students who have had limited access to technology in their K–12 education and who may continue to experience barriers to using technology for learning as college students.

The promise of social justice and transformation that could potentially take place in college writing courses isn't realized unless instructors at the individual level recognize the educational inequities that students experience, take action, and adapt their teaching to support and sustain equity in their own courses. This book describes effective teaching practices that help new college writing teachers as well as instructors who want to change their teaching practices support equitable and inclusive learning opportunities for students. However, we hope it is especially useful for teaching students whose backgrounds and learning experiences are different from those of more educationally privileged students. For a first-year writing course, we define *educational privilege* as having access to resources and cultural capital that supports and sustains smooth transitions to college reading, writing, and learning. Educationally privileged students have not experienced intersectional inequities in their prior learning experiences or faced barriers to going to college, staying in college, and receiving a degree. While all first-year college students experience challenges both inside and outside of school (even more since the start of the Covid-19 pandemic), some students face multiple inequities because of their past educational experiences, language backgrounds, social and cultural identities, life circumstances, access to financial resources, lack of family or social support, and physical or mental health statuses.

Equitable writing courses adapted to student needs take into account the ways college students may be disenfranchised or empowered through their race, class, abled-ness, gender identities, sexualities, first-generation status, language background, or prior educational experiences. Writing instructors can take direct action to address inequities, racism, discrimination, and privilege in their local community, institutional contexts, and courses.[2] Adapting pedagogy for equity and inclusion can sometimes require instructors to rethink their entire approaches to course design, assignments, assessment of student learning, classroom time, online activities, and policies. This type of change can be difficult, disruptive, and uncomfortable. It can be new to recent graduates who may have relied on faculty advisers, program administrators, or department leaders for guidance. It can also require adaptations to teaching that evolve slowly over many semesters and years through collaboration with colleagues.

Similarly, equitable writing programs must recognize the material realities of the majority of college writing teachers—graduate students, adjunct faculty, contingent full-time lecturers—who don't enjoy the full protections of tenure, power, or a voice within an institution. Equitable and inclusive writing programs must account for the consequences of pedagogical, curricular, or assessment practices. This includes assessing how existing practices and potential changes affect teaching and learning conditions in a way that will make it either more or less likely for students to achieve their literacy goals and for instructors to have sustainable, manageable, and equitable working conditions.

---

2. The Community College Research Center has conducted many large-scale national studies on the needs of community colleges and their students and teachers. See, for example, Barnett, Kopko, Cullinan, and Belfield 2020; Bickerstaff et al. 2021; Cullinan and Biedzio 2021; Griffin 2018; Jenkins, Lahr, and Mazzariello 2021; Ran and Lin 2019.

At most institutions, first-year writing serves as a gateway course to any degree because it is often a general education requirement that all students must complete without other options. In other words, when students cannot complete required writing courses, they cannot attain a college degree. First-year writing is thus a site and an opportunity to directly address how institutional cultures create barriers for structurally disadvantaged and historically excluded college students. The stakes are very high for students whose experiences before and during their college writing courses keep them from developing the skills, learning strategies, and rhetorical knowledge writing instructors expect from them, especially if those expectations don't reflect students' access to educational resources and prior learning experiences. This is true regardless of institutional context or type. Reaching all college writers and helping them successfully complete first-year writing depends on critical self-assessment about teaching practices and ongoing efforts to adapt teaching to meet individual and collective student needs.

ADAPTING TO OPEN-ACCESS TEACHING CONTEXTS

Pedagogical adaptability is critical for achieving social justice in writing courses and programs, especially for students who would be excluded from higher education at institutions with admissions standards. Achieving equity in writing studies as a field demands that our teaching and assessment practices account for the students who enroll in literacy courses at community colleges and open-access four-year institutions in addition to university students from communities that have historically been excluded and marginalized in higher education. Writing studies professionals from all types of institutions need to be prepared to teach students who begin college at community colleges because many of them transfer to four-year institutions where university faculty will need to support their continued literacy development. Closing educational equity gaps and achieving social justice in writing programs requires our field to critically examine assumptions about teaching and learning that are often grounded in research and instructional experiences at selective universities. The student populations we have taught and studied and the pedagogies we have developed for open-access teaching are grounded in careful assessment of how to adapt teaching strategies for a wide range of learners who experience structural and academic inequities that create barriers to completing first-year writing courses.

Although most scholarship on college writers focuses on students at more selective research institutions, nearly half of all college students

(49%) enroll in a community college at some point in their academic careers (Community College Research Center n.d.; NSC Research Center 2017). The student population at two-year colleges differs from the traditional but misconceived norm of a first-year US college student who is immediately out of high school, is traditionally aged (eighteen to twenty), and attends school full-time while living on campus and working limited hours. The college experiences of many (but not all) community college students are fundamentally different from those of students at selective institutions. The average age of a community college student is twenty-eight (American Association of Community Colleges 2022), 65 percent of them attend college part-time (American Association of Community Colleges 2022), and they have diverse backgrounds and circumstances. In addition, community colleges are the place where 53 percent of Native American students start college, as do 40 percent of Black students, 50 percent of Hispanic students (Breedlove 2021), and 36 percent of Asian students. The majority of both part-time and full-time two-year college students work (American Association of Community Colleges 2022).

Writing programs at open-admissions institutions have long been forced to confront issues of equity in ways other programs haven't. A scholarly history has documented (and contested) the role of two-year colleges and their literacy programs in social mobility and social justice (see Andelora 2005; Calhoon-Dillahunt 2018; Clark 1960; Giordano and Hassel 2019; Hassel and Giordano 2013; Lovas 2002; Tsao 2005). Community colleges serve the broadest range of students in higher education, ranging from high school valedictorians and students with graduate degrees returning for other credentials to students with limited or interrupted schooling who have nontraditional pathways toward completing high school and enrolling in college. Writing instructors at community colleges need to be prepared to adapt how and what they teach to the student communities their courses serve, which can vary from institution to institution and even within the same program.

All graduate students in writing studies and other subfields of English who plan to stay in academia need to prepare for the possibility that they will teach at a two-year college or an open-admissions university. A large percentage of jobs in the field are at open-access campuses with a teaching-intensive workload focused on first-year writing, developmental literacy courses, or both. To truly serve the majority of students well, graduate students need to be trained beyond a particular pedagogical approach or school of thought. They need to be equipped with flexible habits of mind and the ability to create responsive teaching practices that match the students they have and the courses they teach at a particular moment in time. Rhetorical adaptability develops slowly over time, and instructors continue to learn and apply strategies for adapting their teaching to support students' literacy development in new contexts long after they finish graduate school. However, graduate students can begin to build a foundation for effective, equitable, and inclusive pedagogy by developing a set of teaching skills and strategies they can adapt to new student communities and working environments at open-access institutions and less selective universities.

Teaching first-year writing to support the diverse range of students who take college writing courses requires rhetorical knowledge about audiences, purposes, and contexts for college teaching—and the ability to adapt course design, assignments, instructional activities, and assessment to different teaching situations. Even when an instructor moves from one research institution to another, the conditions for teaching writing change. For this reason, our book has a clear and specific purpose: to help instructors adapt their teaching and learning environments to the overlooked majority of college students who are not considered experienced readers and writers, have not developed the academic behaviors and strategies many instructors expect of them, are encumbered with financial and family responsibilities, and are not able to dedicate nearly all of their time to their studies and the college experience. As a consequence of the Covid-19 global pandemic, even traditionally well-prepared students admissible to more selective campuses often have gaps in learning, academic experiences, and social-emotional growth they would not have had in the past. Likewise, students without educational privilege can and do attend all kinds of college campuses.

Thinking about equitable access to literacy instruction for all students (regardless of their access to educational resources and social privileges) should be the foundation for teaching first-year writing and developing postsecondary literacy programs. Equitable and inclusive teaching for all students requires instructors to move away from personal teaching preferences, and sometimes they have to leave behind what they learned about teaching and literacy from their own experiences as students and as graduate teachers in training. Instead, equity-minded literacy educators center their courses on what students need to know and practice to develop literacy strategies as college readers and writers.

ADAPTING TO EDUCATIONAL REFORM INITIATIVES

Instructors who are new to teaching in different contexts often have to do on-the-job learning to teach unfamiliar types of courses in program structures that are tied to reform initiatives aimed at increasing student retention and college completion.[3] Even instructors who have been teaching in a writing program for many years may have to make major changes to their course design and instruction to adapt to initiatives adopted by their state systems or institutions. Many instructors at two-year colleges and other open-access campuses can anticipate that they will be required to change (if they haven't already) their teaching strategies to accommodate what has become a continual process of mandatory changes to literacy programs and placement processes.

Current national reform movements aimed at reducing the costs of college and time to degree completion have reshaped program development, curriculum, and pedagogy for writing and developmental English programs at community colleges and other open-access institutions (Hassel et al. 2015; Klausman et al. 2016). Some of these initiatives, like co-requisite support courses, come from equity-minded instructional models in our discipline (Adams, Gearhart, Miller, and Roberts 2009; Glau 2007; Grego and Thompson 1996, 2007). However, mandates are often imposed on writing programs and their instructors administratively or legislatively (Rutschow and Schneider 2011; Whinnery and Pompelia 2019). These initiatives include reforming the way students are placed into writing and developmental English courses (Klausman et al. 2016), integrating reading and writing courses (Doran 2019; Saxon, Martirosyan, and Vick 2016a), accelerating students through a writing program more quickly (Adams, Gearhart, Miller, and Roberts 2009), controlling the pathways students take through general education courses (Bailey, Jaggers, and Jenkins 2015), and sometimes eliminating developmental education courses entirely (California Acceleration Project n.d.).

Consequently, pedagogical adaptability often means changing instruction and course design in response to factors that are external to a writing program. The likelihood that an instructor will need to participate in ongoing literacy program reform initiatives increases for those employed at institutions that serve the widest range of student needs. In contrast, instructors who teach at more selective institutions that

---

3. Reform initiatives are literacy program changes that are often mandated by legislation, state system requirements, or top-down institutional decisions. For example, legislation in some states (including California, Florida, and Texas) has reshaped developmental education, writing, and academic reading curricula by requiring co-requisite and integrated reading and writing programs or by requiring the elimination of non-degree-credit courses. Sometimes, reforms are initiated by administrative commitment to particular kinds of philanthropic projects from organizations like the Gates Foundation and the Lumina Foundation.

exclude students based on admissions standards rarely (if ever) have to account for mandated literacy initiatives; they typically don't work in programs that support students with nontraditional educational pathways beyond participating in bridge programs, dual credit high school teaching, or other programs that serve the needs of students who are not yet admitted to the university and may never enroll at that campus full-time. Mandated reform initiatives, along with changes to education because of the Covid-19 pandemic, demonstrate that it is not possible to anticipate minor let alone major disruptions to what we assume are stable teaching conditions. The best way to prepare for uncertain shifts in higher education is to develop flexible strategies and an orientation toward pedagogical adaptability.

Participating in educational reform initiatives and program change work frequently requires faculty to develop new knowledge and skills that will help them advocate for students and other instructors. Reform efforts are often framed as social justice work because they are aimed at limiting students' time in a writing program and reducing coursework that doesn't count toward a college degree. However, some reforms can also be austerity measures aimed at reducing cost while masquerading as social justice accomplishments. Other reforms can be disconnected from the realities of teaching, learning, and the locally situated needs of the diverse student communities an institution serves. Imposed mandates can also remove control from faculty over course offerings, course sequencing, methods for instruction, and sometimes even course content. At other times, literacy program reforms have equity-minded goals but can become inequitable even when they meet the needs of students if they place an unfair and uncompensated burden on instructors' time and workload, especially for already underpaid adjunct faculty working off the tenure track.

From our perspectives and experiences, equitable reform work in writing programs and other types of postsecondary literacy education means that students receive the support and instruction they need for achieving their literacy goals, successfully completing courses, and making progress toward receiving a college degree or other credential. Efforts to fulfill the ideals promised by reforms to college literacy programs are only successful when instructors can translate those aspirational goals to their own teaching. When program changes are disconnected from the experiences of teachers and students, efforts to reform literacy programs can fail to take into account that equity requires that all students have access to educational opportunities and learning experiences that create a foundation for helping them develop as college learners.

Achieving the social justice goals of reform movements and the promise of equity-minded approaches to first-year writing requires instructors in a program to continually adapt their teaching strategies and thinking as the needs of students and their life circumstances change. We hope this book will help instructors and literacy program coordinators who are engaged in equity-minded reform initiatives to ground their work in disciplinary knowledge and inclusive teaching practices.

OVERVIEW OF *REACHING ALL WRITERS*

Drawing from years of our own research, reading, assessment, teaching, and program development work, this book builds on existing writing studies scholarship and brings together effective practices and key concepts for teaching first-year writing, especially (but not only) for instructors who work in open-access learning environments and less selective institutions. This book is designed to help instructors work with all students, not just those who are eligible for admission at selective institutions (although research shows that the strategies in this book also work for those students). Our goal for this book is to create a guide for teaching first-year writing that helps instructors develop strategies for supporting postsecondary literacy development for students from diverse educational, cultural, social, racial, and linguistic communities and backgrounds—in other words, *all* writers. This book is the guide we wanted when we were learning how to teach first-year writing in new contexts outside of the research institutions where we completed our graduate training and had our initial experiences with teaching. We hope it will be a useful resource for all writing instructors.

The teaching principles in this book draw from our own experiences as teacher-scholars, along with student-centered pedagogies and intersectional values. The primary focus of this book is to help instructors improve their teaching and develop flexible strategies for adapting what and how they teach based on the literacy needs of their own students. In *Bad Ideas about Writing*, Seth Kahn (2021) authors a chapter called "Anyone Can Teach Writing," which, as the title suggests, dismantles "the myth that anybody can teach writing." This myth, which Kahn explains as "all too often 'Anybody can teach writing' translates to 'It doesn't matter who teaches writing,' and as a result, nobody needs to pay attention to writing instructors at all," is part of the exigency of this book. The field of writing studies has for many decades worked to establish itself as an independent discipline and has done so through many of the forms of professional distinction that mark disciplinarity—coursework, graduate degrees, independent departments, journals, conferences, and virtual webinars.[4] That being said, instructors have relatively few organized resources for building on their expertise and adapting their teaching to work with a broad range of diverse learners who take writing courses at community colleges, open-access four-year institutions, and less selective universities.

This book bridges the gaps many college writing teachers experience between earning a graduate degree and taking on responsibility for teaching new students in new contexts, including having more autonomy over their courses as they transition to work after graduate school. Many books used to train teaching assistants or new instructors rely on anthologies of peer-reviewed journal articles or excerpts from landmark books on the topic or narrowly focus on preparing a syllabus or on classroom management. *Reaching All Writers* is intended to provide support for instructors who are committed to improving their teaching and building a sustainable approach to a changing environment but also for equitable teaching environments that will increase student retention and learning. Becoming a better teacher is one component of building a culture of access, inclusion, professional engagement, and consistency.

Reaching All Writers has two parts. Part 1: Foundations for Teaching College Writing, consists of this chapter with an introduction to pedagogical adaptability; chapter 2, "Practices for Teaching Effective and Equitable Writing Courses"; and chapter 3, "Thinking Like a Writer: Translating Threshold Concepts in Writing Studies to the Classroom." These chapters provide a foundation for the book's theoretical approaches, disciplinary values, and structural design. Chapter 2 helps instructors reorient their thinking about how to design and teach courses by aligning their expectations with students' diverse academic and literacy needs. Chapter 3 introduces threshold concepts and explains how and why they are useful for understanding the teaching and learning of first-year writing.

Part 2: Threshold Concepts for First-Year Writing examines key threshold concepts instructors and programs can use as a framework for designing first-year writing courses. These chapters focus on foundational concepts that support disciplinary learning for all college writers but especially for students who have limited experience with the

---

4. We use the term *writing studies* rather than composition and rhetoric throughout this book. Writing studies reflects our focus on first-year composition curriculum, assessment, and pedagogy practices, as well as the related fields of professional writing and the central role academic writing plays in many first-year writing courses and programs.

knowledge, skills, and strategies required for successfully completing college writing courses. These essential disciplinary threshold concepts help first-year writers transition to postsecondary reading and writing while also creating a foundation for subsequent learning about literacy:

- Chapter 4: Writing Can Be Taught and Learned
- Chapter 5: Writers Write for Different Purposes and Audiences, and Often in Genres with Predictable Conventions
- Chapter 6: Writing Processes Are Individualized, Require Readers, and Require Revision
- Chapter 7: Reading and Writing Are Interconnected Activities
- Chapter 8: Writers Make Choices about Language within Cultural and Social Situations.

Each chapter includes an overview of a threshold concept, disciplinary background readings, related concepts and principles, practical teaching strategies, assignment or learning activity ideas or both, principles and practices for assessing student learning, and examples from student and instructor perspectives. The suggestions in each chapter can help both new and experienced writing instructors make flexible choices about how to design their courses around key disciplinary concepts while also adapting their teaching strategies to their own working conditions and institutional contexts. Each chapter in part 2 includes opportunities to apply the concept to a variety of student, instructor, disciplinary and program scenarios drawn from experience and research, with prompts to help readers think through how the chapter concepts and scenarios apply to their own local context and situation.

Together, the threshold concepts in the second part of the book help instructors create curriculum, instruction, and assessment models with the goal of supporting students' development as readers and writers in the writing classroom, as well as across the disciplines and beyond college in their literate lives. This book will help instructors prioritize concepts that are crucial for postsecondary literacy and design courses for students with diverse backgrounds and learning needs. No single class can prepare students for all types of literacy circumstances, and all students have literacy needs beyond college. The threshold concepts of writing studies that we discuss in this book (discussed in more detail in chapter 3) provide new instructors with a framework for adapting their current knowledge, training, and preparation to new contexts. They also provide instructors with a starting point for assessing how effectively their curricular and pedagogical approaches serve their students and their programs.

As our introduction to pedagogical adaptability demonstrates, this book's purposes and audiences vary with the context of its readers. This text can be a resource for instructors as they transition from graduate school to full-time teaching, move between institutional contexts, or adjust to changing student populations. We also hope this book helps writing instructors with a variety of options for making choices about how to adapt their teaching to support student learning and literacy development. As instructors move from the graduate programs in which they were trained into full-time or part-time positions across more than one institution, they usually revise and update their course materials to align with the expectations of those departments and to meet the needs of the differing student populations at those campuses. They may also be teaching new course levels—non-degree-credit writing, co-requisite support courses, integrated reading and writing, first-semester writing, second-semester writing, upper-division required writing courses—or in new mediums such as online or blended course models. As writing teachers work to adapt their instructional, curricular, and assessment approaches to these new spaces and students, we see the book as offering them a set of concepts, instructional principles, and resources. We hope this book will help instructors answer their own questions about adapting teaching strategies to support students with diverse learning needs, which might include the following questions.

QUESTIONS FOR REFLECTION AND DISCUSSION:
PEDAGOGICAL ADAPTABILITY AND TEACHING EXPERIENCE
- How have your experiences with literacy shaped your understanding of effective teaching and learning practices?
- What training or experiences have helped you adjust to different teaching contexts?
- How do your teaching practices respond to students' individual learning needs?
- How does your process for course design incorporate flexible and adaptable practices for teaching and learning?
- In what ways does your assessment of student learning reflect the needs of individual students?
- What resources help support your disciplinary approaches to teaching and learning? What other resources do you need?
- What goals do you have for your ongoing growth as a writing teacher?

Reaching All Writers can also support writing program administrators, community college literacy program coordinators, and faculty engaged in collective work to revise programs think about the student populations they are working with, the curriculum they are developing, and the training they offer to new and continuing instructors who teach first-year writing (and sometimes developmental writing, integrated reading and writing, or upper-division courses). This book invites individuals and groups who develop writing courses and programs to consider first and foremost the literacy and learning needs of their students. The threshold concepts and related teaching strategies in this book can provide a framework for articulating core knowledge about writing and writers to support program design work and the development of course outcomes, assignments, learning activities, and course materials.

Finally, this book can help instructors, department chairs, and program administrators at institutions without many writing studies–trained faculty develop their programs, orient new teachers to their courses, and help faculty both on and off the tenure track teach effective, equitable, and inclusive courses. The chapters in this book help ground faculty development work in principles of inclusive teaching and writing studies. We hope that *Reaching All Writers* will equip all stakeholders in conversations about student-centered writing courses with references, disciplinary knowledge, and practical pedagogical suggestions to support their teaching and program development work.

2
PRACTICES FOR TEACHING EFFECTIVE AND EQUITABLE WRITING COURSES

This chapter describes principles and practices for working toward becoming an equitable, inclusive, and effective first-year college writing instructor. We describe teaching strategies that help instructors design equitable and inclusive courses around student learning goals, adapt to varied teaching contexts, and support inexperienced readers and writers who are still developing the literacy skills required for succeeding in college courses.

Adapting teaching to the learning and literacy needs of first-year college students from a diverse range of social, cultural, linguistic, and educational backgrounds requires instructors to use flexible strategies for designing, teaching, and then assessing their writing courses. These practices require knowledge about principles for equitable, inclusive, and effective teaching. Subsequent teaching chapters in the book build on the principles in this chapter and explain how to design activities and assignments that help students learn key threshold concepts for first-year writing that will support their development as critical readers, writers, and researchers.

EQUITY IN COLLEGE WRITING PROGRAMS

How to achieve equity for students in college writing programs is a complex concept that has different meanings, depending on the institutional context. In general, equity in higher education refers to institutional and pedagogical strategies that create equal educational opportunities for all students regardless of their cultural and social backgrounds. This includes fair treatment, equitable access to resources, fair assessments of student learning, and support with learning processes for all students in a classroom, program, or institution (refer to McNair, Bensimon, and Malcolm-Piqueux 2020; Mintz 2021; Suh, Owens, O'Meara, and Hall 2021). Working toward equity and inclusion in a writing course typically means creating conditions for learning, literacy development, and college success that support students from groups that have historically been excluded, marginalized, or minoritized in higher education based on one or more parts of their identities and backgrounds (McNair et al. 2016). This includes (but is not limited to) race, ethnicity, language, gender, sexual orientation, age, social class, social status, country of origin, citizenship, and (dis)ability status.

Equity in higher education is inextricably linked to practices that eliminate or create barriers to higher education attainment (Education Trust 2021). These barriers include the complex factors that support or hinder students from enrolling in college, successfully completing courses, staying in college, and completing a degree or successfully transferring from two-year colleges to four-year universities. Writing programs and instructors play an essential and unavoidable role in creating and maintaining equitable educational opportunities for all college students because first-year writing is often the only universally required course students must complete to attain a degree without an option to take alternative coursework (see Powell 2009, 2014; Ruecker, Shepherd, Estrem, and Brunk-Chavez 2017). Effective writing instruction also supports equity in contexts outside the classroom and higher education by fostering literacy development students can use to achieve their own goals in college, at work, in the community, and in other parts of their literate lives.

Efforts to achieve equity in a college writing classroom or an online learning environment must acknowledge that some students—especially racially and linguistically minoritized students—have been structurally disadvantaged by inequities in society that are a systemic part of educational institutions and entire fields of study (Carnevale and Stroh 2013; McNair et al. 2016). Estela Mara Bensimon, Alicia C. Dowd, and Keith Witham (2016, 1) describe how working toward equitable higher education practices requires an understanding of the ways higher education has created and reinforced inequities for some students: "Effective higher education reform efforts must be infused with an awareness of the ways in which many groups within US society have historically been excluded from educational opportunities, or marginalized within the structures and institutions that house those opportunities. We have characterized this awareness as equity-mindedness—a way of approaching educational reform that foregrounds the policies and practices contributing to disparities in educational achievement and abstains from blaming students for those accumulated disparities."

Many students face barriers to learning or successful course completion in writing courses because social injustices, bias, and discrimination interfere with learning and reduce access to educational resources (Gravely 2021; Page and Scott-Clayton 2015). Students from socially privileged backgrounds typically have access to more educational and financial resources to prepare for college (Mehl et al. 2020). Students who experienced unequal access to financial resources, educational resources, and social power before enrolling in college often continue to experience those inequities as college students. For that reason, designing and teaching equitable writing courses starts with identifying and understanding how inequities influence students' access to an equitable education within the context of the communities and institution in which an instructor works.

Issues surrounding equity are more complicated in open-admissions institutions that serve a broad range of learners who would be excluded from higher education at institutions with selective (or sometimes simply minimal) admissions standards. For example, instructors and program coordinators at four-year research universities might be able to focus on strategies for ensuring that students from historically marginalized communities successfully complete graduation requirements for writing courses in an inclusive and supportive learning environment. In contrast, instructors at community colleges and four-year open-access institutions often need to devote their time to supporting all students through a longer or more intensive sequence of developmental, first-year, and co-requisite writing and reading courses aimed at supporting the needs of first-generation, low-income, and returning adult learners (Boroch et al. 2010). Most instructors at open-admissions institutions teach writing courses in which most (or even sometimes all) of their students have experienced structural inequities that have influenced their prior educational experiences and limited access to social and financial resources to support their literacy development and preparation for college—including students who are inadmissible at institutions with admissions standards.

Variations in student populations, institutional missions, autonomy (and state control), access to resources, admissions policies, and literacy course sequences shape the issues and exigencies that writing programs and individual instructors need to grapple with as they work toward creating equitable, inclusive, and effective courses. This means that much of the required equity work in a classroom or online learning environment depends heavily on the local teaching context—and always requires pedagogical adaptability. Adapting teaching practices to locally situated needs of student readers and writers requires instructors to begin to develop critical awareness of student populations, local communities, and institutional missions early in their careers and whenever they move to new working higher education environments.

Regardless of their teaching contexts, instructors who develop and teach effective writing courses need to become equity-minded practitioners. The Center for Urban Education (n.d.) offers the following definition and outlines the characteristics of equity-minded practitioners in higher education: "The term 'Equity-Mindedness' refers to the perspective or mode of thinking exhibited by practitioners who call attention to patterns of inequity in student outcomes. These practitioners are willing to take personal and institutional responsibility for the success of their students, and critically reassess their own practices." Equity-mindedness requires that higher education professionals take responsibility for addressing educational opportunity gaps and creating conditions for learning that support students who have historically (and continue to be) marginalized in higher education.

Although instructors are responsible for creating equitable and inclusive learning conditions in their own courses, addressing systemic inequities requires ongoing, labor-intensive collaborative work within an entire department or program and across an institution (Casazza and Silverman 2013; Felix et al. 2015; McNair, Bensimon, and Malcolm-Piqueux 2020; Witham, Malcolm-Piqueux, Dowd, and Bensimon 2015). A report from the American Council on Education argues for a shared leadership model for equity in which "organizing teams across campus . . . take collective responsibility in developing and moving the diversity, equity, and inclusion agenda forward" (Kezar, Holcombe, Vigil, and Dizon 2021, vi). The report highlights the reality that eliminating systemic inequities requires institutional change because higher education is inherently inequitable: "Decades of programmatic efforts and interventions have failed to make a difference in the success of racially minoritized, low-income, and first-generation students, whose populations are increasing on college campuses. Higher education remains profoundly inequitable, and institutions have not made the transformational changes necessary to create truly inclusive environments and equitable outcomes for students" (vi). All members of an institution have a responsibility to contribute to institutional equity efforts, including working toward student inclusion, success, retention, transfer, and degree completion. Everyone who works on a college campus can help create a supportive campus environment that helps students know that they belong in college. Members of higher education communities also have a responsibility to contribute to and advocate for equitable and inclusive working conditions for all employees.

However, it's important to note that writing instructors themselves have widely varied working conditions and access to material resources. Writing programs in open-access contexts that enroll high numbers of students from historically marginalized groups often operate within institutions that receive less public funding for student support in comparison to institutions that serve students who have access to more financial and social resources (Kalish et al. 2019; Mullin 2010). Sometimes, instructors face significant inequities on campus because of bias and discrimination based on their racial, cultural, linguistic, or social identities—or because of their employment statuses (Kahn, Lalicker, and Lynch-Biniek 2017; McClure, Goldstein, and Pemberton 2017). Systemic inequities in higher education contribute to a writing program structure at many institutions in which contingent faculty teach a disproportionate percentage of labor-intensive first-year writing courses for low pay (Giordano, Hassel, Klausman, and Sullivan 2021). At universities with graduate programs, graduate teaching assistants are often inadequately compensated and have high teaching loads relative to their other responsibilities (including pursuing their own coursework and research for the purpose of completing an advanced degree). Writing centers and other learning assistance programs can play a significant role in closing educational opportunity gaps for students, but professionals in those learning spaces often lack tenure and employment stability (Geller and Denny 2013).

At two-year colleges, instructors typically teach five or more courses a semester and often teach overloads beyond their contractual obligations (Suh et al. 2021). Adjunct writing instructors at open-admissions institutions often find themselves teaching classes in which a majority of students need intensive, individualized support; at the same time, they lack sufficient resources to provide that support, including a dedicated office space, stable employment, professional respect within an institution, or sufficient co-curricular support services such as a dedicated writing center (Giordano, Hassel, Heinert, and Phillips 2017). Writing instructors with a high teaching load and limited resources in financially constrained institutions may find themselves making strategic choices about the disciplinary best practices they have time to use and the learning support they can manage to give students while also letting go of other practices they can't provide within the constraints of their working conditions (Giordano, Hassel, and Wegner 2020; Giordano and Wegner 2020).

In this book, we describe strategies for designing equitable and inclusive writing courses. But we affirm that the responsibility for creating equitable conditions for teaching and learning begins with state systems, institutions, and writing programs. We acknowledge that individual instructors in some teaching contexts do not have the social privileges and material resources required for making meaningful change to systemic inequities within their institutions even though they can contribute to efforts within their programs and the profession to close educational equity gaps for their own students through effective and equitable teaching practices. Some instructors (especially contingent faculty and instructors who are working as apprentices, such as graduate students) do not have the autonomy to create their own assignments, determine the course schedule and sequencing, or choose textbooks; but all instructors can identify the equitable and inclusive teaching practices that will work in their own courses for their individual circumstances, institutional contexts, and available material resources.

WHAT IS EQUITABLE TEACHING?

Effective teaching is always equitable teaching that supports learning for all students regardless of their cultural, social, linguistic, or educational backgrounds. For the purposes of this book, we define *equitable teaching* as the development and application of teaching strategies that create equal learning opportunities for all students in an environment that acknowledges inequities and actively resists bias and discrimination. Within the context of a writing course and program, equitable teaching means creating conditions for learning that support all students' development as postsecondary writers, readers, and learners. It also means eliminating or changing practices that create barriers to course completion and degree attainment.

We argue that it's not possible to have an effective writing course that meets the needs of only some students—or even most students—while failing to support educational opportunities for students who identify with communities that have historically been and continue to be marginalized in higher education. Developing an equitable writing course includes the following practices:

Strategies for Developing an Equitable Writing Course
- Engaging in careful reflection to identify and work toward eliminating one's own biases as a literacy educator
- Purposefully creating and maintaining conditions for learning that support literacy development and college success for all students, especially those from historically marginalized and minoritized groups

- Recognizing and directly addressing structural inequities within the course, program, institution, and the profession that interfere with learning and educational opportunities
- Using fair and transparent processes for assessment that focus on supporting learning and helping all students achieve the learning goals of the course
- Engaging in ongoing self-assessment to identify and address challenges to learning within the course.

In *From Equity Talk to Equity Walk*, Tia Brown McNair, Estela Mara Bensimon, and Lindsey Malcolm-Piqueux (2020, 2) outline a framework for racial justice in higher education and explain that instructors can move beyond theories about equity to taking action within their own institutional contexts: "Educators with an equity talk and an equity walk critically examine institutional policies, practices, and structures through a lens that questions why inequities exist to change the educational environment to support the success of students—especially students who have been historically and continuously marginalized in our educational systems." This kind of critical reflection needs to happen at both the individual instructor level and collaboratively at the level of a writing program.

Creating equitable and accessible writing courses requires that instructors do more than theorize about social justice or introduce diverse topics into the curriculum. Equitable instructors reflect on how their own teaching practices do or do not create equitable and inclusive conditions for learning and literacy development. They examine their course policies and processes for interacting with students to identify both deliberate and unintentional barriers to successful course completion, especially practices that might privilege students who had and continue to have access to more resources in their prior educational experiences and current lives. They also work toward changing components of their courses (often learned through the ways they were treated as college students) that reinforce and maintain the systemic inequities that have historically provided limited access to the opportunities required for attaining a college degree for students based on their racial, linguistic, social, and cultural backgrounds. This chapter outlines some basic principles for designing equitable and inclusive college courses, and subsequent chapters will provide more specific writing studies strategies for developing courses that support success for all students.

In describing and defining educational equity, Erin L. Castro (2015, 6) argues that "plainly stated, equity in higher education is the idea that students from historically and contemporarily marginalized and minoritized communities have access to what they need in order to be successful." Castro also argues that "to understand equity is to understand power and the ways in which power operates throughout society" (6). Instructors can likewise use this understanding to reflect on their teaching practices and assess the extent to which their pedagogical strategies reduce or reinforce educational equity gaps for students from marginalized and minoritized groups.

The questions below can help you reflect on practices for teaching equitable writing courses:

Reflect on Equity in Your Teaching Context
- What inequities (if any) have you experienced in your own education? How have your own educational experiences shaped your thinking about equity in college writing courses?
- What educational opportunity gaps for students have you noticed in the program(s) in which you work and course(s) you teach? What issues have you identified related to social injustices, bias, and discrimination that influence the access students have to resources for going to college, staying in college, and receiving a degree?
- How has unequal access to financial and social resources influenced some students' opportunities for learning and preparation for college?
- What barriers to student learning and course completion do students in your writing program experience? How do the culture and climate of the program contribute to those barriers?
- What inequities have you noticed in your writing program for instructors or other staff related to aspects of their social and cultural identities, their employment statuses, or both? How do the culture and climate of the institution and program contribute to those inequities?
- Which student communities are missing from or underrepresented in one or more courses that you teach? Which students are excluded from your courses based on institutional admissions criteria, cost of attendance, program policies, and other factors that support students from more privileged backgrounds in your teaching context?
- What are your own priorities as you work toward creating a more equitable teaching and learning environment for students at your institution?

WHAT IS INCLUSIVE TEACHING?

Although inclusion and equity are sometimes used interchangeably to refer to equal access to educational opportunities, *inclusion* in a writing classroom means that students with diverse social and cultural identities and backgrounds are valued and supported within a learning environment. Inclusive courses are designed to support all students in doing their best learning, contributing to the work of the classroom community, and achieving the goals of the course. Writing instructors who use inclusive teaching practices (a) create learning conditions that respect students' cultural, social, linguistic, and racial identities; (b) provide structured learning support that meets students' individual needs; (c) foster safe learning spaces in which students' perspectives are valued; and (d) help students develop a sense of belonging in a classroom or an online community and on campus. Equitable teaching ensures that students have access to educational opportunities; inclusive teaching means working toward helping all students learn and know that they belong in the class and in higher education.

One example of a framework for inclusive teaching in a writing course comes from *Racial Literacy: A Policy Research Brief* from the National Council of Teachers of English (NCTE). In the policy brief, Yolanda Sealey-Ruiz (2021, 6) outlines six stages of racial literacy development that also help describe characteristics of inclusive and equitable literacy educators:

1. *Critical Love*: Make a profound ethical commitment to caring for the communities we work in;
2. *Critical Humility*: Remain open to understanding the limits of our own worldviews and ideologies;
3. *Critical Reflection*: Think through the various layers of our identities and how our privilege and marginalized statuses affect the work;
4. *Historical Literacy*: Develop a rich and contextual awareness of the historical forces that shape the communities we work in but also the society we live in;
5. *Archaeology of Self*: Begin a deep excavation and exploration of beliefs, biases, and ideas that shape how we engage in the work;
6. *Interruption*: Interrupt racism and inequality at personal and systemic levels.

This framework for becoming a racially literate educator illustrates how inclusive teaching starts with caring for our students and critically reflecting on our own biases and limitations. Inclusive teaching isn't primarily theoretical; it depends on our actual behaviors and how we think about, respect, and treat the human beings in the in-person and online learning environments we have stewardship over. Inclusivity and equity in teaching are never disconnected from real relationships and the lived experiences of our students. Becoming inclusive literacy educators is an ongoing, reflective, and challenging process that requires all of us to work toward doing a better job of creating conditions for learning that support all students.

Creating a sense of belonging in a writing classroom requires us to create conditions for learning that clearly communicate to students that they do in fact belong in college. The strategies writing instructors need to use for creating inclusive courses depend heavily on their teaching contexts and the student populations a particular course serves. Examples of inclusive teaching practices include:

- Applying a process-based approach to teaching that provides students with learning support in completing each stage of a project
- Using texts and teaching materials that reflect the diverse backgrounds of students in a course
- Creating online course materials that are accessible to students with disabilities
- Adapting teaching strategies in a course section to account for students' varying levels of college preparation and diverse educational backgrounds
- Eliminating unnecessary gatekeeping elements of a course that prevent students from successfully completing it.

The questions below can help you reflect on practices for creating inclusive learning spaces for your students:

Reflect on Inclusion in Your Teaching Context
- What experiences did you have with inclusive teaching as a student? When were you included? When were you excluded or treated as an "other"? How have your experiences with inclusion and exclusion in educational environments shaped your thinking about teaching and learning?
- What have you done to make an ethical commitment to caring for your students? In what ways might you do better in developing critical love, critical humility, and critical reflection as a literacy educator?
- What limitations are you already aware of in your assumptions and thinking about students and their development as college readers and writers? What challenges might these limitations present for your efforts to create an inclusive learning environment?
- In what ways do your social and cultural identities, privileges, and marginalized statuses influence your approaches to teaching and learning? What challenges and opportunities have you experienced as an educator based on your own multifaceted background? What have

these experiences taught you about creating and maintaining learning environments that respect students' social and cultural identities?
- What steps have you taken to provide structured learning support that meets the needs of individual students? How might you improve your approach to providing individualized learning support?

DIVERSITY AND COLLEGE WRITING COURSES

In contrast to equity and inclusion, *diversity* in a writing course can refer either to the members of a class (or student cohort) or to course content. A course with a diverse community of writers means that students who identify with different social and cultural groups are present in the classroom or in an online learning environment. A *diverse classroom community* includes (but isn't limited to) race, ethnicity, gender identity, socioeconomic status, social class, language, nationality, sexual orientation, religion, (dis)abilities, physical and mental health, age, generational differences, educational background, and political perspectives. A diverse writing program also includes instructors from a variety of different cultural and social backgrounds, including those that represent the student communities an institution serves. When the *content* of a course is diverse, students have access to texts and assignments that represent a range of socially and culturally diverse perspectives. The content of a course can be diverse even when students' backgrounds aren't.

However, a writing course can have diverse students and content without being equitable and inclusive. Equity in college teaching is different from the equal presence of students from different racial, social, cultural, and linguistic backgrounds (Suh, Owens, O'Meara, and Hall 2021, 3). A college writing program can have elements of diversity without being inclusive and equitable if students and instructors are not treated fairly or given equal access to opportunities and resources. A writing course can include class members from diverse backgrounds or have diverse content without being equitable if the instructor's teaching strategies and practices for assessing student learning reinforce inequities that exist in society and higher education, create barriers to student learning, or fail to support student success. Instructors can unintentionally create or reinforce barriers to literacy development and learning when they uncritically transfer writing course curricula, assignments, and teaching practices used at selective institutions (i.e., those that predominantly serve educationally privileged students) to institutions that enroll students from more widely diverse communities that have been traditionally excluded from selective universities. Discrimination and inequality in a writing program or institution can exist even when policies are in place to support equity if those policies are ignored or undermined by instructors, administrators, or students.

MOVING FROM A DEFICIT MODEL TO AN ASSET MODEL FOR WRITING COURSE SUCCESS

A *deficit model* of student learning and success emphasizes the extent to which students do or do not meet instructor expectations or adhere to the culture and conventions of higher education. The NCTE "Position Statement on Writing Instruction in School" (2022) describes how a deficit approach to literacy instruction creates barriers to educational opportunities: "In school settings, writing is often perceived and enacted as a gatekeeping device, which contributes to achievement gaps and other inequities. This happens when writing instruction and assessments focus on the *writing*—the products that are ultimately assessed and evaluated—rather than on the *writers* themselves. Writing instruction and assessments also serve as gatekeeping devices when they are built around deficit notions surrounding students' languages and literacies" (original emphases). The statement also explains that deficit thinking writing instruction is rooted in racism and "Eurocentric ideologies."

In a deficit approach to learning, students (not institutions or instructors) are perceived as mostly or completely responsible for their own success in a course and for their progress toward a college degree. This way of thinking can label some individuals or groups as "good" or "successful" students while learners who don't meet instructor expectations are often viewed as unmotivated, irresponsible, lacking self-control, or lazy. A deficit approach to student learning ignores the ways systemic inequities, bias, and discrimination shape students' opportunities for learning before attending college, and it frames postsecondary readiness in terms of a student's individual responsibility to prepare for college reading and writing while ignoring the cultural and social conditions that provide unequal access to educational resources for many students.

A deficit approach to assessing student writing often focuses on mistakes and correctness (in ways that are typically disconnected from knowledge about how writing and language work) instead of on student learning and literacy development. Deficit thinking about assessment and grading often places responsibility on students to already know about and apply conventions for college writing in a way that is disconnected from their prior experience with writing, their literacy needs and goals, or even what they are learning in the course. Further, a deficit approach to assessment views students' diverse social, cultural, and linguistic backgrounds as problems that interfere with learning instead of as assets they draw from when they use language (Baker-Bell 2020; Davila 2012; Inoue 2015). At its worst, deficit-focused assessment looks for "errors" in student writing (instead of focusing on evidence of learning) through an idiosyncratic and often arbitrary treatment of those errors as a problem to be solved with a low grade, margin comments, or marking on student work (Conference on College Composition and Communication 2020, 2021c). Moving from deficit to asset ways of thinking about student learning can be a complicated process that requires time and critical reflection. Many instructors have asset views for some aspects of teaching and deficit views for other parts of their work as educators.

In contrast, an *asset approach* to student learning and literacy development in a writing course emphasizes strengths in students' reading, writing, and thinking strategies and then draws on those strengths to support students' ongoing learning instead of emphasizing what students don't know or can't do. Part of an asset approach to writing course pedagogy and design is recognizing how systemic inequities shape students' prior and current experiences with literacy and education. An asset approach to teaching uses pedagogical strategies that account for the ways some students experience social privileges that have aligned their literacy experiences with the academic conventions and expectations of higher education while other students haven't enjoyed those privileges. Equity-minded teaching directly addresses educational equity gaps by creating opportunities for students to build on their literacy strengths and demonstrate their learning in ways that reflect their prior learning experiences, access to resources, and cultural and social identities.

An asset model for teaching college writing includes:

- Placing the primary responsibility for learning, student success, and educational attainment on the instructor, writing program, and institution
- Recognizing the individual reading, writing, and learning strengths of all students
- Acknowledging that students learn about literacy and demonstrate that learning in complex ways that reflect their cultural, social, educational, and linguistic backgrounds
- Approaching diversity in students' educational experiences, learning strategies participation in class, process work, and written texts as assets and resources that support learning for the entire class, including the instructor
- Framing learning and literacy development in terms of students' own goals for how they use (and want to use) reading and writing in their literate lives both inside and outside of college

- Proactively reinforcing student learning that supports their individual goals
- Recognizing diversity in the ways students use oral and written language as strengths they draw from for learning.

Instructors sometimes develop deficit ways of thinking about teaching because their own prior educational experiences rewarded academic behaviors that reflect the cultural values of a higher education. People who make it through graduate education in English often do so by adapting to ways of using language and thinking about writing that reward writers by ranking them against each other through grading systems and by reinforcing narrow definitions of what it means to be a successful college writer. Instructors whose primary experiences with writing in college took place in institutions with selective or even moderate admissions standards may need to adjust their thinking when they begin to teach students who would have been excluded from the places where their own learning and early experiences with teaching took place. The assets student writers bring to college from their cultural and linguistic backgrounds are easy to overlook when instructors are new to a student community or when their own educational experiences have purposefully taught them to focus on idealized forms of writing rather than on the writers themselves (National Council of Teachers of English 2022).

CONCEPTS FOR EFFECTIVE TEACHING

Effective college writing instructors engage in ongoing learning and professional development to support their work as postsecondary educators. The following terms and concepts lay a foundation for successful college teaching and help instructors engage in conversations about teaching practices with colleagues in their programs, in the profession, and in other disciplines in their institutions.

Effective teaching means that an instructor uses teaching practices that support student learning and literacy development in a field of study. The instructors' course design, learning activities, assignments, assessment, and feedback strategies help all students achieve the learning goals of the course. Effective teachers also regularly self-assess their own teaching over time to identify which teaching practices work and how to improve as teachers in the context of a course and a program. They support their claims about teaching effectiveness and equity with multiple measures of evidence, which includes (but isn't limited to) informal and formal assessments of student learning, feedback on teaching from students and colleagues, reflective work, and institutional data on course completion.

Evidence-based teaching or pedagogy refers to teaching practices that are supported by credible research. For college instructors, scholarship about teaching includes research on how college students learn (for example, read Ambrose et al. 2010; Doyle 2011; Dunlosky et al. 2013; Eyler 2018; Flippo and Bean 2018), related research on postsecondary teaching (Bain 2004; Nilson 2016), and studies that focus more specifically on teaching and learning in a discipline that also contribute to scholarly conversations in the researchers' field of study (Bishop-Clark 2012; Healey, Matthews, and Cook-Sather 2020; Laird, Shoup, Kuh, and Schwarz 2008). In writing studies, evidence-based teaching draws from both disciplinary theories of writing and research about students' development as college readers and writers (see, for example, Carroll 2002; Sternglass 1997; Tinberg and Nadeau 2010). It also includes interdisciplinary knowledge from linguistics, postsecondary reading, teaching English to speakers of other languages (especially second-language writing), and other related fields of study. By definition, evidence-based teaching in writing courses requires instructors to not only draw from disciplinary writing studies theories and practices but to also base teaching strategies on evidence that they support student learning.

Best practices in teaching are commonly discussed concepts that aren't always clearly defined. The qualifier *best* can be used in varying ways to support different approaches to teaching that may or may not be based on evidence or scholarship. We consider *best practices* to be evidence-based approaches to teaching and learning that draw from peer-reviewed scholarship about postsecondary teaching, disciplinary learning in writing studies, and students' development as college readers and writers. In this book, we also refer to statements from the National Council of Teachers of English, the Conference on College Composition and Communication, and other disciplinary organizations that describe effective teaching practices based on a synthesis or review of scholarship. These statements are typically reviewed and voted on by elected leaders of organizations and sometimes by members.

Critical reflection in teaching describes thinking processes instructors use to learn from their previous experiences and apply them to new teaching situations to improve student learning. Stephen Brookfield (1998, 3) describes critical reflection as "the sustained and intentional process of identifying and checking the accuracy and validity of our teaching assumptions." This includes explicit or conscious assumptions that instructors can identify, along with implicit or unconscious assumptions about students, teaching, and learning. Brookfield explains that "critical reflection happens when we build into our habit of constantly trying to identify, and check the assumptions that inform our actions as teachers. The chief reason for doing this is to help us take more informed actions so that when we do something that's intended to help students learn it actually has that effect" (4–5). This type of self-assessment or self-awareness is essential not only for effective teaching but for adapting teaching strategies to particular teaching situations and responding to student learning needs in equitable and inclusive ways.

Learner-centered teaching (or *student-centered teaching*) focuses activities in a course on what students need and want to learn in contrast to *teacher-centered* education in which the instructor focuses on presenting information to students. Terry Doyle (2011, 7) offers this definition: "Learner-centered teaching (LCT) is about optimizing the opportunities for our students to learn." It means figuring out the best possible ways to get them to do the work. Maryellen Weimer (2013, 26) explains that "experience with learner-centered approaches doesn't just transform students. This way of teaching can also transform what teachers believe about learning and their role as teachers." A learner-centered first-year writing instructor aligns teaching practices with learning goals or outcomes that help students transition to postsecondary reading, writing, and research while also supporting students' own goals for applying their learning to literacy practices both inside and outside of college.

"*Significant learning experiences*" is a phrase developed by L. Dee Fink (2013, 7), who defines it as "learning that makes a difference in how people live—and the kind of life they are capable of living." This type of teaching requires instructors to provide students with multiple and varied types of learning experiences they can connect to their own lives and goals. In first-year writing courses, significant learning experiences arguably help students achieve their postsecondary education goals; connect course learning to their lived experiences with reading, writing, and language; and enhance students' literate lives both inside and outside of school.

Accessibility refers to teaching practices that permit all students (or as many as possible) to access and use learning materials, activities, course websites, classrooms, online learning environments, resources, and technology. For example, Universal Design for Learning (UDL) is a commonly used approach to accessibility in higher education that focuses on accommodating the diverse learning needs and abilities of all students and removing barriers to participation (Behling and Tobin 2018; Burgstahler and Cory 2008; Chardin and Novak 2021). However, *accessibility* also means accommodating the unique learning needs of students with disabilities. Taking steps to create more accessible learning environments for *all* students doesn't exempt instructors from following accommodations and the legally mandated disability rights of individual students (Dolmage 2017; US Department of Justice 2022). In writing courses that are both equitable and accessible, instructors do their best to maintain a learning environment that eliminates barriers to learning for all writers while also ensuring that individual learners with physical, mental, and neurological disabilities receive their accommodations.

Assessment is a broad term that describes all of the practices instructors, programs, and institutions use to measure student learning and evaluate teaching. In *Learning Assessment Techniques,* Elizabeth Barkley and Claire Howell Major (2016, 24) offer this definition: "Within the context of education, the term assessment is used to describe appraisal of knowledge, skills, attitudes, and beliefs that students have acquired, most often as the result of learning in their courses." Almost all postsecondary educators participate in assessment activities at the program and institutional levels (for example, to assess general education or program outcomes to meet accreditation guidelines). However, the most important type of assessment happens at the individual course and classroom level. All effective teaching is grounded in assessment that helps instructors monitor student learning and improve their own teaching.

College writing instructors need to use multiple forms of assessment across a course to ensure that their teaching practices are equitable and effective. This includes *formative assessments,* which are strategies for monitoring and evaluating students' learning and processes in a course (Suskie 2018)—typically for the purpose of making adjustments to teaching, providing feedback, and identifying how to support students individually and collectively. Course-level learning assessment also includes *summative assessments* at the end of a project, unit, course, or program (Suskie 2018). Summative assessments are typically the basis for course grades, and they provide instructors with valuable information for making adjustments to teaching for a subsequent semester. However, they can be less effective than formative assessments in supporting learning for individual students because they often take place after students no longer have an opportunity to respond to and implement feedback. Some types of assessment are connected to grading, but not all grading is learning assessment. For example, many college instructors assign some or even all of students' course grades on factors that are often disconnected from assessing learning and literacy development (for example, attendance, undefined judgments about participation and effort, on-time submission of work, number of drafts completed, and unassessed submission of process work).

PLANNING FOR AND DESIGNING AN EQUITABLE AND INCLUSIVE COURSE

Course design refers to the purposeful planning processes and methods instructors, program coordinators, and curriculum developers use to create courses that help students achieve learning goals and fulfill the purpose of the course. Developing a writing course that both closes educational opportunity gaps and creates an inclusive learning environment for all students starts with effective course design. Equity-minded teaching practices need to be the focus of the entire course rather than an element an instructor adds in piecemeal after planning out the course structure and schedule. While instructors can improve their teaching by working on isolated components of a course to address equity and inclusion (for example, adding readings about linguistic bias or revising writing assignments to clarify assessment criteria), the most effective way to create an equitable and inclusive writing courses is to work intentionally on the overall design to create a course structure that supports literacy development and learning for all students but particularly for those who have historically been excluded from higher education, discriminated against, or marginalized by some approaches to teaching writing courses and assessing student learning. The characteristics of equity-minded course design include the following principles.

The instructor carefully plans for equity, inclusion, and student success. The instructor develops a clear plan for supporting learning and literacy development by identifying how to incorporate equitable and inclusive teaching practices into the entire semester, individual units, assignments, class periods or online modules, learning activities, and assessment/grading practices.

Each component of the course is purposefully designed to support student learning. The teaching practices, reading assignments and activities, writing assignments, process work, and online or in-person class activities are intentionally designed to foster student success and create meaningful opportunities for student learning. Activities in the course are interconnected and carefully sequenced to support students' literacy development over time. In a writing course, this typically means that the instructor strategically designs the course so students complete increasingly more challenging and complex reading and writing activities as they work toward achieving the goals of the course. Purposeful design also means thinking through the progressive goals that take place for students and the instructor over the course rather than in terms of individual class lesson plans or assignments.

The instructor makes in-the-moment adjustments based on critical reflection. Equity-minded writing instructors continually reflect on how their own cultural and social identities shape their perspectives on teaching reading and writing, thinking about learning, and interactions with students. They critically reflect on their teaching strategies, especially assessing the effectiveness of their teaching practices in relation to students' learning and literacy development. They identify barriers to student learning, think through how to reduce those barriers, and then make changes to the course to close opportunity gaps while they are still teaching it.

The course supports disciplinary learning. Equitable writing courses help students do their best learning within the field of writing studies. Effective course activities help students develop the literacy strategies, ways of thinking, and skills required for successfully applying learning about writing, reading, and learning to their own literacy practices. (Subsequent chapters in this book address threshold concepts for supporting disciplinary learning in writing studies.) Because first-year writing at many institutions also serves as the primary gateway to literacy development for college learning in general, writing instructors can also support educational equity by helping students develop rhetorical awareness and flexibility that will help them adapt their reading and writing strategies to other fields of study.

Students engage in learner-centered literacy practices during and outside of class. In an equity-minded writing course, learning activities focus on student learning and students' literacy needs. For example, an instructor might select culturally relevant reading assignments based on the literacy skills and learning strategies engaging with those texts will help students develop. The instructor also breaks larger assignments into manageable steps and actively teaches students how to complete each stage of a larger project. The work students complete outside of class focuses on supporting their development as college readers and writers, and the instructor provides support that helps students transition from instructor-guided work to independent learning.

Assessment activities support student learning. Assessment activities in an equitable and inclusive writing course focus on supporting student learning—not on ranking them against each other or placing value on their work. Graded and non-graded activities for assessing students' progress focus on supporting learning rather than identifying deficits. The instructor uses assessment and feedback practices that help students achieve both the learning goals of the course and their individual literacy goals. This chapter and subsequent parts of the book discuss strategies for designing assessment activities based on student learning.

Course activities help students develop flexible learning processes. Classroom instruction, course activities, and assignments guide students through the learning processes required for success in both first-year writing courses and subsequent writing courses (if any) a student will eventually take in working toward a degree. Instructors provide scaffolded learning support to help students successfully complete smaller steps or stages for course projects and other activities. Students receive multiple opportunities to practice literacy strategies, adapt processes to varied literacy tasks, and receive feedback on their in-progress work.

The instructor's expectations and approaches to teaching are transparent. In an equitable and inclusive writing course, an instructor uses transparent teaching and assessment processes (Feldman 2019; Winkelmes, Boye, and Tapp 2019). The purposes for major components of a course are clear to students and colleagues in the discipline. Course policies, assignment instructions, assessment practices, and grading criteria are written in clear language that first-year college students can easily understand, including those who have experienced limited opportunities for supportive learning about how education works. Equity-minded instructors are also open to new learning about teaching and are transparent about their own challenges as teachers.

The instructor adapts teaching strategies to differing learning environments and modalities. Most writing instructors can expect to teach in different modalities during their careers, which might include in-person (face-to-face), asynchronous online (without a scheduled component), synchronous online (with scheduled videoconference meeting times), and hybrid (a combination of hybrid and in-person) teaching. Effective writing instructors design and teach their courses in ways that account for differences in teaching modalities (Borgman and McArdle 2019; Hewett and DePew 2015), for example, through structuring course websites and developing activities that facilitate learning for students in online courses.

STRATEGIES FOR WRITING COURSE DESIGN

Effective course design for first-year writing requires a variety of different planning activities—for example, designing major writing assignments and related shorter process assignments or activities, identifying the topics to cover and how the instructor will teach them, selecting reading assignments and developing accompanying source-based learning activities, scheduling and sequencing course components, creating in-class or online learning activities or both, determining methods for assessing student learning, developing course policies and guidelines, and creating course learning resources. Equity-minded instructors also need to plan for how to create and maintain an inclusive learning environment and provide support for students who have differing levels of knowledge about how higher education works. Effective course design for first-year writing also needs to account for students' literacy development in relation to the student populations a course serves as well as the role of the course within a sequence of other writing courses at an institution.

Writing instructors have varying levels of autonomy over course design, depending on their institutions, employment statuses, and program policies. Some instructors have complete autonomy while others work within a framework of required program assignments, course components, or both while still making individual choices about most of the course. However, in some programs, instructors have only a small amount of autonomy and are given a syllabus, schedule, assignments, and learning activities they are required to use. Writing instructors also have varying levels of access to program resources for supporting course design. In some programs, instructors are given a fully developed online version of a first-year course (sometimes called a *development shell*) that they can copy directly into a learning management system (e.g., Canvas, Blackboard, Brightspace) and adapt with minimal changes. Development shells are one way writing programs create consistency across course sections while also reducing workload for new faculty, graduate students, and part-time instructors. Other programs provide examples of syllabi, assignments, and other teaching resources that instructors use to design their own versions of first-year writing. Some programs provide few course design resources beyond a course description and program-level or general education learning outcomes for first-year writing. Because of these variations in how writing programs approach course design, instructors need to be prepared to adapt their course design work to the unique workload realities of a particular program (and sometimes a course) as they transition between different institutions or from graduate school to full-time teaching.

Although the most intensive course design work happens when an instructor teaches a new course for the first time or completely redesigns a course in response to program changes, writing instructors use course design principles on a regular basis as they assess what's working and what they might improve in the current semester and the next time they teach a course. Equity-minded writing instructors frequently think through how different parts of a course work together to create effective conditions for student learning. They also redesign parts of their courses as student needs change. One effective way to keep track of ideas for revising and improving a course is through an organized written record (for example, a teaching journal, notebook, spreadsheet, to-do list, or action plan). Because major revisions to courses are labor-intensive, instructors often need to manage their workloads by making small changes to a course incrementally over time through a process of critical reflection, assessment, and revision.

One especially useful framework for designing writing courses is *backward design* (also called backward planning or mapping), which is a process for developing or redesigning courses around student learning rather than topics or content. The backward design approach to teaching comes from *Understanding by Design* by Grant Wiggins and Jay McTighe (1998). Their method of designing individual courses and program curricula focuses on *understanding* and *transfer* (i.e., applying learning from one context to a new learning situation). The term *backward* means that the course design process starts with the end goals of a course—or the learning outcomes students will work toward achieving throughout the course. Instructors then work backward through the course from end to beginning and create assignments and activities that help students complete the overall learning goals of the course.

Wiggins and McTighe (1998) describe three stages of backward design:

1. Identify desired results (i.e., determine what students will learn and demonstrate)
2. Determine acceptable evidence for assessing student learning
3. Plan learning experiences and instruction.

The next three sections of this chapter outline strategies and examples for using backward design to create effective writing courses that focus on student learning.

Stage 1: Developing Student Learning Goals

In the first stage of backward design, instructors *identify desired results* by using existing program learning outcomes or developing student learning goals. Wiggins and McTighe (1998, 12) offer this description of how to "determine acceptable evidence" of student learning: "What will we accept as evidence of student understanding and proficiency? The backward design approach encourages us to think about a unit or a course in terms of the collected assessment evidence needed to document and validate that the desired learning has been achieved, so that the course is not just content to be covered or a series of learning activities."

In first-year writing, the starting point for course design is articulating the reading, writing, critical thinking, research skills, and strategies students will learn, develop, and demonstrate *by the end of the course*. It can also include goals for what students will be able to understand about how language works and then apply to their literacy experiences both inside and outside of school.

Writing courses and programs may have one or more types of student learning goals. *Course learning outcomes* describe what students will be able to do and know by the end of a course. They usually apply to all course sections regardless of the instructor, and they are typically developed by a writing program or English department through a shared governance decision-making process, the work of a committee, or the work of a program administrator. However, some programs use outcomes developed by publishers of a textbook or online learning product. *Learning objectives*[1] are learning goals for a part of the course (for example, an online module, a short writing assignment, or an in-class activity). They typically break down larger course-level objectives into more specific goals an instructor can use to develop course activities and assess student learning in a manageable way. Some programs also have *writing program learning outcomes* for what students will achieve by the end of the entire writing program, which can inform how instructors prepare students for the courses they take after first-year writing. Most institutions also have *institutional learning outcomes* for degree-seeking students (for example, general education outcomes) that are often connected to review processes for regional accreditation.

An *instructor's goals or outcomes for student learning* are developed by an individual instructor. They apply only to an instructor's section(s) of a course. Instructors often have goals for what they would like students to be able to know and do by the end of a course in addition to the learning outcomes developed by a department or program. They also have objectives they want students to work on through a course module, unit, or major assignment as they make progress toward developing literacy strategies required for demonstrating the course learning outcomes provided by their writing programs. Developing student learning goals also provides a way for instructors to address opportunity gaps and incorporate outcomes for diversity, equity, and inclusion into a course if they

---

1. The terms *learning outcomes, objectives,* and *learning goals* are closely related and sometimes used interchangeably. In this book, we use the term *learning outcome* to refer to the end results of student learning for a course. Objectives can also be used to describe the goals of a program or an instructor rather than student learning. We distinguish between student learning goals and the instructional goals instructors have for themselves as teachers.

Table 2.1. Examples of different types of student learning goals or outcomes

Institutional	Writing Program	First-Year Writing	Instructor
Students communicate effectively.	Students write a variety of source-based texts that adapt content, form, and style to the audience, purpose, and requirements of each writing situation.	Students analyze and evaluate the rhetorical features of a text to understand writing strategies used to communicate ideas.	Students make connections between strategies that other writers use and their own experiences as writers.

aren't part of program-level learning outcomes. Subsequent chapters in this book provide examples of knowledge, skills, and strategies instructors might consider when developing their own learning goals for their first-year writing courses. See table 2.1 for examples of different levels of goals and outcomes.

Effective student learning goals are *specific* and *measurable*, which means an instructor can use them to assess students' learning and development as readers and writers through formal assignments and informal assessment activities. Instructors can use measurable learning goals as a tool for evaluating whether their own teaching supports student learning (Barkley and Major 2016) and whether they need to make changes to create a more equitable course. Learning goals for a first-year writing course should also be *learner-centered*, which means they focus on what students need to know, do, and demonstrate. In writing programs that serve a broad range of learners from diverse linguistic and educational backgrounds, learning outcomes and instructor-determined learning goals also need to be *realistic*. They should reflect students' prior literacy and educational experiences. Students should be able to develop the literacy strategies required for demonstrating realistic learning outcomes within the time frame of the course.

The end results of a first-year writing course need to reflect what students will be required to do in subsequent writing courses in a program (for example, intermediate composition, technical writing, or introduction to writing studies). If an institution has two required first-year writing courses, then program-level learning outcomes for first-year writing may be different from those for writing programs that offer a single first-year writing course followed by intermediate composition or another sophomore-level communications general education requirement. Student learning goals also need to account for differences in the role of a writing course in an institution (for example, whether the course is required for transfer to another institution in a state system, for meeting a prerequisite for another first-year writing course, for a liberal arts general education degree requirement, for an applied technical associates degree requirement, or for demonstrating communications proficiencies for a certificate program). The institutional context of a writing course shapes course design decisions.

Stage 2: Designing Assessments of Student Learning

In the second stage of backward design, instructors *determine acceptable evidence* (Wiggins and McTighe 1998) for assessing whether students have learned and achieved the goals of both the entire course and smaller parts of the course (for example, units, modules, or lessons). Instructors identify the types of disciplinary learning activities that create opportunities for students to apply and demonstrate their learning, and then they design specific assignments and other learning activities around student learning goals. The NCTE "Literacy Assessment" (2018a) statement confirms that the central focus of assessment in writing courses is student learning: "Literacy assessments are valid only to the extent that they help students learn."

For writing courses, instructors determine evidence of student learning by planning for and developing writing assignments and other assessable learning activities based on learning goals (Fink 2013). Evidence of learning for first-year writing typically centers on a few different writing projects that (a) give students practice applying strategies for college reading, writing, and research; (b) create opportunities for students to receive instructor and peer feedback; and (c) provide a systematic and transparent way for instructors to assess student learning. Even when a program provides major first-year writing projects, instructors are often still responsible for developing smaller learning activities that will lead to completion of the major projects. Subsequent chapters in this book offer suggestions for a variety of different writing projects and shorter activities focused on threshold concepts for first-year writing.

Like other parts of designing an effective and equitable writing course, writing projects and related activities need to directly address and support the needs of students who enroll in the course. We advocate for an approach to assignment design that moves away from assigning a specific genre of an assignment as a standalone academic exercise (for example, a research paper and a rhetorical analysis) and moves toward designing writing assignments and related classroom activities based on what students will learn from a writing project, including writing skills, reading strategies, process strategies, research methods, ways of using language, and ways of thinking about written texts. Writing assignments should also be flexible and open-ended enough that students have choices as readers and writers in working toward demonstrating their learning for the course.

Backward design (Wiggins and McTighe 1998) can provide useful strategies for designing individual writing projects in addition to an entire course. In a backward design approach to creating writing assignments, instructors—individually or collectively with colleagues—start with the learning goals they want or expect students to develop by the end of the course. They then develop an end-of-semester assignment or activity that brings together learning from across a course and gives students an opportunity to demonstrate their overall learning. For example, instructors or writing programs may use portfolios (Reynolds and Davis 2013; Suskie 2018), general education ePortfolio pages (Yancey 2019), or student reflections (Yancey 1998) for the final assignment.

After determining how to assess students' overall course learning, instructors who use a backward design process identify and design major writing projects for the course, starting with the most complex assignment that builds on earlier learning in the course. They move backward through the course in reverse chronological order to identify earlier writing projects that lay a foundation for helping students work toward the later projects that focus on more challenging student learning goals. As part of designing each writing project, the instructor thinks through strategies for assessing student learning and aligning each assignment with the course's student learning goals. In the next stage of the course design process, instructors break down major writing projects into smaller process activities that students engage in during class, online, or outside of class as they work toward completing each project. The instructor also thinks through strategies for monitoring and assessing student learning for the purpose of providing feedback, evaluating and making adjustments to teaching (Suskie 2018), and helping students learn about their own development as college readers and writers. Course design steps, questions, and examples are outlined in table 2.2.

The most important part of designing writing assignments is determining how to assess student learning. *Assessment of student learning* is essential for determining whether the components of a writing course individually and collectively support students' literacy development. Frequent early assessment activities help instructors determine whether students are successfully transitioning to the expectations and learning environment for the course. Typically, early assessments are low-stakes or non-graded ways for an instructor to get a sense of students' overall needs in a particular course section as well as the unique needs of individual learners as readers

Table 2.2. Example of a writing assignment design process

Course Design Step	Reflection Questions	Examples
1. Find and review required program-level course learning outcomes	What do students need to be able to do and demonstrate by the end of the course? What are the expectations for student learning that apply to all course sections?	Synthesize ideas from a variety of written sources; evaluate the credibility of sources and their relevance to the writer's task, purpose, and audience
2. Optional: identify and record individual instructor learning goals for students	Based on your experience teaching the course and working with the student communities your institution serves, what additional learning outcomes will help students become successful college readers and writers? What learning outcomes will help you close educational opportunity gaps for your students?	Adapt strategies for critical reading based on the audience, purpose, and genre of a text; examine texts to determine what they reveal about cultural assumptions and attitudes toward language diversity
3. Identify the general types of learning activities that will provide students with the opportunity to demonstrate and help you determine whether students have achieved the learning goals of the course	How will you know whether students have made progress toward achieving the goals of the course? What types of evidence of student learning will help you assess students' literacy development and provide students with feedback?	Reading assignments; reading discussions; writing process activities; writing workshops; low-stakes reflections
4. Design the last assignment in the course	What do students need to demonstrate by the end of the course to help you assess their learning and evaluate your own teaching? What types of learning activities will help students bring together their learning from across the course?	Essay reflecting on learning; writing portfolio; ePortfolio page; informal reflection; self-assessment on literacy development

continued on next page

and writers, and they can include in-class activities as well as submitted assignments (Angelo and Cross 1993). Examples of early course assessments include student reflections on their literacy experiences, short written responses to the first writing assignment, and discussions that ask students to share their thinking about reading, writing, or literacy experiences. Instructors who use early course learning activities to monitor students' progress can draw from those assessments to adapt their curricular plans based on the thinking, reading and writing strategies, and literacy experiences that shape students' transitions to first-year college writing.

Subsequent assessment activities normally focus on monitoring students' incremental literacy development across a course as they

Table 2.2—continued

Course Design Step	Reflection Questions	Examples
5. Work backward through the course to design each of the major writing projects, starting with the final project and ending with the first project	What major writing projects will help students demonstrate the learning goals of the course? What projects will help students apply and practice fundamental strategies for college reading and writing? What writing projects will help close educational opportunity gaps for your students?	Primary research project on writing or literacy communities; analysis essay exploring rhetorical strategies used for a website selected by the student writer; database research project that explores a literacy issue selected by the students through multiple sources
6. Determine transparent and equitable methods for assessing learning for each writing project	How will you know whether students have achieved the learning goals for each project? What are the most equitable strategies you can use for assessing each project? How can you use assessment practices to ensure that all students have an opportunity to succeed in the course?	Essay rubric based on learning outcomes; completion checklist for writing process activities; student reflective note or other self-assessment
7. Break down each large project into smaller learning activities	What reading and writing skills and strategies do students need to practice in multiple ways across a course? When and how do you need to create low-stakes opportunities for students to demonstrate their learning and receive feedback?	Group discussion on thesis statements; in-class writing about a source for a writing project; workshop for using databases to find and evaluate research sources
8. Determine equitable and transparent ways to assess students' literacy development across the course	When and how should you assess student learning and provide formative feedback for in-class and take-home activities? What types of feedback will help students achieve the learning goals for both the course and each writing project? When and how do you need to assess students' literacy development to improve and adjust my teaching practices?	Informal in-class feedback on writing process work; whole class peer review for thesis statements; assessments of low-stakes responses to readings; discussions about what is and isn't clear about assignments

engage in increasingly more challenging and complex literacy tasks. Assessments of student learning during a writing course typically include submitted major writing projects, which instructors use to determine the extent to which students are on track to achieve program-level learning outcomes for the course—including key goals that prepare students for the next course in the writing program sequence. However, the most important assessment activities that take place during a course are those that focus on processes and strategies for reading comprehension, critical reading, writing, research, and other types of literacy tasks.

Process-based assessment activities create opportunities for students to apply and practice learning about literacy while also helping an instructor self-assess, monitor, and adjust their teaching strategies. They also create a clear and systematic way for instructors to provide students with feedback on their learning and for students to learn how to give each other feedback. Examples include regular in-class instructor and peer feedback as part of structured writing workshops, informal evaluation of students' submitted writing process work and responses to readings, discussions during scheduled one-on-one writing conferences, and class discussions that help students identify their successes and challenges in working toward achieving the goals of the course and their own learning goals.[2] Each of these types of assessment activities is most effective when specifically designed to assess student learning. In other words, the course activities are created intentionally to help students practice and demonstrate their progress toward developing the learning strategies required for achieving the goals of the course.

The NCTE (2018) position statement "Literacy Assessment" states that assessment should be "meaningful to the learner." For that reason, equitable and inclusive assessment activities also provide students with opportunities to identify, monitor, reflect on, and self-assess their own literacy goals through both writing and discussion activities. Instructors can also strategically ask students to provide feedback on their experiences in the course through informal notes to the instructor, reflection assignments, and online surveys. These types of assessment activities help an instructor focus a course not only on program-level goals but also on what students would like to do in a course based on their own literacy needs and educational goals. It's important to use a variety of different measures of reflective activities across a course that give students the flexibility to think about their literacy development and then make adjustments to their goals, priorities, and learning strategies.

At the end of the course, assessing student learning typically focuses on assigning a course grade. Instructors usually assess a final project that helps students bring together their learning from across the course through a portfolio, a reflection, or an assessable writing project. The final assignment in a course affords instructors opportunities to provide each student with individual encouragement, respond to writing from

---

2. Read Angelo and Cross (1993) for examples of strategies for incorporating assessment into classroom learning activities.

the perspective of a reader, and offer feedback on strategies from the final project that an individual student can apply to the next writing course. The end of a course is also the most important time for an instructor to critically self-assess their own progress as a literacy educator. Carefully assessing students' work for the final assignment helps an instructor identify where and how to make adjustments in a course to improve student learning, provide learning support, and make changes to assignments. Instructors can then create an action plan or a to-do list for revising the course. Instructors also need to pay close attention to students who didn't complete the course or achieve their own stated learning goals. Critical reflection can help an instructor identify and adjust parts of the course that created barriers to student learning or that reinforced opportunity gaps for some students.

Grading is sometimes the most important part of assessment for students and sometimes the only part of assessment that is visible to learners. However, attaching a value to students' work through a grade doesn't necessarily result in actual assessment of student learning if the practices used for grading aren't connected to student learning goals. In other words, some grades can be labels placed on students' experiences in a course without actually evaluating what a student learned and did. Inequities in grading often occur when the practices for grading aren't transparent to students (Feldman 2019), when students are evaluated on criteria that are different from what they were taught and practiced in a course (which is sometimes the case for writing assessment based on grammar and style), and when grading standards are achievable by only some and not all students.

Alternative ways of grading can sometimes be reproductions of existing hierarchies that create opportunity gaps for students if they don't result in feedback for students or assessment that improves teaching and learning. Examples of assessment methods in writing studies that move away from traditional grading include specifications grading (Nilson 2015), ungrading (Blum 2020), and labor-based contract grading (Carillo 2021; Inoue 2019). Using these methods for grading doesn't remove an instructor's responsibility to assess student learning by monitoring students' progress toward achieving course goals, providing individualized feedback, and engaging in self-reflection to evaluate and improve a course.

Stage 3: Planning Student Learning Experiences
In the final stage of backward course design, instructors plan out the learning activities, instruction, and resources they will provide to support

students in achieving and demonstrating learning (Wiggins and McTighe 1998). Even instructors who are required to use a program syllabus and assignments normally have considerable autonomy over this part of the course development process. Carefully designed learning experiences help students successfully complete each interrelated component of the course while also connecting learning to their individual educational and personal literacy goals. In this stage of the course design process, instructors work toward creating significant learning experiences (Fink 2013) that will help students develop as college readers and writers.

Intentionally planning course activities around learning support is one of the most effective ways to design an equitable and inclusive writing course that helps all students do their best learning and achieve the goals of the course. *Scaffolding* in instruction and course design means breaking down a larger project into small, short learning activities. Each activity focuses on at least one course learning outcome and helps students work toward completing the major assignment in incremental steps. Examples of scaffolding in a writing course include mini-lessons on writing studies concepts connected to a larger project, discussions about reading assignments used as sources in writing projects, workshops that focus on a writing strategy, and discussions that encourage students to share their in-progress writing. Scaffolding can also include short, low-stakes assessment activities that provide students with opportunities for individualized feedback before submitting a project for a grade. Effective scaffolding helps inexperienced college readers and writers develop literacy strategies required for successfully completing first-year writing and preparing for other writing courses.

Another key part of planning for learning support is purposeful *sequencing*, which is the process of purposefully organizing scaffolded assignments in a strategic order that supports student learning. It includes scheduling and pacing activities to keep students on track to successfully complete course units and major projects. Sequencing can also refer to the strategies instructors use to arrange assignments and activities across an entire course to help students develop increasingly complex academic and disciplinary literacy skills. This creates a course structure in which learning activities and writing projects are interconnected, with student learning building on previous activities, as illustrated in table 2.3.

Activities for this type of writing project would typically be sequenced and scheduled over a month or more of a full-semester writing course. The instructor would use each activity as an opportunity to monitor student learning and make adjustments to course planning and instruction. Table 2.4 sketches out the types of learning experiences instructors

Table 2.3. Example of scaffolding and sequencing for a project

Activity	Learning Purpose
Introductory in-class discussion and online instructions	To introduce the project, learning goals, research methods required for successfully completing the project
Small group in-class or online brainstorming discussion	To help students understand the assignment requirements; to generate ideas for their project and search terms
Guided hands-on library database practice in class or online video activities	To help students develop proficiency in using library tools to find credible sources; to provide individualized support with finding sources
Take-home activity or online discussion	To help students find, read, and evaluate research sources, using the research strategies practiced in class
Small group or whole class citation activity	To help students create a working bibliography; to help students choose and practice using a documentation style
Small group or whole class reporting	To help students report on and discuss their research findings; to teach and discuss strategies for incorporating secondary research into an essay; to help students learn from other students' research
Direct instruction and low-stakes in-class or online writing practice	To help students identify and use strategies for incorporating research sources into a writing project
Essay planning workshop	To provide students with feedback on their essay planning and in-progress writing (often with students at varying stages of the process); to help students learn about the varied ways writers plan for and structure essays
Essay draft workshop	To provide students with feedback on a draft; to help students learn to read and respond to the work of other writers
In-class or online micro-revision activity	To give students support with revising a targeted part of a writing project; to model effective strategies for revision
Reflection on learning from the project (standalone assignment or part of a portfolio)	To help students identify and articulate their learning from the project; to help students reflect on and trace their own development as college writers

might include in a first-year writing course to help students achieve learning goals and develop as college readers and writers.

DRAWING FROM DISCIPLINARY PRINCIPLES FOR FIRST-YEAR WRITING COURSE DESIGN

A key component of equitable and inclusive teaching in any field of study is designing courses around disciplinary concepts and skills that support students' learning in that discipline and prepare them to take

Table 2.4. Example of building support around learning goals

Types of Learning Support	Examples of Learning Experiences	Critical Reflection Questions
Direct instruction	Classroom lessons Online learning pages Discussions	What foundational knowledge do students need to understand and apply to achieve each learning outcome?
Support for transitioning to college learning	Course orientation activities Technology orientation Discussions about learning	What do students in my teaching context need to know about expectations for college learning in my course and on my campus?
Reading activities	Assigned texts Reading activities Written responses to texts Feedback on reading	What types of reading assignments help students achieve course learning outcomes? What scaffolded experiences with reading do students need to have to successfully complete writing projects and the course?
Writing process activities	Writing process activities Low-stakes writing Instructor feedback Instructor conferences Online writing workshops In-person writing workshops	What activities will break down a longer writing project into smaller parts of a process? What kinds of activities will help students develop and adapt flexible writing processes?
Research activities	Library resources orientation Project management activities Research process activities Reading activities for sources	What activities will help students learn about expectations for college research? What activities help students develop and adapt research processes for differing purposes?
Collaborative learning experiences	Peer review In-class discussions Online discussions Collaborative projects	What activities will help students develop strategies and processes for working with other readers and writers?
Self-assessments/ reflections	Notes to introduce writing Reflective discussions Low-stakes reflections Requests for feedback Midterm reflections Final reflection essays Portfolio reflections	What activities will help students learn how to monitor and assess their own literacy development? What teaching strategies help students identify their own needs as readers and writers?
Access to external resources	Online learning resources Writing center collaboration Access to additional campus services Technology support	When and how can I help students learn how to access institutional resources that will help them succeed in the course and stay in college?

subsequent courses in the same discipline and apply college learning to real-life contexts outside of school. In particular, introductory courses like first-year writing need to lay a foundation for future learning in the field, provide students with opportunities to practice the literacy skills that help them move from novice to expert (Sommers and Saltz 2004), and help them begin to have experiences with ways of thinking that support students in applying their learning to their lives both inside and outside of school. For that reason, effective writing courses need to be grounded in foundational disciplinary knowledge that supports students' transitions to college literacy and learning.

The CCCC position statement "Principles for the Postsecondary Teaching of Writing" (2015) provides instructors with a starting point for identifying what to teach and emphasize in a writing course by outlining eight guiding disciplinary principles for "sound writing instruction" that instructors and writing programs can use as a framework for designing their courses:

1. Emphasizes the rhetorical nature of writing
2. Considers the needs of real audiences
3. Recognizes writing as a social act
4. Enables students to analyze and practice with a variety of genres
5. Recognizes writing processes as iterative and complex
6. Depends upon frequent, timely, and context-specific feedback from an experienced postsecondary instructor
7. Emphasizes relationships between writing and technologies
8. Supports learning, engagement, and critical thinking across the curriculum.

The position statement also lists "enabling conditions" that help instructors teach effective writing courses:

- Provides students with the support necessary to achieve their goals
- Extends from a knowledge of theories of writing
- Is provided by instructors with reasonable and equitable working conditions
- Is assessed through a collaborative effort that focuses on student learning within and beyond writing courses.

The position statement (CCCC 2015) provides examples of different types of disciplinary knowledge instructors can draw from to critically reflect on their own teaching practices and to develop student learning goals, writing assignments, and learning activities.

Instructors can also develop their own guiding principles in consultation with colleagues to reflect the literacy and learning needs of the students within their local teaching contexts. In our own teaching, we also add the following guiding principles for effective writing instruction to the CCCC list:

- Adapts course content, teaching strategies, assignments, and feedback to a local teaching context and needs of students in a course
- Designs courses to support students from varied social, cultural, linguistic, and educational backgrounds
- Connects reading and writing activities to support postsecondary literacy development within the context of an institution and its student populations
- Provides students with individualized feedback for both reading and writing
- Uses multiple measures to assess the effectiveness of teaching, including equity and inclusion
- Adapts teaching strategies to differing modalities of instruction.

The chapters in the second section of this book explain how to incorporate disciplinary principles and other foundational writing studies concepts into a course through a threshold concepts framework that emphasizes disciplinary knowledge and teaching strategies that support learning and literacy development for first-year college readers and writers.

EQUITABLE AND INCLUSIVE TEACHING CONCEPTS FOR FURTHER STUDY

As we close this chapter, we think it's important to highlight key concepts that provide college writing instructors with a theoretical and practical foundation for effective, equitable, and inclusive teaching. These concepts can offer instructors a starting point for identifying how they might improve their learning about teaching through further study and professional development. They can also help instructors participate in faculty development activities and conversations about equitable and inclusive teaching with faculty on their campuses from other disciplines. Some of these terms may be familiar to instructors who have a formal background in diversity, equity, inclusion, and social justice. However, even instructors with a solid theoretical background need to be able to identify practical strategies for applying equity-minded principles to their work as college teachers.

The following terms are helpful for understanding and assessing the role of equity in the work of a college literacy educator.

Positionality is a theoretical concept for explaining how an individual's cultural and social identity shapes their power, social position, biases, and perceptions (Hearn 2012; Ortiz et al. 2018). Positionality influences teaching and working conditions for every college writing instructor. Examples include interactions with students, social privileges based on educational attainment and professional status, perspectives on students and learning, access to power within an institution and the profession, and perspectives on disciplinary issues and professional conversations. Writing instructors who are used to thinking about positionality as researchers and as graduate students may need to shift their thinking to identify and critically reflect on how positionality influences their work as teachers.

Social privilege is a theoretical concept that describes the benefits and advantages some people have access to based on one part of their cultural or social identities or both (for example, race, gender, sexual orientation, class). Identifying and analyzing privilege is one way of accounting for inequities in higher education that disproportionately affect students from some groups and communities. Students and colleagues can enjoy some privileges in one part of their lives while experiencing inequities and a lack of privilege in other areas. Creating equitable writing courses requires instructors to recognize how their own social privileges shape their attitudes about teaching and learning (Barnett 2013), as well as how students' social privileges—or a lack of them—influence a classroom or online learning environment and students' available educational resources. Instructors also need to consider how privilege shapes the institutions in which they work, including which communities have access to or are excluded from higher education within their teaching contexts.

Intersectionality refers specifically to discrimination and injustices some individuals experience based on overlapping parts of their social and cultural identities (Mitchell, Simmons, and Greyerbiehl 2014; Runyan 2018). They often face forms of bias, discrimination, and inequities that differ from the experiences of people who do not have those same intersectional identities. Legal scholar Kimberlé Crenshaw (2015), who developed the concept in 1989, described her work as an "attempt to make feminism, anti-racist activism, and anti-discrimination law do what [she] thought they should—highlight the multiple avenues through which racial and gender oppression were experienced so that the problems would be easier to discuss and understand." Intersectionality for college students can refer both to (a) how a student experiences a course, learning environment, and campus because of intersectional identities and (b) how others perceive and treat the student. Equity-minded writing instructors work toward understanding how intersectionality shapes the higher education experiences of their students and colleagues.

Implicit or unconscious biases are assumptions, beliefs, attitudes, and preconceived opinions that aren't part of an individual's conscious awareness (Staats, Capatosto, Tenney, and Mamo 2017). The Kirwan Institute for the Study of Race and Ethnicity (2012) explains that "these biases, which encompass both favorable and unfavorable assessments, are activated involuntarily and without an individual's awareness or intentional control. Residing deep in the subconscious, these biases are different from known biases that individuals may choose to conceal for the purposes of social and/or political correctness. Rather, implicit biases are not accessible through introspection." Everyone has unconscious biases, which are shaped by an individual's cultural and social experiences. Equity-minded college writing instructors need to work to identify how their own biases and assumptions affect their attitudes toward students, their thinking about learning, their beliefs about literacy development, and their thinking about what defines a "good student" and "good writing."

Culturally responsive teaching is a term developed by Geneva Gay to describe an approach to teaching that draws on students' cultural knowledge and prior experiences to make learning relevant to those from diverse social and cultural backgrounds. Gay (2018, 32) explains that "a very different pedagogical paradigm is needed to improve the performance of underachieving students from various ethnic groups—one that teaches to and through their personal and cultural strengths, their intellectual capabilities, and their prior accomplishments." Gloria Ladson-Billings (1995, 2021) coined a similar term, *culturally relevant teaching*, which focuses on strategies that affirm students' cultural identities while supporting their learning. Culturally relevant teaching enhances learning by drawing on students' cultural strengths and reference points (Chávez and Longerbeam 2016; Hammond 2014). *Culturally sustaining teaching* is another closely related term for describing approaches to education that affirm and maintain students' cultural, linguistic, and racial identities with a focus on equity, access, and accountability for the communities an institution serves (Alim and Paris 2017).

Stereotype threat is a concept developed by Claude M. Steele and Joshua Aronson, which Steele (1997, 614) describes as "the social-psychological threat that arises when one is in a situation or doing something for which a negative stereotype applies." Steele's (2010) research on students suggests that an individual's performance and behavior can be affected by the threat of not doing well because of a negative stereotype. Fear or anxiety connected to negative stereotypes about a cultural or social group can result in students' underperforming in college courses, including when the stereotype is not clearly stated in a situation. *Impostor phenomenon* is a related concept for describing how even accomplished people can doubt their own abilities and feel like frauds. Stereotype threat and impostor phenomenon make learning challenging for students (Cisco 2020) and contribute to the feeling that they don't belong in college.

Microaggressions are subtle or indirect forms of discrimination and bias. In their book *Microaggressions in Everyday Life*, Derald Wing Sue and Lisa Beth Spanierman (2020, 8) provide this definition: "Microaggressions are verbal and nonverbal interpersonal exchanges in which a perpetrator causes harm to a target, whether intended or unintended. These brief and commonplace indignities communicate hostile, derogatory, and/or negative slights to the target." They further explain that "microaggressions theory values the target's perception in identifying harm, as perpetrators often are unaware that they have engaged in an exchange that demeans the target" (8). Microaggressions create a hostile learning environment for students.

Antiracist pedagogy means using teaching strategies that actively resist racism. Antiracist literacy educators recognize that racism in students' prior educational experiences and current life circumstances creates inequities in higher education, and they take action to reduce barriers for students who experience discrimination, bias, and educational inequities because of their race. They also critically reflect on their own teaching practices and make a commitment to change the culture of their classrooms, online learning environments, and campuses. Antiracist pedagogy can also include directly teaching students about racism (Brookfield 2018) and using teaching strategies to help students develop racial literacy (Sealey-Ruiz 2021).

A *teacher-scholar* is a college instructor who is fully engaged in a discipline as both a researcher and an educator. George Kuh, Daniel Chen, and Thomas F. Nelson Laird (2007) describe the characteristics of a teacher-scholar: "Teacher-scholars are committed to high-quality undergraduate education, pursue an active program of research and scholarship, and are presumed to enliven and enrich their teaching and the student experience by incorporating insights from their own research into their instructional activities, student advising, and related work." Effective teaching is as much or more of a priority for teacher-scholars as are research and publication. From our perspective, engaging fully in the work of a teacher-scholar and integrating disciplinary scholarship with knowledge about evidence-based teaching practices and proficiency in college teaching is a key part of becoming an equity-minded writing instructor. Creating conditions for effective learning requires a career-long commitment to engagement in a profession, ongoing work to apply and adapt disciplinary learning to teaching, and continual critical reflection.

QUESTIONS FOR REFLECTION AND DISCUSSION: PRACTICES FOR TEACHING EFFECTIVE AND EQUITABLE WRITING COURSES

1. How can backward design support student learning in your writing course?
2. What are your current plans for assessing student learning and providing feedback to students? How are they related to providing grades for course credit? How can you make the feedback and assessment approach you use more equitable?
3. Consider table 2.4 "Example of Building Learning Support around Learning Outcomes." What types of learning experiences might you add to your course(s) to help students achieve learning outcomes?
4. How do you use scaffolding and sequencing in your course? How might you revise or add additional scaffolding and sequencing to improve student learning?
5. At the end of this chapter, we asked you to review several disciplinary concepts that can help provide a foundation for equitable and inclusive teaching. Select one or two of these concepts and consider how you might apply them to your educational environment.

3
THINKING LIKE A WRITER
Translating Threshold Concepts in Writing Studies to the Classroom

This chapter explains how threshold concepts in writing studies inform the theoretical approach and evidence-based practices in this book. We begin by reviewing the evolving definition of first-year writing within the disciplinary research of writing studies and the interrelated components of its outcomes, curriculum, and pedagogy. We then provide an overview of threshold concept research and what it offers academic disciplines and writing studies. Then we introduce a framework of threshold concepts for first-year writing that support students' development of "thinking like a writer" and ways of knowing in writing studies.

As a near-universal requirement for students, first-year writing (FYW) has to balance core disciplinary principles alongside responsiveness and evolution. Complicating this tension, FYW teachers have varying degrees of expertise and experience with writing studies as a discipline. Some may be graduate students working in a writing program during graduate school, some may be non-tenure-track faculty, and some are professors with training in literary study or creative writing; still others are full-time faculty who are also pursuing advanced degrees in the field or teaching in multiple disciplines (in many two-year colleges). A relatively small percentage of FYW teachers are writing studies scholars who are engaged in disciplinary research and writing.[1] At the same time, students enter FYW courses with years of literacy education in the K–12 setting and

---

1. Though Emily Isaacs's *Writing at the State U* (2018), a study of 106 universities, does not include two-year colleges, it provides some sense of the composition of the staffing of first-year writing instructors. In terms of *who teaches FYW most*, respondents indicated that in 27.4 percent of programs, tenure-track faculty taught the majority of FYW courses, while 18.9 percent identified indefinitely renewable lecturers as the majority of instructors. The greatest number, 35.8 percent, noted that adjunct faculty taught the most FYW courses (with 8.4% identifying full-time lecturers on limited terms and the same number, 8.4% identifying graduate students as teaching most of their first-year writing courses).

with varying levels of familiarity with the kinds of rhetorical skills and genres they will be asked to tackle in college courses. Writing studies interest in more carefully describing and naming the moves, genres, and skills is evidenced by the professional documents that have been produced, endorsed, and circulated over the last two decades, including the *Framework for Success in Postsecondary Writing* (Council of Writing Program Administrators, National Council of Teachers of English, and National Writing Project 2011), and the *Writing Program Administration Outcomes Statement for First-Year Composition* (Council of Writing Program Administrators 2014). The field of writing studies and its members grapple with articulating what can often feel like a slippery target.

As a result, it is often difficult for writing programs and their instructors to make connections between what is happening in the field and what should be happening in the classroom. What, exactly, should students know and be able to do after they complete a course or a course sequence in college composition? Just as the field has struggled to define postsecondary writing, so have instructors struggled to understand appropriate starting points for their composition courses, despite national efforts such as the Common Core State Standards (2022) to articulate benchmarks for graduating seniors in English language arts. What concepts and experiences can instructors expect students to have? Even students who arrive with a conventional secondary education have diverse experiences with literacy. Beyond the disciplinary canon of studies on selective student populations, what do typical, nontraditional, linguistically diverse, first-generation, or structurally disadvantaged students already know? Finally, how can instructors engage with students whose experiences are not necessarily aligned with the expectations of postsecondary writing classrooms?

Using threshold concepts as a framework, disciplinary texts like *Naming What We Know* (Adler-Kassner and Wardle 2015) have successfully identified and explained many of the concepts writing studies scholars agree are central to disciplinary knowledge and understanding. However, using these concepts alone for teaching FYW, designing curriculum, or informing pedagogical approaches re-creates the gap between disciplinary scholars and writing (and often teaching) novices in FYW classrooms. Instead, *Reaching All Writers* builds on existing knowledge about threshold concepts to distill "entry-level" understandings for FYW. The goal of using threshold concepts in this way is to offer a flexible and adaptable framework for FYW teachers, a framework that can be customized to instructors' backgrounds and priorities and can apply to a wide range of postsecondary teaching and learning contexts.

Likewise, this theoretical framework of disciplinary threshold concepts provides a foundation for understanding the disciplinary research and reasoning that informs equitable, student-centered approaches for a diverse range of learning needs of first-year writers.

DISCIPLINARY STATEMENTS AND FIRST-YEAR WRITING

The research and practices in this book emerge from disciplinary knowledge established through national organizations' position statements about writing. Most notably, the *WPA Outcomes Statement for First-Year Composition* (Council of Writing Program Administrators 2014) identifies five broad areas of skill/proficiency that students should develop in a first-year writing course or courses:

- Rhetorical knowledge
- Critical reading, writing, and thinking
- Processes
- Knowledge of conventions
- Composing in electronic environments

The outcomes statement has tremendous national reach and serves, for many writing programs, as a foundation for their own program goals and outcomes.[2] The outcomes continue to be updated and revised as disciplinary knowledge evolves. However, as an outcomes-based document, the statement focuses more on skills and less on the conceptual knowledge required for developing those skills and building a foundational knowledge of writing. Likewise, while there is much disciplinary consensus about these skills, there is little advice about how teachers can effectively teach and assess them.

The *Framework for Success in Postsecondary Writing*, by contrast, supplements outcomes and skills with what it terms habits of mind or dispositions. These dispositions reflect what the authors explain as "experiences with writing, reading, and critical analysis that serve as foundations for writing in college-level, credit-bearing courses. Students who come to college writing with these habits of mind and these experiences will be well positioned to meet the writing challenges in the full spectrum of academic courses and later in their careers" (Council of Writing Program Administrators, National Council of Teachers of English, and National Writing Project 2011, 2). The *Framework* lists and

---

2. For example, in Isaacs's (2018) study of first-year writing programs at 106 public universities 22.6 percent of them had adopted the *WPA Outcomes Statement for First-Year Writing.*

defines eight habits of mind that help students work toward achieving success in postsecondary writing: curiosity, openness, engagement, creativity, persistence, responsibility, flexibility, and metacognition. The *Framework* serves particularly useful functions for first-year writers, though as habits of mind rather than ways of seeing, thinking, and knowing from a disciplinary perspective, they can be challenging to relate to teaching or assessment of student learning. Furthermore, it could be argued that they are not discipline-specific and that these habits of mind apply across a range of fields of study. Last, multiple critiques have been offered about the potential of the *Framework* to reify white supremacist and neoliberal cultural logics and other imposed habits of mind that are neither desirable nor sustainable for some student populations and instructors (Gross and Alexander 2016; Inoue 2019; Kalish et al. 2019).

One goal of this text is to synthesize and contextualize the *Framework* and other foundational texts in ways that are classroom-adaptable and that account for the literacy experiences of diverse student populations—for example, committed to fulfilling the principles in the National Council of Teachers of English's (NCTE) "Students' Right to Their Own Language" position statement (1974; affirmed 2014) and "Definition of Literacy in a Digital Age" statement (2019). Other important documents include updates to NCTE's position statement, "Teaching Composition: A Position Statement" (1984), to create an updated disciplinary set of practices for teaching writing. The revised position statement, "Understanding and Teaching Writing: Guiding Principles" (2018b), draws from the threshold concepts in *Naming What We Know* (Adler-Kassner and Wardle 2015) to outline a basic set of principles for "teaching written language to students, largely in school, from pre-kindergarten through graduate school."

NCTE's (2018b) "Guiding Principles" for teaching writing at every level of education intersect with the research about how threshold concepts help first-year writers develop new ways of thinking about writing. For example, "Principle 2.1: Everyone is a writer" provides a clear overview of how to help student writers develop an understanding of the threshold concept that writing can be taught and learned: "Everyone has the capacity to write. Writers are not static. They develop skills and enhance their writing skills throughout their writing lives; thus, writers grow continually. Becoming a better writer requires practice. The more writers write, the more familiar it becomes" (Adler-Kassner, Baca, and Fredricksen 2014). Throughout part 2 of *Reaching All Writers*, we address the ways instructors can draw from the "Guiding Principles" and other disciplinary statements that provide a framework for teaching writing and strategies for helping students cross thresholds into a more advanced understanding of writing and their own work as writers.

Foundational documents from disciplinary professional organizations serve as important points of reference for new instructors of writing because they reflect the consensus of research and experience in the field. Indeed, they have guided the research we have conducted on student learning that informs this text. And while they continue to evolve to reflect new disciplinary knowledge about teaching and student learning, they frequently provide standards without processes, directions, or context—the very things instructors who are working through different teaching challenges need. The first-year writing threshold concepts we identify and unpack in part 2 of this book articulate specific and adaptable strategies to support teachers in their syllabus construction, curriculum development, policy setting, instructional activities, and assessment values.

IT'S ALL CONNECTED: OUTCOMES, CURRICULUM, PEDAGOGY, ASSESSMENT, AND STUDENT LEARNING

So many experiences in our collective professional lives have identified the gaps and often misalignment among the various component parts of course and program outcomes, curriculum, instructional policies and practices, assessment of student learning, and the learning needs of all students. These misalignments create barriers for students and instructors alike. The goal of *Reaching All Writers* is to provide a framework that will help instructors make effective connections among four key components of effective instruction and course design: outcomes, assessment and evidence of student learning, curriculum, and pedagogy.

Outcomes: In writing courses in particular, outcomes are often framed as proficiencies writers will demonstrate by the end of the course. Outcomes might also be framed as competencies or other specific skills because they describe an aggregate of student learning defined by programs, courses, instructors, and professional organizations. For example, the *WPA Outcomes Statement for First-Year Composition* spells out outcomes underneath categories like Critical Reading, Thinking, and Composing, or "Processes" that are further broken down. For example, in Rhetorical Knowledge, a student would be expected to "learn and use key rhetorical concepts through analyzing and composing a variety of texts," while in the category Processes, a student writer would be expected to "develop flexible strategies for reading, drafting, reviewing, collaborating, revising, rewriting, rereading, and editing" (Council of Writing Program Administrators 2014). Determining how and whether a student has achieved that learning outcome is part of assessment.

Assessment and Evidence of Student Learning: Connecting course content, instructional approaches, and learning outcomes requires each instructor (or sometimes programs) to answer the question, How will we know? Or, what counts as evidence of student learning, and what will *demonstrate* that students have achieved the learning outcome? For writing courses, this might be a specific type of assignment that asks students to do a rhetorical analysis, or it might be a portfolio of assignments that target or demonstrate multiple—or even all—of the outcomes. The principles of backward design (Wiggins and McTighe 1998)—or starting from what students know, do, or understand, as discussed in chapter 2—constitute a framework from which to design subsequent curricular and pedagogical activities that will move students from where they are and toward the learning outcomes for the course.

Curriculum: The curriculum is the sequence of activities, materials, and assignments that will take students from the beginning to the end of the course and also to the achievement of the learning outcomes for the course. While individually created curricula may reflect sets of activities or readings that emerge from personal affinities for those topics or activities, an effective curriculum is a sequence of actions and labor asked of students that can and should move them purposefully toward the learning outcomes provided for instructors or that have been devised by the program or larger supervisory body that may have made determinations about what students "should know" or do after they have completed a writing course or courses in a teaching context. Carefully prepared materials and organization of the learning experience constitute one important connection between outcomes and instruction.

Pedagogy: At some point, all teachers have probably been asked to develop a teaching philosophy, and individual instructors' teaching philosophies can and should drive their pedagogies. Likewise, the pedagogical approaches should reflect the expertise and experience of the instructors and help students move through the course in a scaffolded way so their knowledge, skills, and demonstration of both happen in ways that are useful to students, show intentionality of design, and provide and produce meaningful results for both learners and teachers.

Building the connections among all of these components requires a set of choices and a level of expertise that takes time for new teachers to accumulate or for experienced teachers to adjust. One of the tools for making these connections visible is threshold concepts, what have been described as "ways of seeing, thinking, and knowing" or what the experts in teaching and learning who have studied them have called "portals" that unlock key ways of seeing within a discipline that makes it possible for a learner to progress to new levels of knowledge, dispositions, or habits of mind.

THRESHOLD CONCEPTS IN ACADEMIC DISCIPLINES

Both Scholarship of Teaching and Learning (SOTL) research and recent disciplinary discussions in writing studies have focused on threshold concepts, but this is still a relatively new way of writing about disciplinary knowledge. Threshold concepts represent disciplinary ways of thinking and knowing that are unique among specialized communities of knowledge and frequently capture the unstated values, practices, and epistemologies of disciplinary practice. SOTL research on disciplinary learning like David Pace and Joan Middendorf (2004) and Jan H. F. Meyer and Ray Land's (2003) working paper represent some of the earliest non-disciplinary scholarship about threshold concepts. Meyer and Land (2003, 1) establish what has remained the most commonly reproduced definition:

> A threshold concept can be considered as akin to a portal, opening up a new and previously inaccessible way of thinking about something. It represents a transformed way of understanding, or interpreting, or viewing something without which the learner cannot progress. As a consequence of comprehending a threshold concept there may thus be a transformed internal view of subject matter, subject landscape, or even worldview. This transformation may be sudden or it may be protracted over a considerable period of time, with the transition to understanding proving troublesome. Such a transformed view or landscape may represent how people "think" in a particular discipline, or how they perceive.

The "threshold" is a metaphor for unlocking, crossing, and inhabiting a new knowledge space, making a new (disciplinary) way of understanding possible for learners. If learners do not acquire this understanding, they cannot move toward a more advanced understanding. For some disciplines, this can be phrased as a single word or short phrase, such as "complex numbers" in engineering, "variation" in biology, or "intersectionality" in women's and gender studies; threshold concepts can also be a complete sentence like "Writing is a social and rhetorical activity." Among scholars, it is generally agreed that threshold concepts are transformative, troublesome, irreversible, integrative, bounded, discursive, and reconstitutive (Cousin 2006). In other words, students find them difficult to understand, but once they do, the threshold concepts transform their disciplinary understanding in a way that is integrated into other ways of knowing in the discipline, replaces previous ways of knowing, and even impacts students' ways of discussing disciplinary concepts. As Land and colleagues (2006, 195) explain: "It has long been a matter of concern to teachers in higher education why certain students 'get stuck' at particular points in the curriculum whilst others grasp concepts with comparative ease . . . what might teachers do in relation to the design and teaching of their courses that might help students overcome such barriers to their learning."

Further scholarship explores what happens to students who develop a liminal understanding or "a suspended state of partial understanding" of a threshold concept (Land, Meyer, and Baillie 2010, ii). Related research that uses student "bottlenecks" to identify foundational or threshold concepts includes the Decoding the Disciplines approach, which takes as its foundational practice the identification of learning bottlenecks and naming mental tasks that can help students navigate those bottlenecks (Middendorf and Pace 2004; Middendorf and Shopkow 2017). All of this research has informed the way disciplinary researchers have worked to identify threshold concepts for writing studies.

The initial theorizing of threshold concepts has evolved in defining their features, complicating how we identify them, and exploring methods for coming to disciplinary consensus. There does not seem to be a single "authorized" way to decide what constitute definitive threshold concepts in a field. In fact, that work has typically taken place independent of disciplinary organizations or position statements and has emerged from a range of methodologies. Essentially, initial forays into the definitional process typically follow a model that includes professional consensus building, including dialogue among expert teacher-scholars in the field. This process allows disciplinary experts to draw from both their own experience of having crossed those thresholds and their direct observation of student roadblocks or bottlenecks. That being said, threshold concepts seem to emerge organically—through scholarly publications and articles and from professional networks—rather than from disciplinary organizations or groups (Barradell and Peseta 2014; Walker 2013).

Because it is not a fully developed area of the field, research on how threshold concepts relate to practical questions like assessing student learning is still emerging. However, as instructional and professional development tools, threshold concepts stand on their own even without a firm decision on these questions. Distilling knowledge that explains "what we know" about writing and the transfer of knowledge in writing—in the case of our discipline—has been an effort decades in the making, and articulating threshold concepts in writing studies at an increasingly refined level is one way to continue to build that toolkit for writing students and teachers. Threshold concepts help instructors connect their classroom choices to the core disciplinary concepts for the purpose of helping students move past learning roadblocks and barriers that are common as writers develop.

HOW WRITING STUDIES HAS GRAPPLED WITH DISCIPLINARY CONCEPTS FOR FIRST-YEAR WRITING

Composition and rhetoric, or writing studies, has evolved as a discipline over the last fifty years, as discussed in multiple landmark books (Berlin 1987; North 1987; Ruiz and Sanchez 2016; Skinnell 2016). During this time, a robust history of inquiry and foundation of knowledge in the discipline have been built, drawn in part from literary studies, rhetoric, and communication. As the field has evolved, one of the central emphases of disciplinary work has been on the first-year writing class and attention to the goal of the core part of the curriculum—one of the few classes required of students in US higher education (Ritter 2009). Our own research into threshold concepts as well as our experiences mentoring new instructors in writing instruction suggest that both students and instructors benefit from organizing writing classes conceptually (Hassel and Launius 2017; Phillips et al. 2019). The roots of this conceptual work build on the scholarship about disciplinary knowledge that has given rise to the Teaching for Transfer and Writing about Writing approaches to FYW and informed disciplinary and professional statements like the *WPA Outcomes Statement for First-Year Composition*.

Some of the earliest disciplinary research related to threshold concepts is drawn from Anne Beaufort's *College Writing and Beyond: A New Framework for University Writing Instruction* (2007), which moved theories about writing transfer and disciplinary knowledge forward. Beaufort identifies overlapping domains of knowledge that shape a writer's approach to and experience of writing. The "Elon Statement on Writing Transfer" offers this definition: "Writing transfer is the phenomenon in which new and unfamiliar writing tasks are approached through the application, remixing or integration of previous knowledge, skills, strategies, and dispositions" (Elon University Center for Engaged Learning 2013, 4). Best known is Beaufort's model identifying how distinct areas of knowledge overlap in any given writing task and work together as discourse community knowledge (figure 3.1).

Figure 3.1. Anne Beaufort's conceptual model from College Writing and Beyond

Extending some of Beaufort's work is Stuart Blythe (2016), who offers a kind of synthesis of prior transfer work, sketching out distinct models of transfer that offer schema for describing the ways writers adapt to new situations. Scholars concerned with transfer—for example, Elizabeth Wardle (2007), Dana Lynn Driscoll and Jennifer Wells (2012), Hassel and Giordano (2009), Mark Blaauw-Hara (2015), Howard Tinberg (2015b), and Sonja Andrus, Sharon Mitchler, and Howard Tinberg (2019)—have all contributed to the development of theories about transfer in writing studies.

Teaching for Transfer (TFT) as a pedagogical approach in writing studies emerged from Beaufort's theoretical foundation, spearheaded by Kathleen Blake Yancey and colleagues (Yancey et al. 2018, 2019). Using research from learning theory by D. N. Perkins and Gavriel Solomon (1988) on the more theoretical work about how writers transfer knowledge, Yancey, Liane Robertson, and Kara Taczak worked toward developing a curriculum of *teaching for transfer* for specific use in writing studies research and classrooms; their 2014 *Writing across Contexts: Transfer, Composition, and Sites of Writing* grounds its arguments in theories of transfer and small study of writing students using a TFT curriculum that requires three key components: a focus on writing concepts, use of reflective practice, and students' development of a theory of writing. The TFT approach has been subsequently scaled and tested in other institutional contexts and levels of college writing coursework, including basic writing, advanced writing, and TA prep courses and in two-year colleges and regional comprehensives. More recently, Andrus, Mitchler, and Tinberg (2019) aim to translate the TFT curriculum for a basic writing or first-year writing curriculum at open-admissions institutions. TFT's structure—around three interconnected principles—includes writing studies vocabulary or terminology (e.g., audience, genre, rhetorical situation, reflection), which is related to but not the same as the threshold concepts approach. In this way, TFT draws from some similar impulses as threshold concepts and Writing about Writing, blending the elements of shared rhetorical terminology with specific pedagogical practices and a common assignment/writing task (developing a personal theory of writing).

Developing alongside TFT is the Writing about Writing (WAW) pedagogical approach to curriculum, which emerged from an article by Douglas Downs and Elizabeth Wardle (2007). Downs and Wardle first advanced the notion of a curriculum focused on a writing studies–based curriculum, a related curricular and theoretical model to TFT and threshold concepts. WAW has evolved from the earliest model by Downs and Wardle as introducing students to disciplinary research and scholarship from rhetoric and composition (launched in the 2007 article in a sophomore-level writing course at a public research university), including independent student research projects focused on a writing studies line of inquiry. WAW has since more explicitly connected its learning project to threshold concepts, with Wardle as a co-editor of the *Naming What We Know: Threshold Concepts of Writing Studies* collection (Adler-Kassner and Wardle 2015) and the *Writing about Writing* textbook (Wardle and Downs 2020), which blends both critical and content instruction. Section I offers what Wardle and Downs see as the threshold concepts in writing studies, revised with an emphasis on an undergraduate student audience:

- Writing is impacted by prior experiences.
- Writing helps people make meaning and get things done, but there are always constraints.
- "Good" writing is dependent on writers, readers, situation, technology, and use.
- Writing is a process, all writers have more to learn, and writing is not perfectible.

The rest of the volume assembles foundational and current scholarship in writing studies so that the curriculum approach of *Writing about Writing* is supported with original research in the field.

We see all these approaches as valuable efforts to make visible the disciplinary knowledge that equips writers to approach a range of tasks and equips instructors with pedagogical content knowledge to structure courses in ways that will foster the greatest growth in student writers—whether first-year writing, advanced writing courses, writing studio (or other forms of co-requisite support), or basic writing. We are interested specifically in the threshold concepts approach to writing because we believe it creates a central focus that is part dispositional (like the *Framework for Success in Postsecondary Writing*) and part outcomes-focused (like the WPA Outcomes Statement) while giving instructors a touchstone for course design that is flexible enough to operate across programs and courses.

Threshold concepts also provide a way to articulate disciplinary learning in ways that do not use a student deficit model or prescribe overly narrow definitions. For example, the WPA Outcomes Statement creates a set of academic standards that work for most FYW programs. However, recent scholarship has also aimed to gather data on and theorize about whether the current standards and principles that have or are guiding writing program administration in the field are, in fact, effective. For example, research findings by Gabrielle Garcia de Mueller and Iris Ruiz (2017, 35), in their qualitative study on the relationship between race and writing program administration, revealed that

> Most participants in the study affirmed that POC [people of color] students are not served well in support, pedagogy, or assessment and that there are no clear administrative strategies to combat racism and colorism; however, participants also suggested that they believe they are doing well in the classroom. Some participants were able to point to concrete methods they were using in their courses to address race, while others rated their strategies as effective but their narrative explanations conflicted with their self-rating. This conflict seems to suggest that some white/Caucasian instructors might have good intentions but lack the critical knowledge to address race and ethnicity.

Even more troubling, "White respondents think diversity strategies are effective while in general POC do not, creating a clear disconnect in perceptions about how successful writing programs address differing levels of racial and linguistic diversity of their student bodies" (Garcia de Mueller and Ruiz 2017, 36). We emphasize this point because, as instructors who have taught for decades in open-admission two-year colleges, we know that 40 percent of all college students attend such institutions and that students of color across racial groups are more likely to attend two-year colleges. Culturally responsive and social justice–oriented curricula are essential areas of attention in higher education broadly but are of greater impact and importance in two-year colleges and less selective four-year universities. While these may be the majority of students at access institutions, they inhabit every writing classroom. An effective curriculum must be designed to reflect the needs of all writers.

Many instructors will benefit from substantially rethinking their teaching approaches and learning goals to adjust to new student populations, and this may happen recursively and continually. This especially includes part-time and adjunct instructors and all instructors who graduate from a graduate teaching position to any position at a different type of institution that is not a research-focused university (private liberal arts, open-admission, or two-year college; regional comprehensives). For most writing instructors, it is unlikely that the curriculum, instruction, or assessment practices they cultivated during their graduate training can be directly mapped onto the new site of learning and it *is* likely that the resources, context, and material support will be different from their graduate education experiences.

Threshold concepts in first-year writing can be a professional development resource, a touchstone for reflection, and a set of core principles for new instructors and instructors in training who are building the pedagogical framework that will support their professional growth across stages of their careers. They can also serve as a text that supports instructors as they transition to new writing ecologies and need to adjust their teaching approaches to a new set of students, colleagues, program goals, and institutional contexts.

THRESHOLD CONCEPTS IN WRITING STUDIES

The work that first addressed threshold concepts in writing studies is Linda Adler-Kassner, John Majewski, and Damian Koshnick's "The Value of Troublesome Knowledge: Transfer and Threshold Concepts in Writing and History" (2012), which reported on research across two general education courses: one in writing, and another in history. The publication of *Naming What We Know: Threshold Concepts of Writing Studies* (Adler-Kassner and Wardle 2015) extended this work to begin sketching out what these transformative and troublesome concepts are within the field, broadly. The largest umbrella concept is "Writing Is an Activity and a Subject of Study," with five sub-concepts delineated (and supporting concepts that elaborate on those five):

1. Writing is a social and rhetorical activity.
2. Writing speaks to situations through recognizable forms.
3. Writing enacts and creates identities and ideologies.
4. All writers have more to learn.
5. Writing is (also always) a cognitive activity.

These five concepts are intended to launch the scholarly conversation about the disciplinary knowledge that cuts across levels and subfields.

Recognizing that writing studies is an expansive discipline that encompasses a wide range of areas of inquiry, methodologies, and academic program areas, our own interest—like that of many researchers and teachers who use threshold concepts—is as a way of seeing, thinking, and knowing. That is, threshold concepts are intended to capture the way disciplinary experts approach the subjects and objects of inquiry in the field. So, for most fields, the introductory course in that discipline serves as a gateway to that field—Sociology 101, Political Science 101, and the like—and also serves the particular function within the college curriculum of giving students a foundation in the disciplinary lenses. What helped Downs and Wardle's Writing about Writing curriculum gain so much traction in writing studies in the early 2000s is the recognition that first-year writing courses often focused less on helping students develop a disciplinary foundation in how writing works (the bailiwick of composition and rhetoric for several decades) and more on the process and practices of writing. Adler-Kassner (2012, 132) as well, in an address to the Council of Writing Program Administrators, framed this as a "no vampires policy," asserting that "writing classes, especially first year classes, must absolutely and always be grounded in Writing Studies, must always be about the study of writing" (as opposed to selected themes individual instructors center their courses around).

This shift in thinking about what happens in the college curriculum and how it is connected to the functions and epistemologies of the discipline underpins the goals of *Reaching All Writers*. To a certain extent, the threshold concepts outlined in *Naming What We Know* (Adler-Kassner and Wardle 2015) focus on advanced disciplinary literacy (Shanahan and Shanahan 2012) in writing studies—or the knowledge and ways of thinking within the discipline that experts and advanced learners have developed—in contrast to the more fundamental concepts that can open a portal to new ways of thinking about writing for beginning, novice college writers.

THRESHOLD CONCEPTS FOR FIRST-YEAR WRITERS: "THINKING LIKE A WRITER"

We first introduced a version of threshold concepts for first-year writing courses in the chapter "Thinking Like a Writer: Threshold Concepts and First-Year Writers in Open-Admissions Classrooms" (Philipps et al. 2019) in *(Re)Considering What We Know: Learning Thresholds in Writing, Composition, Rhetoric, and Literacy*, edited by Adler-Kassner and Wardle (2019). Intending to distill the key threshold concepts *Naming What We Know* (Adler-Kassner and Wardle 2015) brought to scholars in 2015, we adapt a set of streamlined concepts that are a tool for instructors and program administrators. The threshold concepts have emerged from our own systematic research and inquiry into student learning at a two-year institution, our previous published work, and the scholarly conversations initiated by *Naming What We Know* and *(Re)Considering What We Know*.

In part 2 of *Reaching All Writers*, we explore the following threshold concepts (see table 3.1) that lay a disciplinary foundation for diverse first-year college writers and transform their thinking about how writing works—primarily writing processes and writing instruction. The wording of these concepts purposefully uses language that is accessible to first-year college students. However,

Table 3.1. Threshold concepts for first-year writing courses

1. Writing can be taught and learned.
2. Writers write for different purposes and audiences, and often in genres with predictable conventions.
3. Writing processes are individualized, require readers, and require revision.
4. Reading and writing are interconnected activities.
5. Writers make choices about language within cultural and social situations.

the concepts are not designed to be used by instructors in a single lesson or unit. Rather, they are concepts that instructors repeat directly and indirectly throughout a course or an entire writing program through intentional course design, reading activities, process work, and formal writing assignments. By definition, threshold concepts serve as gateways to thinking and learning in a field, and it takes time for students to develop their thinking about threshold concepts and apply and integrate them into their own experiences with literacy.

In part 2, we provide a theoretical overview and rationale for each threshold concept based on relevant scholarship and our own research on student writers at open-admissions, two-year campuses. We describe what students need to know about student learning to teach each concept and what first-year college students need to know about it for their own development as readers and writers. We also provide examples and offer practical teaching suggestions and resources for incorporating each concept into the design of a first-year writing course. Even if an instructor doesn't want to directly discuss threshold concepts in a writing course, the concepts we have identified lay a foundation for designing any writing course around the needs of diverse students and the learning that supports their development as college readers and writers. We view these concepts as a framework for effectively teaching first-year writing courses at any type of institution.

From our research and experience, the first-year writing threshold concepts developed in this book are complementary to the other disciplinary documents that aim to articulate the skills, dispositions, and learning objectives of first-year writing we have referenced in this chapter. However, as faculty with careers spent primarily at open-admissions campuses working with students whose educational pathways may not be well aligned with the different benchmarks for college-level writing, we see an important need for additional tools to help instructors navigate among diverse instructional environments, student populations, and course levels. Furthermore, we see these concepts as an architecture on which to develop curricular, instructional, and assessment practices that are suitable to their local ecologies but also attuned to the national organizational statements about what students should be able to do or habits of mind they should have at the start and end of first-year writing.

In this chapter we have drawn from and distilled disciplinary and SOTL research to explain our theoretical framework for *Reaching All Writers*. Threshold concepts help articulate the disciplinary ways of thinking and knowing that are troublesome for students and that frequently prevent them from making progress with learning. At the same time, threshold concepts are ways of thinking and knowing that are second nature to most disciplinary practitioners in the writing classroom. Our disciplinary threshold concepts reflect the values and assumptions of experiences and skills that instructors have mastered and that are often unconscious components of our teaching practices. By using threshold concepts as a framework for part 2 of *Reaching All Writers*, we hope to allow instructors to examine their disciplinary beliefs and values, unpack the ways our disciplinary understandings inform our teaching, and make stronger and more effective connections among disciplinary outcomes, curriculum, pedagogy, and assessment that support the learning of all students.

QUESTIONS FOR REFLECTION AND DISCUSSION:
THINKING LIKE A WRITER

- What have been the most transformative learning experiences for you as a writer? What aspects of the experiences made them transformative for you?
- What aspects of your own writing and writing process are you (still) working to improve? What practices or resources support you in this work?
- What does "thinking like a writer" mean to you? How are those ideas reflected in your curricular and pedagogical choices about teaching writing?
- Which "Threshold Concepts for FYW" do you consider your teaching strengths? Why?
- What aspects of "Threshold Concepts for FYW" do you recognize as challenges for yourself as a teacher? Why?
- Which "Threshold Concepts for FYW" do you identify as challenges for your students?
- What other barriers or thresholds do your student writers struggle with overcoming or crossing? How are they related to the "Threshold Concepts for FYW"?

PART 2

Threshold Concepts for First-Year Writing

4
WRITING CAN BE TAUGHT AND LEARNED

This chapter provides an overview of the threshold concept writing can be taught and learned and shows how this concept supports an equitable approach to reaching all writers. The chapter begins by reviewing key disciplinary research and professional statements to help instructors connect related writing studies concepts to their own teaching. Reflective prompts and strategies help teachers frame their teaching, feedback, and assessment practices and help students understand that they can learn and grow as college writers.

Writing can be taught and learned is an important threshold concept for helping students develop an awareness of their own capacities for learning and growth as writers, especially those enrolled at community colleges and other access institutions. Students in these environments commonly have challenging prior learning experiences with reading and writing, which makes it important for them to learn that writing is something that can be improved upon through experience and practice. In the 2016 statement "Professional Knowledge for the Teaching of Writing," the National Council of Teachers of English (NCTE) names this principle for effective teaching across all levels of literacy education: "Everyone has the capacity to write; writing can be taught; and teachers can help students become better writers." The idea that everyone can become a successful writer and achieve their own goals for postsecondary literacy is perhaps the most foundational concept for students to learn in first-year writing.

Yet writing anxiety and student mind-sets that they are "not writers" abound in research about composition. Even students who performed well in secondary education often find themselves challenged by new writing tasks they encounter in postsecondary contexts. Jan H. F. Meyer and Ray Land (2006. 23) discuss the moment "when a student for the first time becomes conscious that they are, or are beginning to think like[,] an accountant, chemist, economist, historian, lawyer, mathematician, physician, statistician, and so on." We applied this idea to writing in our chapter in *(Re)considering What We Know* (Adler-Kassner and Wardle 2019): "In our framework, thinking like a writer—not like a writing studies scholar or compositionist but one who is actively engaged in making conscious decisions about writing choices (the beginning of moving toward disciplinary competence)—starts with the students' belief that they can be writers regardless of their past academic experiences" (Phillips et al. 2019, 63–64). Likewise, "thinking like a writer" also starts with instructors believing that all students can develop postsecondary literacies given the opportunity, support, and resources they need. *Writing can be taught and learned*, on its surface, may seem like an easily achievable concept to grasp and master. However, it can be very difficult for students to unlearn what they have been told about writing and their own work as writers. Likewise, it can be challenging for instructors to change and to continue to adjust expectations about the knowledge and experiences students bring with them to the classroom, as well as how students' social, cultural, linguistic, and educational backgrounds affect classroom learning.

DISCIPLINARY RESEARCH ABOUT HOW WRITING IS TAUGHT AND LEARNED

The threshold concepts introduced in *Naming What We Know* (Adler-Kassner and Wardle 2015), such as "writing is not natural," "writing is informed by prior experience," and "all writers have more to learn," speak to the constructed and iterative nature of writing instruction and writer development. Disciplinary statements also emphasize the developmental nature of literacy education from K–12 to postsecondary environments. For example, the NCTE (2018b) defines writing as the social and rhetorical act of creating composed knowledge, which takes place across a variety of contexts and purposes. The NCTE outlines key principles for understanding writing, including "everyone is a writer" and "writers bring multiliteracies, and they bring cultural and linguistic assets to whatever they do." These principles acknowledge that acts of composition are universal but individualized, and writers are continually learning and relearning as they enter new rhetorical contexts (National Council of Teachers of English 2018b). The implications of the concept *writing can be taught and learned* are paramount for writing instructors: without internalizing, actualizing, and continually committing to this principle, no writing teacher can be effective in their classroom.

College writing instructors sometimes need to challenge their own beliefs about how writing is learned, including the idea that students' writing abilities are fixed or fully developed or that proficient college writing is possible only for students who have had eighteen years of a particular kind of literacy instruction. It is easy for instructors to forget that every writer, no matter their skill or experience, will struggle with new or different writing tasks. For example, as Chris Anson (2016) documents, even exceptionally skilled writers can become struggling writers when faced with a new task, situation, purpose, and audience. Anson writes that "we must see every writer, and every context into which the writer moves, as a unique amalgam of situation and human agency. Some contexts may appear at first glance to involve relatively 'near-transfer' situations (who would think that an accomplished writer would flounder over a simple summary?) but on closer inquiry surprise us with their complexity" (540). Anson ultimately reveals that the subject of his case study is, in fact, Anson himself, reframed as "Martin" in a type of autoethnography. What the self-study reveals is how often expert writers encounter new genres and audiences that are challenging and that writing teachers (who are often rather skilled and accomplished communicators themselves) would do well to recall such a situation as they instruct first-year students who are encountering multiple new academic genres for the first time.

All writers grapple with unfamiliar or more complex writing tasks, and recognizing this fundamental truth is essential for effective writing instruction. The NCTE statement "Professional Knowledge for the Teaching of Writing" (2016) acknowledges the ways learning about writing and growth in writing is individual and varies based on literacy contexts: "Students are different from one another, and they bring to the experience of writing a wide range of resources and strengths. At the same time, any writer can be positioned as weak, struggling, or incompetent. All writers need to learn multiple strategies and modalities to compensate for moments when they feel stuck or defeated, to get on with the business of composing."

Disciplinary research demonstrates that although members of our profession may know that students are unique and that they must learn new writing strategies for unfamiliar situations, new and experienced instructors alike may struggle to apply an intellectual and theoretical understanding of this reality to specific classes and students. For example, research by Dylan Dryer (2012, 441) shows that new graduate teaching assistants participating in his study "consolidated their authority as teachers by refusing those students the very particular struggles, conflicts, and tensions that illustrate that academic writing is less a 'standard' and more a messy agglomeration of sociohistorical and material conventions." Put another way, new writing instructors had difficulty transferring their self-awareness of how they adapted their understanding of academic writing to their first-year writing students' struggles. Because teachers have often mastered or forgotten the struggles with writing they experienced as students, they frequently overlook students' challenges. Instructors also might not recognize the writing challenges of students whose educational experiences are different from their own.

Likewise, many new instructors may believe that a knowledge of and adherence to a perceived standard written English is an important way to teach writing or maintain academic rigor. However, research on error has consistently shown that (a) error is often more a matter of individual reader judgment than a factual reality (Williams 1981); (b) student writers do not make more or substantially different errors than previous generations of students (Lunsford and Lunsford 2008); and (c) many writing teachers themselves are not proficient at differentiating among error, usage, grammar, and other linguistic terminology (Hartwell 1985). Instructors may believe they are evaluating grammar mistakes when, in fact, they are expressing a usage preference. These examples from scholarship illustrate that writing instructors can have preconceptions about teaching and learning that they need to examine and unlearn and that even writing instructors need to learn more about writing and how language works.

WHAT INSTRUCTORS NEED TO KNOW ABOUT EXPECTATIONS AND STUDENT LEARNING

Teacher expectations for college student writing and learning can be rooted in inequities and enculturation that make educators implicitly biased toward some students (Staats, Capatosto, Tenney, and Mamo 2017). It is important to examine these expectations and assumptions to uncover and address these biases, especially since some students have been experiencing them constantly throughout their literacy development. Racism, classism, linguistic bias, ethnocentrism, sexism, ableism, heterosexism, and other forms of discrimination have profoundly shaped many students' literacy experiences. Structural inequities in education and communities contribute to students' attitudes toward literacy and beliefs about their own capabilities as readers and writers. Some students arrive at college not knowing that writing can be learned because their prior learning experiences have taught them that teachers do not value their work as writers. Some students have internal beliefs about themselves as writers based on their educational and linguistic experiences. Others experience stereotype threat (Steele 2010) that creates fear and anxiety about academic performance and writing because of negative stereotypes connected to one or more parts of their cultural, social, and linguistic identities. Literacy educators need to critically reflect over time about how their own words and behaviors toward students can create, reinforce, and maintain students' negative thinking about their work as writers and their potential as college learners.

The inequities many college students experience are often not apparent to an instructor. Financial and social inequities limit students' access to resources more privileged students enjoy in their K–12 education for developing literacy skills, using technology, and learning strategies that would normally provide them with a smooth transition to postsecondary reading and writing. This includes (but isn't limited to) students from rural or underfunded schools, learners with inconsistent and interrupted schooling, students with undiagnosed or inadequately accommodated disabilities, those who have experienced violence and trauma, and learners who have had or continue to have housing and food insecurity. They experience daily realities that influence their mental, emotional, and material resources. Students' material realities and privileges (or lack of them) often shape their transitions to college reading, writing, and learning. Instructors' beliefs about and expectations for students' postsecondary literacy development need to account for the inequities and material realities their own students experience.

The questions in table 4.1 are helpful for guiding reflection on the relationship between literacy experiences and beliefs about student learning.

The answers to these questions and other related experiences might influence approaches to course design, writing assignments, learning activities, and assessment practices. Assumptions about student learning might lead to biases, reinforce restrictive thinking about writing and learning, and make it difficult for students to develop the belief that they can grow as writers. In contrast, the answers to these questions may reveal effective strategies for helping students develop confidence in their own learning processes and work as writers.

Teachers of writing need to directly address their beliefs about writing and other forms of literacy as teachable skills, especially because the history of writing has frequently positioned writing as a talent associated with good writing products and therefore with good writers. Jill Parrott (2017) tackles the myth that "Some People Are Just Born Good Writers." As Parrott writes: "Some of this idea—that writing is a

Table 4.1. Reflect on experiences and assumptions about learning and writing

Reflect on Your Own Experiences	Think about Student Learning
What was your emotional relationship with reading and writing as a student? How did you feel about assigned reading and writing tasks? What sorts of emotions did you experience before, during, and after the process of working on writing projects?	How has the emotional relationship you had with reading and writing as a student influenced your beliefs and assumptions about what college students should be able to know and do as readers and writers?
Which cultural, social, linguistic, and educational experiences in your life shaped how you learned about writing and how you developed as a writer?	What are your assumptions about how students learn about writing? What are your assumptions about the learning experiences that help students develop as writers?
What do you consider to be "good" or "effective" writing? How is your thinking about what is and isn't good writing shaped by your own cultural, social, racial, and linguistic identities?	How do your perceptions of "good" or "effective" writing influence your behaviors as an instructor? How do those perceptions influence the tone and words you use to discuss writing with students?
Consider the material conditions of your own literacy learning, including access to financial and educational resources. How did those conditions shape your literacy development and experiences with learning?	In what ways do your students' material conditions shape their literacy development and learning? What changes do you need to make to your teaching to adjust your expectations to account for how your students' material realities affect their experiences with learning?
When you were a college student, what did you do when you needed help with writing tasks? When you didn't ask for help, what were the constraints preventing you from getting help? To what extent were your experiences with asking for help as a student shaped by your cultural background and social privileges (or a lack of them)?	What are your assumptions about what students should do when they need help with writing? How do those assumptions influence the ways you do and do not provide support to individual students in your courses? What cultural and social factors have influenced your assumptions about how and when students should ask for help with writing?

talent set in stone—can be directly correlated to the history of writing instruction itself," observing that throughout the history of writing instruction in educational institutions, "language instruction came to be about nation building (compelling members of various communities to adopt and adapt to a homogeneous identity wrought through linguistic conformity)" (71).

As disciplinary scholars have demonstrated, much of early writing instruction in the late nineteenth and early twentieth centuries, particularly at the college level, focused exclusively on products and on the conformity of those written products to a standardized set of language norms. Parrott (2017, 72) notes that this "reinforced the idea of writing as a skill some people just had. Essays were usually written once and were done, for good or ill. Students who were privileged to be of the right socioeconomic, national, or ethnic background already wrote to the university's standards because they were part of the group in power who set the standards."[1] Both the process and the product of literacy development are linked to cultural norms and values that privilege dominant groups. Literacy education that reaches all writers must acknowledge and address cultural assumptions and social privileges that shape perceptions about what is and is not good writing.

Teachers of writing should also consider how their pedagogies, course design, and assessment practices help students believe they can learn and grow as writers. For example, courses that emphasize instructor assessment for a single written product (typically an academic essay) may reinforce the idea that student writers who are part of a dominant social, cultural, or linguistic group (or who have adopted the language and writing standards of those groups) have a kind of natural talent or gift for meeting the standards of an external authority—a teacher, department, or institution. These types of beliefs about writers can reinforce, as Parrott (2017, 74) says, "the deeply held idea in the collective psyche that only some lucky people are good writers. If a person thinks their writing ability is stuck in place, improvement is incredibly difficult, further solidifying as a self-fulfilling prophecy the belief that they are a hopeless cause." As writing instructors, we can continually interrogate our participation in practices that perpetuate the belief that some students can't or won't become good writers because that assumption is rooted in discrimination and bias based on race, linguistic background, disabilities, educational background, social class, and other aspects of college students' social and cultural identities.

We see a direct connection between inequitable teaching practices that harm students from historically excluded communities in higher education and the politicized myth that some students shouldn't go to college because they can't be taught or aren't talented enough. Like many writing instructors, we have witnessed the lasting impact of these harmful beliefs when our community college students tell us that previous teachers or authority figures have directly told them that they aren't "good at writing" or aren't "college material." We've also taught (and in some cases have been) students who believe they have very little to learn in writing courses because they think they already know everything there is to know about writing, since prior educational experiences have reinforced the idea that they are "better" or more talented writers than other students. Students' literacy development at all levels of educational experience with writing is limited if they don't believe they can learn more about writing.

---

[1]. See also Berlin 1988; Brereton 1995; Douglas 1976; Horner 1990; Kynard 2013; Ritter 2009.

To support students in their learning, instructors can provide opportunities for them to draft and produce writing that is imperfect, that allows them to make mistakes, that encourages them to take risks, and that provides feedback on how to improve and to try again. Disciplinary scholarship, including *Naming What We Know: Threshold Concepts of Writing Studies* (Adler-Kassner and Wardle 2015) and *Failure Pedagogies: Learning and Unlearning What It Means to Fail* (Carr and Micciche 2020), has addressed the role of "failure" and acknowledged that failure can be socially constructed, disproportionately attributed to particular literacy performances, and emotionally difficult. Allison Carr and Laura Micciche (2020, 3) note that "failure is always modified by body experience and forms of knowing" and, importantly, that "failure has been wittingly and unwittingly appropriated to advantage those most likely to be insulated from risks associated with pursuing or embracing failure as a creative strategy." In this way, it's important for instructors to be aware of advice to "try, try again" or else feedback to students that is focused on correcting errors and finding problems may reinforce previous negative experiences students have had as writers.

It is also important to acknowledge that failure (perceived or experienced) can be profoundly demoralizing and disheartening for students and that repeated exposure to negative feedback from writing teachers can signal to students that they are unlikely to achieve their own or others' goals for their writing. We have heard instructors and colleagues express the belief that, for example, assigning low grades to student texts they view as flawed or unsuccessful will motivate students to do better on subsequent tasks. In fact, our years of experience (see, for example, self-efficacy research by Albert Bandura [1997]) tell us that such experiences are just as (if not more) likely to lead students to disengage, give up trying, and sometimes drop out of a class or college altogether.

To self-assess how teaching supports the concept that writing can be taught and learned, instructors can reflect on the ways learning activities and assessments reveal assumptions about literacy development and all students' capabilities for growth. The questions and examples in table 4.2 provide an opportunity to evaluate how components of first writing courses do or do not provide opportunities for students to understand and apply the concept that writing can be taught and learned.

Each component of a writing course may reflect beliefs and assumptions about how writing is taught and learned. Reflection on and purposeful engagement with the theory and practice of the concept *writing can be taught and learned* is fundamental to effective, equitable, and inclusive teaching.

Table 4.2. Reflect on components of your writing course

Teaching Practices	Critical Reflection Questions	Examples of Course Components
Providing opportunities for revision	What opportunities do students have to revise and improve their writing? How might you incorporate scaffolded and carefully sequenced opportunities for students to learn from revision?	Structured revision of essays Portfolio or ePortfolio Assignment resubmissions Required revision(s) Optional revision(s) No opportunities for revisions
Developing assessment activities	What writing is assessed in your course? What is the relationship between assessment and grading? How might you incorporate more opportunities for low-stakes and non-graded writing?	Individual writing assignments (essays) Drafts Outlines Portfolios or ePortfolios Group work Discussions
Using texts as models and examples of writing	What examples of "good writing" are your students being provided or encountering in the classroom? To what extent are your examples of writing relevant to first-year college students? How might you use a more inclusive array of writing to broaden students' understanding of "good writing"?	Scholarly writing Other published writing Digital texts Textbook examples Student academic writing Student non-academic writing
Teaching students about how language works	How do you teach students about usage, grammar, and style? What strategies do you use to address students' negative preconceptions about error? How do you help students develop flexible strategies for adapting their language usage to varying communication contexts?	Social and cultural nature of language usage Descriptive and prescriptive grammar Grammatical choices Meaning of words in context Style choices Adapting formatting to context Adapting documentation styles to academic fields of study
Assessing writing conventions	To what extent do you value writing conventions when you assess student work? What does your approach to teaching conventions reveal about your beliefs and assumptions about writing and student learning? What adjustments do you need to make to how you approach conventions to create equitable learning opportunities for students from diverse cultural, educational, and linguistic backgrounds?	Directly grading students on conventions Focusing on conventions for revised drafts Providing recommended resources/support Including as a minor component of course grade Treating as a secondary/lower-order concern Considering relevancy to a student's goals
Creating opportunities for feedback	What opportunities do students have to receive feedback to improve their writing? What do the types of feedback you provide suggest about your assumptions about how students develop as writers? What adjustments do you need to make to your feedback practices to help students understand that writing can be learned?	Final revised drafts Complete rough drafts In-progress work Project development and planning In-class support Peer response activities In-class writing workshops

WHAT STUDENTS NEED TO KNOW ABOUT *WRITING CAN BE TAUGHT AND LEARNED*

As disciplinary texts discuss, students' prior literacy experiences and their beliefs and feelings about those experiences inform their understanding of themselves as writers. In *Naming What We Know*, experts' version of this disciplinary understanding is "all writers have more to learn" (Adler-Kassner and Wardle 2015, 59). In *(Re)Considering What We Know* (Adler-Kassner and Wardle 2019), we show that to foster that expertise, novice students—which includes the wide range of learners found in first-year writing—should be taught how to think about themselves as writers and learn the ways writers think of writing before they can develop this understanding independently. Students benefit from hearing directly about how writing can be taught and learned. More important, perhaps, they need to see how this concept can apply specifically to them as learners, to what they are being asked to do in the classroom, and to how they are being asked to do it.

In table 4.3, we identify four key concepts students need to know to envision their possibilities as writers and help them develop their thinking about the threshold concept *writing can be taught and learned*.

Students can come to understand that learning writing is possible if these concepts are integrated into a course repeatedly, using a variety of methods. For example, instructors can discuss concepts directly, include them in learning activities, and show them to students by demonstrating these ideas in practice. By integrating clear messages about how writing development occurs into course design, students should be able to see how learning activities, writing assessments, and feedback reflect the concept that writing can be learned—regardless of students' background, experiences, or current circumstance.

DESIGNING COURSES THAT HELP STUDENTS LEARN ABOUT THEMSELVES AS WRITERS

Effective writing course design helps students discover that *all* learning about writing and literacy contributes to their own growth as writers. Students sometimes have preconceived and narrowly focused ideas about what learning is in a writing course, or they have difficulty making connections between writing studies concepts taught in a course and their own experiences as writers. They need structured activities that help them reflect on their own literacy development and scaffolded support that helps them recognize that learning is different for different people and different projects. Instructors can create opportunities for

Table 4.3. Student-centered concepts for learning about writing

Concept	Learning Purpose
1. Writing is not an innate gift or quality but a skill that can be developed with practice and feedback.	Students with anxiety about their own writing need support to identify how their own learning goals, purposeful writing process tasks, and responses to feedback can help them develop as writers.
2. Expectations of and feelings about writing are influenced by prior learning and experiences—both positively and negatively. Writing anxiety is common and can vary across writing situations and contexts.	College students come with a wide range of prior experiences that make it more or less possible for them to engage in new types of learning; for example, students who have received primarily critical feedback on issues of sentence-level correctness may have one kind of anxiety, while students who have struggled to adapt to new writing tasks may have anxiety around starting unfamiliar types of writing projects.
3. Writers do not produce perfectly formed pieces of work on the first draft—writing products are the result of a process.	Students need to understand that writing processes are messy and that writing failures or setbacks are a normal part of effective writing processes. They can make choices and take actions as part of their writing processes to work through challenges in a writing project.
4. There are multiple strategies for writing, composing, revising, and editing that can help develop writing for different audiences and purposes. Engaging and participating in different writing strategies is how students learn to become effective writers.	There is no single linear writing (or research) process that works for every student, and students benefit when they are taught multiple strategies to use throughout the process of approaching a writing task; expert writers make choices about how to deploy different process tools and strategies depending on their unique needs and the specific demands of the task and situation.

students to learn about writing and themselves as writers through three different types of guided learning.

Big picture learning about writing focuses on concepts, strategies, and tools for writing that can help all first-year college students learn about how writing, revision, and written language work. This includes the threshold concepts we cover in this book and other parts of a course that give students a vocabulary for talking about reading, writing, research, language, and literacy. Big picture learning also includes activities that give students guided practice and experiences with working through a writing project, making choices as a writer based on the audience and purpose of a literacy task, providing feedback, and responding to feedback through revision. These parts of a course support learning about writing for every student in the class regardless of their prior experiences with writing.

Small picture learning about writing is our way of thinking about the learning that happens incrementally in a course as students learn from their experiences with literacy when they complete learning activities and short writing tasks. This type of learning helps students apply and adapt conceptual learning about writing to literacy tasks while also expanding their learning about writing as they gain insights and strategies from their own experiences as writers and readers. For example, the simple act of recognizing that a sentence isn't clear and then revising it for readers is a small learning moment. Another example might be when students are discussing a text together and notice a strategy a writer uses or have an insight about how literacy works. Some students may have difficulty recognizing these learning moments unless they have opportunities to reflect on their work as writers and discuss their learning processes with an instructor and other students. Small picture learning about writing is as essential to students' postsecondary literacy development as is learning about the big picture concepts and strategies that are typically the primary focus of a first-year writing course. Small moments with writing experiences contribute to big picture learning and help students know that they can learn and grow as writers.

Individualized learning about writing refers to the learning each unique student does in first-year writing to transition to college-level writing and achieve their own literacy goals. Effective, equitable, and inclusive first-year writing courses have a course design that intentionally takes into account the reality that college students have widely varying experiences with writing, cultural and linguistic backgrounds, access to educational opportunities and resources, and academic and career goals. They also have unique needs, interests, and perceptions about writing. The design of a writing course needs to provide flexibility with the options students have for completing learning activities, a structured way for students to receive individual support with completing assignments, and individualized feedback. Examples of course design strategies that support individualized learning include planning for incremental and formative feedback at key points across a course, including instructor conferences in a course schedule, and providing varied and targeted online resources to support independent learning.

Instructors can help students develop conceptual knowledge and apply it to their own learning experiences by incorporating learning about writing recursively throughout a course through direct instruction and through learning activities that are intentionally designed to help students develop confidence as writers. Table 4.4 outlines five important course components that help students develop knowledge about the ways writing can be taught and learned: revision, feedback, reflective writing, resources, and policies.

Table 4.4. Developing learning about writing by design

Course Design Component	Purpose	Examples of Teaching Strategies
Revision activities	To help students learn to understand that revising is the most important component of improving as a writer To provide students with practical strategies illustrating the relationship of revising to composition and drafting To show that effective writing processes involve change and revision To confirm that expert writers revise more (not less) than novice writers To emphasize that revision is a crucial *part of* the writing process, not a *failure of* the process	Design courses around portfolios or ePortfolios Assign low-stakes or non-graded revision activities (individual activities, small group work, discussion) Model and discuss examples of revised work Provide direct instruction on specific revision strategies relevant to the writing assignment Give students time in class to make small changes to their work (micro-revisions) and discuss them with the class
Feedback	To provide opportunities for students to use reader and instructor input to improve their work To teach students that all writers learn from reader feedback To help students identify their strengths as college writers from the perspectives of readers To provide students with strategies for revision and for applying learning from their work on a current project to future literacy tasks	Design in-class learning activities around multi-stage writing review and feedback from peers and instructor (e.g., topic, outline, draft, revision) Provide regular informal in-class instructor feedback on in-process work Facilitate online and in-class process workshops Offer in-person and virtual one-on-one instructor conferences
Reflective writing	To help students develop meta-cognition and meta-awareness of their writing products and processes To cultivate students' meta-linguistic knowledge To make visible to readers the composing processes that produced a text To review their writing and identify progress with learning as well as their continued goals for growth	Assign regular low-stakes reflective assignments throughout the course Create reflective writing and discussion activities that help students self-assess meta-cognitive learning Assign author's notes to help students reflect on their writing processes and products Ask students to identify their needs through written requests for feedback included with draft work
Resources and support	To teach students how to access and use resources that provide individual support for reading and writing To affirm that using resources and support is a regular practice of successful and self-directed learners To be assured of their problems or concerns that can be addressed by the instructor, campus, institution, or others	Keep track of resources requested by students Build a resources module in course learning management system; add to it regularly based on student needs and research Devote class time to resources—classroom, institution, campus, or external Remind students that resources are there to be used at all times, not only when students are struggling

Continued on next page

Table 4.4—continued

Course Design Component	Purpose	Examples of Teaching Strategies
Course policies	To align pedagogical and program values with the learning and assessment opportunities students experience To show students that classroom policies are transparent and accessible To assess progress with the course outcomes or assessments related to learning	Include classroom, department, and institutional policies in syllabus, LMS, and course documents Create grading policies focused on student learning and progress with the course outcomes; minimize or eliminate compliance-focused grading (e.g., attendance, lateness) Provide opportunities for students to make up for missed learning

As we have discussed in this chapter, many writers have either been directly taught or indirectly learned the incorrect idea that there is a single, narrow definition of "good writing," especially academic writing. In actuality, there is no single definition of good writing except the extent to which a text meets audience expectations and fulfills a writer's purpose within social and cultural communication contexts. Writing instructors can create opportunities to undo learning and beliefs about writing as an inherent or fixed talent through teaching practices that affirm that everyone has the capacity to learn and grow as a writer. Examples of strategies that explicitly teach students about their own abilities to develop as writers include the teaching strategies listed in table 4.5. In addition to supporting students' growth as writers, each of these strategies also helps instructors create an inclusive learning environment that focuses on student learning and respects the work of all writers.

Strategies for incorporating the way writing can be taught and learned into a first-year writing course also include sequenced, low-stakes (especially non-graded) opportunities to practice writing different types of texts in different ways. The NCTE statement "Professional Knowledge for the Teaching of Writing" (2016) affirms the role of practice in students' literacy development: "Writing instruction must include ample in-class and out-of-class opportunities for writing, including writing in digital spaces, and should involve writing for a variety of purposes and audiences, including audiences beyond the classroom. Teachers need to support students in the development of writing lives, habits, and preferences for life outside school. It is useful for teachers to consider what elements of their curriculum they could imagine students self-sponsoring outside school. Ultimately, those are the activities that will produce more writing." For students at community colleges, open-access

Table 4.5. Teaching strategies that support writing development

Direct instruction	Actively discuss and teach students how bias and discrimination can influence the beliefs and assumptions about writing that students learn from educational experiences
	Clearly communicate to students that your classroom or online learning environment is a community in which the work of all writers will be treated with respect
	Normalize the idea that all students and all writers sometimes need help with completing writing projects; incorporate frequent reminders about campus support services into the course
	Affirm throughout the course that writing processes often entails working through multiple iterations, which is a normal part of the writing process and not a failure of effort
Discussions about examples	Discuss examples of student planning, drafts, and polished work to illustrate how the process for a project evolves over time (with permission); illustrate how writing processes continually move toward meeting the needs of readers and writers
	Discuss examples of student writing that is "good enough" to fulfill the purpose of an academic writing task while still not complying with rigid beliefs about sentence-level errors (with permission)
	Share and discuss examples from the instructor's own in-progress and draft work, including challenges and mistakes
Writing assignments	Assign reflective writing assignments across a course to help students trace and reflect on their development as readers and writers
	Share examples of student work that illustrate how students approached an assignment and writing processes in different ways (with permission)
Other learning activities	Invite former first-year writing students (especially those from the communities represented by the class) to talk with the class about the strategies they used to complete writing process activities and assignments
	Assign students to complete advice for future first-year writing students, such as a letter or crowd-sourced guide to first-year writing to be shared with students the next semester

colleges, and other institutions that serve those who are excluded from institutions with selective admissions standards, opportunities to practice writing include scaffolded learning support from the instructor and other students built into each activity.

ASSESSMENT PRACTICES TO TEACH STUDENTS THAT *WRITING CAN BE LEARNED*

Because the idea that *writing can be taught and learned* is holistic and involves meta-cognition, direct assessment of students' beliefs about writing typically aren't a main component of a composition course (or even a main learning objective expressly related to the course outcomes). At the same time, all of students' learning related to writing is correlated with attitudes and beliefs about writing that are communicated to students through writing assessment practices.

"Writing Assessment: A Position Statement" (reaffirmed in 2022) explains that "writing assessment is useful primarily as a means of improving teaching and learning. The primary purpose of any assessment should govern its design, its implementation, and the generation and dissemination of its results" (Conference on College Composition and Communication 2006). This means instructors need to use assessment practices that help them reflect on and improve their teaching. Assessment in writing courses should directly support student learning about writing and literacy, including helping students apply concepts they have learned in class (or through online instruction), practice using a range of reading and writing strategies, and reflect on their own growth and development as writers. Both the assignments (and other assessment activities) instructors ask students to do and their responses to those assessments are essential parts of teaching students that writing can be learned. Effective and equitable assessment becomes a meaningful learning opportunity, especially for students whose work has been treated in disrespectful ways through rigid grading practices and negative feedback.

How Learning Works (Ambrose et al. 2010) and the NCTE statement on "Professional Knowledge for the Teaching of Writing" (2016) concur about the purpose and effect of feedback. Feedback on student work must take place at points that are process-appropriate. As the NCTE (2016) writes, feedback during the "process of writing—formatively—[is provided] in order to offer timely assistance during the composing process." Likewise, Susan A. Ambrose and her colleagues further break down different types of opportunities to learn and the kinds of feedback that help learners develop proficiency in a skill or disciplinary habit of mind. Deliberate practice, for example, offers students a chance to try out a new skill, and instructional scaffolding supports students' efforts. Formative, targeted, and summative feedback constitute instructor interventions that can direct student efforts in productive ways. For college writers in particular, this strategic type of feedback is essential because so many students are attempting new types of writing practices and unfamiliar genres they have not previously undertaken.

The assessment practices instructors use to grade students' work and provide feedback communicate both stated and implied messages about writing, literacy development, and the value of students' work and experiences as writers. Writing instructors can take proactive steps to help students develop the threshold concept that *writing can be taught and learned* through written feedback, formative in-class and online feedback on in-progress work, and one-on-one teaching in writing conferences. For example, providing positive comments about what students are doing well helps them identify when they have made successful moves as writers that communicate effectively with an audience and fulfill the purpose of a literacy task. Instructors may take it for granted that students can identify how they are successfully applying learning to their writing, but students may not be aware of their own development as postsecondary writers, especially if they have had negative and inflexible comments or low grades on their writing in their prior educational experiences.

Another strategy for helping students think about their own learning as writers is to provide feedback on the choices a student might make for a current writing project while also providing comments that point forward to applying learning to upcoming projects (or at the end of a course, to the next writing course). Effective feedback and assessment practices that help students understand their own learning processes and literacy development take place incrementally across a course in activities that go beyond formal assessment of submitted work, including class discussions, oral and written responses to informal writing, reflective writing activities, conversations with small groups, and online discussion facilitation.

Students are sometimes enculturated to believe that writing can't be taught and learned because of the ways teachers or graders have assessed their writing and provided comments on their work. For that reason, equitable and inclusive first-year writing instructors need to use assessment as a tool for helping students unlearn negative beliefs and assumptions about both writing and the strategies experienced writers use. Feedback that reinforces a deficit approach to student writing is used not only in writing courses but in other disciplines as well, and instructors often resort to correcting errors or negative comments because of their own experiences with receiving feedback as students. This type of feedback is often misaligned with student learning goals in a course.

Table 4.6 gives examples of feedback practices that can create or reinforce the idea that writing ability is innate, fixed, or unchangeable. The chart also provides examples of more inclusive and equitable alternatives that support writing development for students from a range of diverse educational and linguistic backgrounds.

In changing feedback and assessment practices, instructors may need to move away from practices they developed based on the models of assessment they experienced as students, including how instructors responded to their writing. This shift may require an instructor to move away from using feedback to justify or explain a grade, replacing it with feedback that supports student learning and literacy development.

Table 4.6. Strategies for responding to student writing

Student Learning Need	Responses That Reinforce a Deficit Approach to Writing	Responses That Support Literacy Development
Supportive feedback	Writing comments that denigrate the quality of writing or effort of the writer ("You obviously didn't work hard enough on this"; "This writing is sloppy")	Use an inclusive tone and language that respects each writer's work; send messages that encourage positive thinking about growth in writing
Guided feedback	Using restrictive language that limits students' writing choices ("you should," "you must," "I would like you to," "do ____")	Provide specific but flexible suggestions to help the writer develop a targeted area of the text based on strategies they are learning in the course and their requests for feedback
Transparent assessment based on course learning	Requiring, commenting, or assessing students on criteria not discussed or learned in the course	Focus feedback and assessment on learning goals and writing strategies students have been working on in the course and on the goals they self-identify
Help with challenging parts of a text	Telling students to revise or fix part of a text without explaining how or why ("fix your commas")	Give students supportive suggestions for flexible strategies they might use to revise the text or apply learning to a future writing project
Help adapt writing to the purpose of an assignment	Listing factual statements about writing strategies and moves the student didn't use	Provide students with resources and models for learning about adapting writing to the purpose of the assignment
Identify effective writing strategies	Explaining what the instructor likes about the content or the writing	Identify successful strategies and moves the student makes in a text
Student-centered revision strategies	Identifying what the instructor wants from a text as a reader	Provide feedback that cultivates rhetorical awareness and gives options for students to make choices as writers
Support with developing and finishing a writing project	Penalizing incomplete and short drafts	Design scaffolded in-class or online support for completing writing projects that work for students who are at various stages in the process
Flexible strategies for using language	Marking errors on a hard copy or electronic document	Provide feedback based on a student's literacy goals; create structured support for revision and editing
Support with learning citation styles	Grading based on MLA or APA compliance; conflating citation errors and academic plagiarism	Offer low-stakes opportunities to practice using citation styles; provide resources and examples; explain the rhetorical purpose of citation styles
Feedback from peers	Structuring peer review activities to focus mainly on an instructor's expectations or academic conventions; creating a workshop environment that makes students think their objective as a reader is to notice and correct mistakes	Create a flexible workshop structure that helps students respond to each other's work as authentic readers; teach and model how to engage in effective and inclusive peer review

Effective, equitable, and inclusive teaching means using assignments and other assessment activities to strategically create meaningful learning opportunities for students instead of as a way to grade, sort, or place judgment on students' work and academic behaviors. This type of teaching requires critical reflection on assessment practices that might reinforce the inequities some students have experienced in previous writing courses and may continue to experience in other college courses.

Part of teaching students that all writers are capable of learning requires instructors to eliminate assessment practices and activities that create barriers to student learning and course completion. Here are some examples (among many others) of how instructors can self-assess their approaches to assessment, identify inequities, and then create change that results in meaningful learning opportunities for students:

- *Carefully evaluate the purpose of each assessment activity and component of a course grade.* Revise activities that are disconnected from students' literacy development and the goals of a course (or students' own learning goals).
- *Eliminate high-stakes assignments or other assessment activities that account for most of a grade* and replace them with low-stakes process work and ongoing opportunities for revision. For example, quizzes on MLA citation style or comma rules are not connected to students' writing.
- *Identify parts of a course that are challenging for some students;* create learning activities that will help students successfully complete those activities, or eliminate them from the course if they aren't essential for the purpose and goals of the course.
- *Remove high-stakes timed writing and tests that privilege students who have more experience with working within time constraints.* Develop activities that help students demonstrate their learning over time, such as portfolios of student work.
- *Identify course policies that affect grades* (for example, attendance, late work, and makeup work policies). Assess each policy for equity and inclusion. Remove components of grading that are disconnected from the work and learning students do in the course, and seek flexible ways to allow students to show their proficiency with the course material and goals.
- *Eliminate participation points and other grading practices that depend on a subjective judgment of students' academic behaviors or a student's cultural knowledge* of how education works in the United States. Create opportunities for students to engage in low-stakes discussions about writing and classroom or online literacy activities.

In addition to self-assessing and changing teaching practices, helping students understand and believe that all writers are capable of learning and developing sometimes includes creating opportunities for students to write about or explicitly discuss the ways the criteria used to judge their performance in other English courses or classes in other disciplines reinforce educational inequity. This includes analyzing and discussing incorrect ideas about how writing is taught and learned, discriminatory treatment of students' language, restrictive thinking about students' capabilities as writers, and other forms of deficit thinking. A first-year writing course has the potential to become a safe space and a learning environment in which students can develop knowledge and strategies for actively resisting messages from other instructors that question the idea that every writer is capable of learning or that disconnect assessment from learning.

As we conclude this chapter, it's important to note that even though all students are capable of learning about writing and developing as writers, some students require significant support, which may go beyond what an individual instructor can provide in first-year writing. Sometimes instructors need to help some, most, or all of their students access resources that will help them become successful in writing courses. Depending on the instructional context, that help might include a writing center or other learning center, a federally funded Equal Opportunity Center, such as a TRIO program, a disability resource center, a language lab for multilingual students, and other types of academic support resources. The resources available to students will vary, unfortunately, according to the financial resources or public funding that supports student learning at an institution.

Not all students will be able to achieve the student learning goals of a writing program within the time frame of a semester or term. Sometimes students might be misplaced in a course when other options (or even a different program like English as a second language [ESL]) might be a better fit for their learning needs. Some students don't complete a writing course and need to retake it regardless of how the instructor has designed the course, created learning opportunities, and offered individual support. There are a range of reasons why an individual student might not have the resources, time, or mental bandwidth to do work they would otherwise be capable of doing in a first-year writing course—for example, chronic illness, mental health issues, deaths of loved ones, legal issues, caregiver responsibilities, housing and food insecurity, or full-time employment. Even when a student appears to be avoiding writing and not participating in the course, instructors need to shift their thinking away from judgments about students' behaviors to a careful consideration of how systemic inequities, trauma, and often unseen life circumstances can interfere with learning.

Sometimes the students who need the most support with understanding that writing can be learned and that they are capable of developing as writers are the students who aren't doing much writing. The actions a first-year college instructor takes to communicate with and teach students who aren't doing coursework (and who eventually don't finish the course) can make a difference in students' perceptions about whether they might be able to continue their college education at another point in life. Even if students leave and never return to college, they can still have significant learning experiences in a writing course that help them understand their capacities for future learning about writing in their literate lives outside of school.

APPLYING AND CONNECTING
Student Perspectives: Beliefs about Writing and Learning

Two contrasting examples from one of our grant projects (Phillips et al. 2019, 220) show varying levels of understanding of the concept "writing can be taught and learned." In an early-semester self-assessment essay, one writer illustrates how some first-year students have difficulty viewing writing as a skill they can learn and develop over time: "People do not always enjoy writing. Some people can't stand the thought of reading and writing. People will do whatever they can to try and avoid doing either of these tasks. Some think that writing and reading is too much. They don't want to take the time to do either of them. I am most defiantly [*sic*] one of those people. My past experiences have not been very pleasant. I have not had fun with my past writing. For that reason I do not enjoy it now, and don't look forward to it." Another student with different prior literacy experiences demonstrated an understanding of this threshold concept early in the course: "Writing is an activity that can never be perfected. For all the different styles of writing, there is always room for improvement and growth" (219).

Reflecting on Student Perspectives
- What can you learn about teaching college writing from these two contrasting student perspectives on writing?
- What teaching strategies and learning activities might you use to help students like the first writer develop an understanding that writing can be taught and learned?
- How might you support students in applying knowledge about this threshold concept to their own work and processes as writers?

Instructor Perspectives: Adapting to Student Challenges and Needs

In Holly and Joanne's research study "First-Year in the Two-Year," instructors shared their experiences with adapting to their first year of teaching literacy courses for a widely diverse range of learners in an open-admissions context (Giordano and Hassel 2023). Representative examples from participants' reflective writing about teaching and learning included these insights:

- I do feel that I've grown as a teacher through this experience. If nothing else, I've become more acutely aware of how many overlapping challenges my students are facing, and I've become more focused on creating meaningful learning experiences for them in the present moment.
- Questions that I have are mostly around how we can better support our students in a new era of academia. I think we need to start centering marginalized people in the classroom or we will constantly be trying to address these things as they come up which doesn't work. I guess my question is, how can we do this? I feel that it is in our best interests as an institution to support marginalized students first and I guess I'm just not sure how to do that or where we can allocate resources.

These examples illustrate that writing instructors (and other postsecondary literacy educators) can experience intersections between their own new learning about literacy and their students' experiences with learning.

Reflecting on Instructor Perspectives

- What have you learned from your own experiences with teaching new courses and working in new contexts that can help you understand that everyone (including professional writing instructors) has more to learn about writing and literacy?
- What strategies have you used to create meaningful learning experiences for students in your own teaching context(s)? How have you adapted your teaching to meet the needs of students who experience challenges with learning, which might create barriers to helping them understand that they can learn and grow as college readers and writers?
- In your teaching context and local community, which students have historically been excluded from higher education or experienced inequitable access to educational resources? Why do educational exclusion and inequities make it difficult for some students to understand that writing can be taught and learned?
- What actions might you take in your teaching context to center your teaching on students' needs and support their literacy development? What perspectives, assumptions, and practices might you need to change as a literacy educator?

Instructor Perspectives: Dual Credit High School Students

Like many first-year writing teachers, some instructors in our "First-Year in the Two-Year" project (Giordano and Hassel 2023) taught in dual credit programs for high school students. These programs can take different forms at different institutions, including students enrolling directly in college courses at a campus, instructors teaching high school students online, or students receiving instruction directly in their high school programs. One project participant taught a course half of whose members were high school students and experienced a wide range of skill levels in a single course section. Another discussed challenges with teaching during the early days of the Covid-19 pandemic: "The particular high school I worked at, it sounded like their move online left students completely overwhelmed by—they were kind of expected to do schoolwork around the clock; experiencing the grief; let up a lot in that class."

Reflecting on Instructor Perspectives
- How might the presence of high school students in a college writing classroom shape students' expectations for teaching and learning? What differences between high school and college learning environments might require writing instructors to adapt how they teach the concept "writing can be taught and learned"?
- What teaching strategies might you use now (or in the future) to help high schools create a foundation for students' ongoing learning in college both in their dual credit experiences and when they enroll in college as degree-seeking students?
- How did pandemic disruptions alter the learning experiences of K–12 students? What might college writing instructors do to support college students who had disrupted educational experiences in high school?

Program or Disciplinary Perspectives: Dual Credit Program Expectations

Professional organizations like the Two-Year College English Association (TYCA), the Conference on College Composition and Communication (CCCC), and the National Association of Concurrent Enrollment Partnerships have set out guidelines for dual credit programs. Locate and read the CCCC, TYCA, CWPA and NCTE's "Joint Position Statement on Dual Enrollment in Composition" (2019).

Reflecting on Program or Disciplinary Perspectives
- What expectations does the statement set out for the kinds of learning that will take place in these types of courses?

- In what ways do you see this threshold concept reflected (or not) in the guidance offered by these two organizations?
- In what ways does your own program/institution address the learning that will take place in a dual credit writing context and how students are prepared or assessed before, during, and after their completion of those courses?

QUESTIONS FOR REFLECTION AND DISCUSSION: WRITING CAN BE TAUGHT AND LEARNED

- When and how do you provide students with direct instruction that helps them learn about writing and their own capacity for literacy development? At what points of your course might you add to, revise, or enhance the way you help students learn about writing?
- How do the components of your course work together to provide students with incremental and sustained support in learning about writing and applying that learning to their own writing?
- What types of structured learning activities do you provide to help students learn and practice writing strategies that support their literacy development? What changes might you make to your course to create significant learning experiences for students?
- What informal and formal practices do you use for assessing student learning? What are the beliefs and assumptions behind those practices? To what extent do your assessment practices enhance, hinder, or create barriers to students' understanding and application of the concept that *writing can be taught and learned*?
- To what extent are your assessment practices connected to learning about writing and literacy development? What assessment practices do you need to eliminate, change, or improve to support students' literacy development both for college learning and for their literate lives outside of school?
- What stated and implied messages do your feedback practices communicate to students about their capacity for learning and growth as writers? To what extent do your feedback practices help students develop the capacity to make independent choices about their own work as writers? What changes do you need to make to your feedback practices to support students' incremental development as writers?
- What teaching practices do you use to support students whose prior experiences have given them limited perspectives on their own capacities for growth as writers? What practices might you use for helping those students expand their thinking about writing, develop strategies for achieving their goals as writers, and apply learning from the course to their own work as writers?
- What teaching practices do you use to help students learn when they believe there isn't much for them to learn in a first-year writing

course? What strategies might you use for helping those students understand that all writers have more to learn about writing?
- How does the concept *writing can be taught and learned* inform your own work as a writer? How has your thinking about your own capacity for learning shaped the way you view yourself as a writer across varying literacy contexts and purposes? In what ways might you learn more about writing? In what ways would you like to develop as a writer?

5
WRITERS WRITE FOR DIFFERENT PURPOSES AND AUDIENCES, AND OFTEN IN GENRES WITH PREDICTABLE CONVENTIONS

This chapter provides an overview of the threshold concept writers write for different purposes and audiences, and often in genres with predictable conventions. We explain why learning how to adapt reading and writing based on context, audience, purpose, and genre is critical for developing academic literacy at the college level. The chapter includes an overview of key disciplinary statements and scholarship to help instructors understand rhetorical awareness and adaptability, and we also describe concepts that help students develop rhetorical awareness. The chapter offers teaching strategies and learning activities for helping first-year college students develop rhetorical adaptability.

One important part of teaching first-year writing and other postsecondary English courses is helping students understand how college reading and writing are different from the literacy tasks they have completed in their K–12 education, in the workplace, and in their lives outside of school. College students need to recognize the complex differences among reading, writing, and research conventions used in the varied fields of study for their coursework. To move from novices to advanced college learners (Sommers and Saltz 2004), students need to build on a growing rhetorical awareness as they learn how to adapt their strategies as readers and writers to changing literacy contexts and tasks.

The threshold concept *writers write for different purposes and audiences, and often in genres with predictable conventions* is essential for college students to develop and apply as they transition from beginning to more advanced college writing throughout their undergraduate experiences. This concept may also take the longest to develop for some students because it encompasses many other first-year writing concepts and requires sustained practice. The ability to write for diverse purposes, multiple audiences, and different social and cultural contexts typically

https://doi.org/10.7330/9781646425372.c005

evolves after students have had significant experience reading complex texts and writing for many different situations. For college learning, this can mean adapting reading and writing strategies across disciplines, courses, and course levels. For that reason, no single assignment or activity in first-year writing will ensure that students develop this threshold concept and apply it to their own writing. This chapter details how disciplinary concepts related to rhetorical knowledge are complex and intersect with every part of a writing course.

The *Framework for Success in Postsecondary Writing* defines *rhetorical knowledge* as "the ability to analyze and act on understanding of audiences, purposes, and contexts in creating and comprehending texts" (Council of Writing Program Administrators, National Council of Teachers of English, and the National Writing Project 2011, 6). In this chapter, we describe two different types of rhetorical knowledge: rhetorical awareness and rhetorical adaptability. We define *rhetorical awareness* as knowledge of a communication situation (context, audience, purpose, and genre) combined with an understanding of how to use that knowledge to read and write texts. We define *rhetorical adaptability* as the ability to adjust reading and writing strategies, processes, and ways of thinking to the demands of a unique literacy task. Designing first-year writing course around the concept *writers write for different purposes and audiences, and often in genres with predictable conventions* means designing instruction and learning activities that help students develop rhetorical awareness as readers and writers through scaffolded learning activities across an entire course so they can adapt their literacy strategies based on the context and purpose of reading, writing, or research tasks.

DISCIPLINARY RESEARCH ABOUT RHETORICAL AWARENESS AND ADAPTABILITY

Landmark research studies and meta-analyses in writing studies lay a foundation for helping first-year writing instructors understand issues connected to rhetorical awareness and rhetorical situations. For example, foundational work by Sondra Perl (1979) and Nancy Sommers (1980) as well as more recent research by Sommers and Laura Saltz (2004) emphasize the different mental models that are used by experienced writers versus novice writers, with experienced writers focused more intently on taking on a "reader's perspective" and having developed an internalized sense of audience awareness. Novice writers, in contrast, emphasized correctness and a narrower understanding of an imagined audience, one they were writing *to and for*, with attention to meaning and communication. Another foundational article is Lisa Ede and Andrea Lunsford's "Audience Addressed/Audience Invoked: The Role of Audience in Composition Theory and Pedagogy" (1984). Like Walter Ong's "The Writer's Audience Is Always a Fiction" (1975) this landmark article pushed the earlier understanding of audience in a rhetorical situation to audiences as mental models that are constructed as "knowable" readers or listeners. More recently, Lunsford (2015, 21) discussed the writing studies threshold concept "writing addresses, invokes, and/or creates audience" and explained that rhetoric and writing studies scholarship has "extended [an] understanding of audience, explaining how writers can address audiences—that is, actual, intended readers or listeners—and invoke, or call up, imagined audiences as well."

Further research on audience and student learning (Britton 1970; Britton et al. 1975; Hillocks 1986; Melzer 2014) has directed scholarly attention toward writers' instructional strategies and classroom experiences and how various pedagogical approaches can help cultivate an internalized sense of audience awareness that will move developing writers toward a more advanced grasp of rhetorical knowledge. Research by Hassel and Giordano (2009) illustrates the challenges students can face in transferring knowledge and adapting writing strategies for different audiences and purposes even across sequential courses in the same writing program.

More recent writing studies work suggests that first-year writing instructors need to account for diverse cultural, social, racial, and linguistic contexts and audiences when teaching students about rhetorical awareness and responding to their students' work as readers. For example, April Baker-Bell (2020) expands disciplinary knowledge about audience and context by arguing for a materially situated understanding of language that names and values Black language, one that rejects code switching as necessary or even effective in written discourse. Jamila Kareem (2019) presents a set of learning outcomes for first-year writing built on language diversity and an understanding of it should be foundational goals for first-year writers. Vershawn Ashanti Young and Aja Y. Martinez (2011) bring together voices in an edited collection who move from "code switching," an understanding of language and discourse as relatively stable "codes" that a speaker or writer moves back and forth between, to "code meshing," where communicators occupy and use multiple codes simultaneously.

Additional studies can help writing instructors understand the importance of rhetorical awareness of genre conventions for college writers. Anis Bawarshi and Mary Jo Reiff's book-length study, *Genre: An*

Introduction to History, Theory, Research, and Pedagogy (2010, 5), comprehensively synthesizes history, theory, and methodologies of naming and studying genre toward a larger goal of recognizing that genre conventions "reflect and coordinate social ways of knowing and acting in the world." Charles Bazerman (2009, 504; see also Bazerman 2015) analyzes the genre of an experimental report in science to illustrate the connection between developing rhetorical awareness and adapting to academic genre conventions: "The student must understand and rethink the rhetorical choices embedded in each generic habit to master the genre. Although genre may help stabilize the multiform rhetorical situation of scientific writing and may simplify the many rhetorical choices to be made, the writer loses control of the writing when he or she does not understand the genre." Anne Beaufort (2007) traces one student writer from his first year to workplace post-graduation, arguing for explicit instruction in genre analysis and knowledge to make it more likely that writers will "transfer" their knowledge beyond a specific writing task.

Developing students' rhetorical awareness of genre conventions is complicated by the research of Elizabeth Wardle (2009). She argues that many of the writing "genres" taught in first-year writing classes are actually better characterized as "mutts" because they do not reflect authentic social, historical, and disciplinary conversations in the ways texts assigned in other discipline-specific introductory courses do. In operating outside of a recognized academic activity system, first-year writing courses may be more effectively focused on helping students learn how writing works in the university rather than suggesting that students learn how to write for college, something Wardle argues is not achievable.

Scholarly work on disciplinarity can also help first-year writing instructors understand how college writers adapt their literacy strategies for varying disciplinary audiences, contexts, and purposes in general education courses and in their chosen programs of study. The concept of disciplinarity is intended to define what it means to be an academic area of study. Rita Malenczyk and coauthors (2018b, 336) summarize the pressing question in writing studies focused on the relationship among knowledge, practice, and expertise: "Our teaching practices and course content must reflect our research and our understanding of what writing is and does—which is only possible if those employed to teach writing courses are familiar with and draw upon that research."

There is no shortage of scholarship and research that has tackled the question of what constitutes disciplinarity of rhetoric and composition—or writing studies, as Douglas Downs and Elizabeth Wardle (2007) popularized (also see Olson 2002). Efforts to concretize what writing studies is and does have focused on tracing its history of inquiry (Berlin 1987; North 1987); emphasizing shared disciplinary knowledge (Adler-Kassner and Wardle 2015; Hairston 1982); defining its research foundations (Olson 2002; Rosner, Boehm, and Journet 1999), graduate programs, and degrees (Lauer 1984); and analyzing federal recordkeeping (Phelps and Ackerman 2010). Each area of study in which students read and write for college tends to have shared values that emerge from this similar type of negotiation, with conventions that become established over time and have common features. Helping students understand written academic discourse as situated within not only audience, purpose, and genre but also disciplinary conventions equips them to unpack, analyze, and reproduce the genre conventions of texts they read and write in college.

WHAT INSTRUCTORS NEED TO KNOW ABOUT TEACHING RHETORICAL AWARENESS

Scholarship on threshold concepts aimed at experts can help instructors identify and understand how to help students develop rhetorical knowledge and apply it to their work as writers. *Naming What We Know* (Adler-Kassner and Wardle 2015) includes two threshold concepts related to rhetorical awareness and adaptability. The first concept is "writing is a social and rhetorical activity." Kevin Roozen (2015, 18) explains why this concept is essential for writing courses: "If teachers can help students consider their potential audiences and purposes, they can better help them understand what makes a text effective or not, what it accomplishes, and what it falls short of accomplishing." A second threshold concept is "writing speaks to situations through recognizable forms." Bazerman (2015, 35) describes why this learning concept can be challenging: "Writing . . . addresses social situations and audiences organized in social groups and does so through recognizable forms associated with those situations and social groups. But with writing we have fewer here-and-now clues about what the situation is, who our audiences are, and how we want to respond." Research and theory by Bawarshi (2003) and Bawarshi and Reiff (2010), Carolyn R. Miller (1984), and Amy Devitt (2015) have offered additional insights into the role of genre within writing and rhetorical knowledge.

The *Framework for Success in Postsecondary Writing* argues that "study of and practice with basic rhetorical concepts such as purpose, audience, context, and conventions are important as writers learn to compose a variety of texts for different disciplines and purposes" (Council of

Writing Program Administrators, Conference on College Composition and Communication, and the National Writing Project 2011, 6). This commitment is echoed in the "Principles for the Postsecondary Teaching of Writing" (Conference on College Composition and Communication 2015), which describes two major principles for rhetorical awareness and adaptability. First, "Sound writing instruction emphasizes the rhetorical nature of writing." The statement explains this principle by describing how writers adapt their strategies to specific contexts: "To be rhetorically sensitive, good writers must be flexible. They should be able to pursue their purposes by consciously adapting their writing both to the contexts in which it will be read and to the expectations, knowledge, experiences, values, and beliefs of their readers" (Conference on College Composition and Communication 2015). A first-year writing course that emphasizes rhetorical awareness integrates discussions and activities that focus on audience and purpose throughout the entire course rather than simply addressing it as an isolated topic that students learn about in a lesson or part of a course. The second principle is that "sound writing instruction considers the needs of real audiences" (Conference on College Composition and Communication 2015). The statement describes the relationship between having an awareness of audience and students' postsecondary literacy development: "Writers grow by envisioning and learning to write for a variety of audiences. These include audiences in different postsecondary disciplines and those outside of the academy. In practice, this means that writers develop heightened sensitivities to the needs of a range of audiences by considering expectations and values of audiences and purposes that writing might serve for them" (Conference on College Composition and Communication 2015). Effective first-year writing instruction depends heavily on literacy educators who can ground their teaching practices in disciplinary scholarship about rhetorical knowledge and how writers develop and apply rhetorical strategies to varying literacy tasks and contexts.

WHAT STUDENTS NEED TO KNOW ABOUT RHETORICAL AWARENESS AND ADAPTABILITY

First-year writing instructors need to define, explain, and illustrate basic terms for discussing rhetorical knowledge, including *audience, purpose, genre,* and *context.* Some students learn these words in high school, but instructors still need to review them and explain how they apply to college reading and writing. Other students may not know how these terms apply to their own experiences with literacy. Instructors can also support students' developing abilities to adapt their writing to different audiences and purposes by introducing and discussing disciplinary terms that may be new for most students. Table 5.1 provides an overview of key terms that help writing instructors discuss their rhetorical choices as readers and writers,

In addition to knowing terminology that will help them discuss issues related to rhetorical knowledge, students also benefit from discussions of other concepts that lay a foundation for helping them understand that *writers write for different purposes and audiences, and often in genres with predictable conventions.* The following concepts can help first-year college students develop rhetorical awareness and adaptability as readers and writers.

Concepts for Developing Rhetorical Awareness and Adaptability
1. Rhetorical knowledge is an essential part of reading and writing.
2. Reading and writing are contextual.
3. Context gives meaning to words.
4. College readers need to adapt their reading strategies based on the purpose of a reading task and requirements for related coursework.
5. Writers adapt their writing strategies and processes for different writing purposes.
6. Writers assess the needs of their readers and adapt their writing to an audience.
7. Sometimes readers are identifiable, but sometimes they are unknown.
8. Writers adapt the form, content, and style of a text to a particular genre.
9. Genre conventions are flexible and depend on context and audience.

Rhetorical knowledge is an essential part of reading and writing. Writers use rhetorical knowledge to adapt their writing to specific audiences, purposes, and genres. Readers use rhetorical knowledge to make sense of what they are reading.

Reading and writing are contextual. First-year writers need to know that writing is situated within a social, cultural, and historical context. Readers use information about context to make sense of what they are reading and adapt their reading strategies to a particular reading task. Writers draw from an understanding of the context for a writing situation to adapt their writing to a particular audience, purpose, and genre.

Context gives meaning to words. Words and phrases have meaning in the specific context of a text, including an entire text, chapter, section, paragraph, and sentence (i.e., words communicate ideas to an audience in relation to other words in the same text). Readers draw from what

Table 5.1. Key terms for understanding rhetorical choices

Term	Definition for First-Year Students	What Students Need to Know
Rhetorical knowledge	The Framework for Success in Postsecondary Writing (Council of Writing Program Administrators, Conference on College Composition and Communication, and the National Writing Project 2011, 6) defines rhetorical knowledge as "the ability to analyze and act on understandings of audiences, purposes, and contexts in creating and comprehending texts."	The term *rhetorical knowledge* gives students an umbrella for understanding other concepts that can help them develop and increase rhetorical awareness.
Rhetorical situation	For the purposes of first-year writing, a rhetorical situation includes the context, the writer, the audience, the purpose, the content or message, and the language or words the writer uses. Related language to use with first-year students can include *reading situation, writing situation*, and *communication situation*.	Rhetorical situation is a concept students can use to discuss and learn about both the context for a specific literacy task and the components of a communication situation.
Rhetorical strategies	For *reading*, rhetorical strategies are approaches to reading, analyzing, and making sense of a text that draws from a knowledge of context, audience, purpose, and genre. This concept also refers to how readers make choices based on their own or assigned purposes for reading and adapt how they read to different reading situations. For *writing*, rhetorical strategies refer to moves and choices writers make to adapt their writing based on the context, audience, purpose, and genre for a writing task.	For first-year college students, it can be helpful to think about rhetorical strategies in more specific ways for particular literacy tasks by identifying and discussing *reading strategies, writing strategies, learning strategies*, and *communication strategies* (which can include spoken and nonverbal communication).
Rhetoric	For the purposes of first-year writing, students might think about rhetoric as effective communication. Instructors might also teach them that rhetoric is a field of study in the context of explaining that reading and writing can be subjects of study. (See the meta-threshold concept "Writing Is an Activity and a Subject of Study" in *Naming What We Know* [Adler-Kassner and Wardle 2015, 15–16].)	First-year writers do not need extensive knowledge of the vocabulary used for discussing rhetoric by experts or students in higher-level courses. They benefit from a study of communication and language that focuses on terms that are already part of their academic vocabularies from prior educational experiences.

they have already read in a text to make sense of new sections of a text. Writers need to have rhetorical awareness of context at the paragraph and sentence levels to provide background information to readers and write clear sentences that effectively communicate their ideas.

College readers need to adapt their reading strategies based on the purpose of a reading task and requirements for related coursework. All reading tasks require rhetorical knowledge that guides readers in how to approach a written text. Experienced readers adjust their reading strategies for the unique demands of a reading task and for the text itself—in other words, varying how they read both for their own reading purposes and for the purpose, genre, and difficulty level of the text.

Writers adapt their writing strategies and processes for different writing purposes. College writers need to adapt their writing strategies and processes for each unique writing situation. Students also need to be able to identify and respond to varied purposes for writing across multiple disciplines.

Writers assess the needs of their readers and adapt their writing to an audience. Thinking about real (or imagined) audiences and responding to their needs is one of the most important skills for helping students develop the rhetorical awareness required for college writing. Effective writing requires students to think both concretely and imaginatively about how readers will encounter a text.

Sometimes readers are identifiable, but sometimes they are unknown. For some writing situations, a writer can anticipate the needs of known readers they encounter in everyday life who may or may not provide them with feedback. Students also need to understand that they often write for and anticipate the expectations of an unknown (or imagined) audience of readers who might encounter their writing that they share publicly (for example, in an online forum or a school newspaper).

Writers adapt the form, content, and style of a text to a particular genre. Developing rhetorical awareness of genre (or type of text) and genre conventions offers students both flexibility and boundaries for learning common kinds of texts writers produce regularly in a range of consistent contexts. As readers, first-year students need experience with identifying the features of a text that help readers identify its genre conventions. As writers, they need repeated practice with adapting their own writing to varied genre conventions.

Genre conventions are flexible and depend on context and audience. The form of a text is connected to rhetorical awareness of context and audience. Therefore, students need to know that genre conventions are flexible and contextual and that they change over time. To develop rhetorical adaptability, college students need to recognize that genre conventions (especially conventions for fields of study) provide a framework for organizing a text, making choices about content, and adjusting their writing style and strategies to recognizable forms. At the same time, they need to know that genre conventions aren't rigid, inflexible rules that writers always follow. Genre conventions are negotiated within social contexts and adapted to the needs of an audience.

Table 5.2 can help instructors consider how to teach students about different purposes for reading and writing.

Table 5.2. Purposes for reading and writing

Purposes	What Students Need to Know	Teaching Considerations
A writer's own purpose (reasons for writing)	All writing has one or more purposes that are determined by a writer (for example, to make a request to an employer, ask a family member for money through a text message, record experiences for personal use through journaling, or share an idea with a friend through social media).	In college courses, students normally have their own writing purposes and learning goals for assigned tasks, which might differ from an instructor's objectives for an assignment.
General rhetorical purposes for a text	In some writing courses, discussions about the purpose of a text focus on general rhetorical categories—for example, to inform, persuade, entertain, analyze, compare, narrate. When a writing program requires this approach, students need to be able to define and illustrate each type of writing.	Broad categories can be useful for helping students understand the relationship between purpose and writing strategies, but they are limited and insufficient for helping students adapt their writing to the demands of more specific purposes and reasons for writing. Students benefit from a more flexible approach to learning about writing purposes.
Assigned purposes for a text	For college writing and frequently in workplace writing, texts typically have purposes that are provided to a writer by the parameters of an assignment or writing task. For example, the purposes of a research-based writing assignment might be to independently locate research sources, incorporate them into a writing project, analyze those sources in connection to a thesis, and demonstrate learning about an issue within a field of study.	Each component of an instructor's learning goals for an assignment—in combination with a student's own writing purposes—can require a different set of reading and writing strategies. College writers need to adapt their writing strategies and processes not only to a general writing purpose but also to very specific purposes attached to the learning goals and instructor expectations for each task. Assigned purposes can be clearly stated or implied, which means they may or may not be clear to a student.
Readers' purposes for reading	In addition to developing an awareness of their own reasons for writing and the stated purposes of a text, writers also need to think about why readers read their texts and what they might do with them—which may be different from their reasons for writing.	In a college writing course, students typically write for more than one purpose. They read each others' texts to complete peer review activities (and sometimes to get ideas about how to do an assignment) while instructors typically read the same texts to assess student learning and monitor literacy development. In a typical workshop-based writing course, students write for two audiences that have very different reading purposes and potentially for other audiences external to the course.

GETTING STARTED WITH FOCUSING A WRITING COURSE ON RHETORICAL AWARENESS

First-year college students come to their postsecondary courses with a wide range of prior experiences with literacy, language, and education.

It's important for writing teachers to anticipate that students will have varying levels and types of knowledge about audience, purpose, and genre. Their understandings of varied contexts and audiences for reading and writing are shaped by their cultural, linguistic, educational, and social backgrounds. Knowledge of the student communities a writing program serves is an essential part of identifying what and how to teach students about rhetorical knowledge. Similarly, different institutions have their own educational missions as well as mechanisms for placing students into first-year (or developmental) writing courses, developing curriculum, and assessing students' development as writers. Learning about these distinct features of a writing program or department is an important first step in thinking about how to design courses and learning activities that will help students explore rhetorical adaptability in first-year writing and develop strategies for applying rhetorical knowledge to their learning in other disciplines and their literacy experiences outside of school.

An early assessment can help first-year writing teachers understand the diverse literacy experiences students bring to their classrooms. This assessment might include any of the low-stakes learning activities described in the section "Strategies for Teaching Rhetorical Awareness and Adaptability" later in this chapter or a simple diagnostic writing assignment that allows students to reflect on their reading and writing contexts. The rhetorical awareness and adaptability students bring to their college composition courses will reflect their previous experiences with literacy, including their home environment, their K–12 learning, their workplace, community or public spaces, and digital/online platforms. Giving students opportunities to share their prior experiences in these literacy contexts can help writing teachers design learning activities that will be relevant to their own students.

Likewise, twenty-first-century college students face an increasingly complex literacy landscape both in college and in their literate lives outside the classroom. As communicators, they have opportunities to create messages using an infinite array of technological and social media tools with a similarly infinite set of audiences. With this reality in mind, we recommend the following approaches to designing courses to support new uses of technology and changing literacies:

- Create activities to support rhetorical awareness that go beyond the identification and analysis of rhetorical appeals
- Assign reading and writing tasks across modalities to reflect the frequency with which students read and write digitally
- Provide a flexible approach to texts that will help students develop a range of reading and writing strategies in their future academic

courses—not to prepare them for every academic subject but rather as sets of principles, questions, and heuristics they can deploy when they encounter new types of texts.

Ultimately, the success of a course design and pedagogy that emphasizes rhetorical analysis rests on an instructor's own preparation to explain the purpose and value of understanding how texts work (and make meaning) as well as their continued growth in reading and writing a variety of texts.

COURSE DESIGN PRINCIPLES FOR TEACHING RHETORICAL AWARENESS AND ADAPTABILITY

Helping students develop proficiency in rhetorical awareness and adaptability needs to be a central part of course design for first-year writing. "Principles for the Postsecondary Teaching of Writing" is one of the primary disciplinary documents from the Conference on College Composition and Communication (2015) focusing on how to teach college writing. The statement argues that "instructors emphasize the rhetorical nature of writing by providing writers opportunities to study the expectations, values, and norms associated with writing in specific contexts. This principle is fundamental to the study of writing and writing instruction. It informs all other principles in this document." In other words, most guiding disciplinary principles for teaching writing build on rhetorical knowledge, which means that effective writing course design depends heavily on pedagogical approaches that focus on helping students develop rhetorical awareness as readers and writers. The following course planning strategies can help instructors build rhetorical awareness and adaptability into the overall design of a course, especially as they plan for reading and writing assignments before a course starts.

Planning for Writing Assignments

Perhaps the most important part of helping students develop the ability to adapt their own writing to different audiences, purposes, and genres (or forms) is structuring a first-year writing course around increasingly more challenging projects written in different genres. The easiest way to build rhetorical flexibility into a course is to organize it around a few major writing projects in different genres, with shorter, more informal low-stakes work that serves as prewriting or process work for the longer projects. Each writing assignment can ask students to use different strategies for both reading and writing. The writing assignment example in this chapter describes suggestions for creating an analysis assignment that helps students develop rhetorical awareness; other chapters of the book provide options for other types of source-based writing.

In planning a course, instructors might also create multiple low-stakes, informal writing activities to provide students with opportunities to adapt the content and style of a piece to the requirements of a particular assignment. In addition to longer and more formal writing projects, examples of low-stakes assignments include reflective writing, non-graded in-class responses to readings with varying types of prompts, practice essays, take-home work that responds to texts or explores a writing studies concept, handouts for other students, blog posts, short reports on research findings, and short collaborative work that leads to a longer writing project.

First, first-year students need experience with writing assignments that provide them with enough flexibility to structure their ideas and adapt their writing based on an audience, a purpose, and the content they want to communicate to readers. Traditional modes that are sometimes part of college writing textbooks (e.g., exposition, narration, description, definition) may be occasionally useful for describing moves writers do in parts of a text, but they are artificial forms of writing—not genres that normally exist outside of a writing course as standalone texts. Students need more experience with making choices about how to adapt the form of a text to a writing purpose and the needs of an audience than modes or other types of formulaic writing provide.

Second, first-year writers need structured experiences with adapting their writing to an authentic audience and not artificial, invented audiences created only for the assignment. Typically, the primary audience for an academic text is an instructor (or a grader), and instructors need to pay close attention to their own expectations as an audience while creating assignment instructions. Students need to develop rhetorical awareness that will help them adapt to expectations of instructors in many different disciplines. But authentic readers for college writing can also include class members, writing center consultants, family members who read their work, readers of institutional ePortfolios, or a public audience for work shared online through a website or a blog.

Planning for Reading Assignments

Another key part of centering a course on rhetorical awareness is selecting assigned texts that (a) provide students with practice reading texts that require varying strategies and (b) help facilitate discussions, learning activities, and writing assignments that focus on developing an awareness of context, audience, purpose, and genre. Sometimes this requires an instructor to shift away from texts they enjoy as readers to focus the course on readings. Here are four strategies for text selection that support rhetorical awareness.

First, assign readings written in different genres for varying audiences and purposes. All three of these disciplinary statements argue for offering students variety in the types of texts they read because a crucial part of developing rhetorical awareness and adaptability is practicing reading, analyzing, and writing about texts with different forms, audiences, and purposes. This can include texts about writing and language that are frequently used in college writing course; instructors might also consider academic texts from other disciplines, articles for general audiences that report on research, web pages, both argumentative texts and informational texts written for different audiences, and scholarly research articles that students discuss before doing independent research.

Second, select texts that help students explore a variety of reading strategies that develop rhetorical adaptability in their work as writers. Most activities and assignments in a first-year writing course that focuses on rhetorical awareness need to be based on texts (both assigned and independently selected through students' research). When selecting texts for a first-year writing course (whether from online texts, Open Educational Resources, or a required program textbook), instructors need to consider what students will do with assigned readings as readers, what the instructor will do with texts in the classroom or for online discussions, and how students will write about texts through their formal and informal work for the course. To do this effectively, an instructor needs to think about the reading strategies students need to develop to successfully complete writing assignments. For example, to teach students how to analyze the evidence writers use to make arguments, instructors might select several texts that use evidence in different ways (e.g., supporting arguments with original research, secondary sources, examples or a narrative). To teach synthesis, instructors need to assign a few different texts with shared topics or similar concepts. By planning for how students will use texts and then selecting texts based on goals related to the rhetorical strategies they teach, writing instructors can support new college students' developing rhetorical awareness while also making it easier to develop effective source-based learning activities and writing assignments.

Third, carefully sequence reading assignments based on students' developing rhetorical awareness as readers. Many first-year students have had limited experience with analyzing the rhetorical features of nonfiction texts before they come to college. Even more experienced readers come from high school English courses that focus primarily on literary texts. Students benefit from reading less complex and shorter nonfiction texts early in a course to work on identifying and analyzing the features of a text by indicating its main point(s), claims, context, audience, purpose, and genre conventions. Many first-year students also need practice with shorter, more readable texts to learn how to analyze and evaluate the evidence writers use in relation to audience, purpose, and genre—along with how those parts of a text establish its credibility for readers. Instructors can then add increasingly more complex texts later in the course after students have become familiar with identifying and discussing and responding to the rhetorical features of earlier reading assignments. For example, an instructor might assign news articles or other texts that report on research for general audiences early in a course before introducing students to scholarly texts written by experts for other experts on the same topic.

Fourth, plan for teaching students about how online reading differs from reading books and other printed materials. First-year college students need experience adapting their reading strategies based on how a reading situation varies depending on whether a text is published online or available in a book or other printed (hard-copy) format. Instructors can assign both online and print texts to use for discussions and learning activities that help students analyze differences in identifying rhetorical strategies of websites compared to print texts. Even if all readings for a course are online, instructors can select different types of online texts—for example, website homepages, online articles, and articles in PDF format that were originally published in print format. Students also benefit from identifying and analyzing rhetorical features of texts available through open web searches compared to the types of sources and how they are organized in library subscription databases. Instructors need to be aware that students might access readings in different ways within a course and adjust assignments accordingly (see Cohn 2021 for teaching strategies related to digital reading).

PRINCIPLES FOR DESIGNING WRITING ASSIGNMENTS FOR DEVELOPING RHETORICAL AWARENESS

Rhetorical analysis is a frequent type of writing assignment for first-year writing. Some courses are structured so that a rhetorical analysis assignment is a single unit of the course or a standalone essay that focuses on analyzing a required course text through a narrowly focused lens of rhetoric terms like ethos, logos, and pathos (emerging from Aristotelian and other traditions of classical rhetoric). This approach can be limiting in its value for teaching students about rhetorical awareness if it is disconnected from both their experiences as readers and other writing assignments for the course. Our experience has been that first-year students often have trouble connecting a traditional rhetorical analysis assignment to their work in other courses when it is approached as a standalone activity with narrowly focused rhetorical terms for guiding their thinking as readers. Such an approach to rhetorical analysis reduces a writing project to a task to complete in a single course rather than a framework for thinking about the texts students use as readers and writers for varied purposes both inside and outside of school. To develop rhetorical awareness as readers, students need to be able to identify, think about, and evaluate the varied strategies writers use to communicate with readers. For that reason, rhetorical analysis assignments that limit students' reading and writing experiences to three or four features of a text (especially concepts an instructor selects and requires) are inadequate for helping students develop rhetorical adaptability.

In this section, we outline a more expansive and flexible approach to analysis assignments that help inexperienced college readers and writers develop rhetorical knowledge about how writers adapt their writing strategies based on a rhetorical situation.

Principle 1: *An effective rhetorical analysis assignment focuses on flexible critical reading strategies that students can apply both to their college coursework and to reading experiences in their literate lives outside of school.* Analysis assignments that build rhetorical adaptability in reading while also fostering development in critical reading are based on students' own experiences as readers, including what they notice in a text about the strategies a writer uses to communicate with readers. One important way for students to develop rhetorical awareness in reading is to provide them with flexibility and autonomy that encourages them to independently identify, analyze, and illustrate how writers adapt their strategies based on audience, purpose, and genre. This typically means offering individualized guidance and scaffolded support instead of using a checklist approach to rhetorical analysis that requires all students to look at and discuss a limited or rigid set of features of a text (in contrast to adapting their reading and writing strategies for an assignment based on the text itself and their own thinking as readers).

Principle 2: *A learning-centered rhetorical analysis assignment builds on and strengthens the literacy skills and strategies students develop throughout a* *course.* Assignments that build rhetorical awareness draw from the learning students do earlier in a course and inform their subsequent reading and writing tasks. An effective analysis assignment is also inextricably connected to what students learn and do in their work as readers and writers in a course. Instructors can provide opportunities for students to develop rhetorical awareness by asking them to analyze the strategies writers use to communicate with an audience. Then students can complete an informal or formal writing assignment that creates an opportunity for them to write about the rhetorical strategies they notice as authentic readers of a text.

Principle 3: *Student-centered analysis assignments that support reading comprehension and critical reading development for inexperienced college readers focus on students' insights as readers about rhetorical strategies rather than narrowly focused elements of a text predetermined by an instructor.* Analysis assignments that require students to focus only on preassigned parts of a text (like ethos, logos, and pathos) without permitting other types of analysis do not resemble an authentic reading experience or the types of textual engagement students do throughout their literate lives. They also don't model for students the processes more experienced readers use to understand, evaluate, and critically engage with a text. For example, some students might need or want to spend time analyzing how writers support ideas with evidence or exploring how an author's writing strategies are situated in a cultural, cultural, or disciplinary context.

Principle 4: *Students benefit from choosing which texts to write about, which may be assigned course texts, research sources, or websites—depending on the assignment.* When instructors require the entire class to write about the same text, students don't have an opportunity to practice identifying texts that meet their needs as writers based on an assigned writing task. Giving students options for text selection adds an additional layer of experience with adapting their learning strategies to the requirements of a writing task. When students in a course share and discuss an analysis of different course texts, they learn about a wider variety of rhetorical strategies and ways of reading texts.

Principle 5: *Before students start a formal rhetorical analysis assignment, they often need multiple opportunities to discuss the rhetorical features of texts.* Identifying the audience, purpose, genre, and main point(s) of a text collectively as a class needs to be a routine starting point for reading discussions and other activities. Students also need practice identifying and discussing the strategies different writers use to achieve varied writing purposes, which they might do through discussion activities or low-stakes assignments in a class session or online class discussion.

Principle 6: *For a student-centered and rhetorically flexible analysis assignment, what students choose to focus on varies, depending on the texts they select and their own thinking as readers.* Related in-class discussion activities can focus first on reading strategies that apply to analyzing the rhetorical features of all texts (for example, identifying the context for publication, genre, purpose, audiences, main point, supporting points, and types of evidence). But the second and more important part of in-class activities might focus on students identifying, analyzing, and sharing the unique features of a text that indicate how a writer communicates with an audience, makes an argument (if relevant to the text), and supports and develops ideas with evidence. In particular, students can practice identifying features and qualities that are typical of particular genres (e.g., individual blog posts versus sponsored or organizational blogs, magazine articles, opinion versus informational news stories, scholarly journal articles). Based on the texts they select, students can then discuss, share, and write about a range of strategies writers use to adapt form, content, and style to an audience and a purpose and learn from each other's work as well as from their own writing projects.

Principle 7: *An analysis assignment that develops rhetorical awareness focuses on analyzing and not summarizing.* Instead of summarizing large sections of a text, students focus on analyzing a text and then make choices about what to select to illustrate the writing strategies they have identified. Students frequently struggle with distinguishing between summary and analysis, and they need practice making choices about what to selectively summarize to support an analysis in relation to a particular task.

Principle 8: *After students complete a rhetorical analysis assignment or unit, they need ongoing experience with critically analyzing the rhetorical features of texts.* The work that comes after an analysis assignment is important for helping students to continue developing rhetorical awareness. For example, students might work on one or more subsequent writing projects that ask them to analyze independently selected sources to use in their work as writers.

EXAMPLES OF WRITING ASSIGNMENTS FOR DEVELOPING RHETORICAL AWARENESS

Ideally, a rhetorical analysis assignment helps students develop and demonstrate competence with critical reading and writing—particularly with analyzing the features of a text that demonstrate how writers adapt their writing strategies based on the context, audience, purpose, and genre of a text. Identifying the rhetorical features of a text can be challenging even for experienced readers without scaffolded learning support. An analysis assignment also provides students with an opportunity to adapt their own writing to an assignment that focuses closely on their thinking as readers, in contrast to other types of writing that focus on making arguments or reporting on information from sources.

Instructors might take several different approaches to designing a writing assignment around rhetorical awareness. This can include assigning an analysis assignment around sources for a subsequent writing project or asking students to analyze texts they encounter in their lives outside of school. Any of the following suggested assignments can be assigned as either major writing projects or as smaller, low-stakes activities with accompanying class discussions. They can also be completed as collaborative group activities.

Option 1: Analysis of a Source for a Subsequent Writing Project

ASSIGNMENT: Analyze a research source that could potentially be used as a source for a subsequent research or writing project. Evaluate the credibility of the text as a source for college writing by analyzing the author's writing strategies, research methods, and evidence.

PURPOSES: An analysis assignment based on a research source helps students develop or strengthen the rhetorical awareness they need for finding and evaluating credible sources for college writing projects. This type of assignment helps students learn to identify how writers adapt their evidence and strategies for communicating with readers within the reading, writing, and research conventions of a field of study.

Option 2: Annotated Bibliography for a Research Project

ASSIGNMENT: Create an annotated bibliography for a research project that includes several different sources. For each source, write annotations that summarize the text, analyze its credibility as a source for writing, and evaluate its usefulness for the writing project.

PURPOSES: An annotated bibliography that includes an analysis and evaluation component can help students evaluate the credibility of texts as sources for writing, assess the usefulness of a text for their own writing purposes, and pay close attention to the varied ways writers use evidence to support their assertions.

Option 3: Website Analysis

ASSIGNMENT: Write an essay that analyzes a website selected by the student. Discuss how the sponsoring company, organization, or author uses writing and visual images to communicate with readers and achieve the purpose(s) of the website.

PURPOSES: A website analysis assignment provides students with an opportunity to practice reading online texts; develop rhetorical awareness of the features of online texts (which can be different from print texts); analyze how visual images work with written text to communicate with readers; explore the strategies websites use for informing, persuading, and potentially manipulating an audience; and analyze the strategies the sponsoring organization uses to achieve its purpose for a particular audience.

Option 4: Analysis of Assigned Texts for a Field of Study

ASSIGNMENT: Write an essay that discusses the assigned readings or other texts for another course (or from first-year writing if selected by the student). Analyze what the texts show about the reading and writing conventions for a field of study.

PURPOSES: Analysis assignments that draw from work students do for other courses help them make connections between their learning about rhetorical strategies and the genre conventions of a field of study. This type of assignment also develops an awareness of disciplinary literacy while also helping students think more purposefully about transfer and how to apply learning from first-year writing to their work as readers in other courses. Another variation on the same assignment is to give students the option to analyze texts from their workplaces or community activities.

Option 5: Analysis of a Scholarly Text within a Field of Study

ASSIGNMENT: Write an essay that discusses a scholarly article or research report. Analyze what the author's research methods and writing strategies suggest about how knowledge is produced and shared within a field of study.

PURPOSES: This assignment helps students begin to develop an awareness of how fields of study have unique reading, writing, and research conventions. They also learn how to adapt their reading strategies based on the genre conventions of different types of research articles—especially if students select their own research article and discuss their analysis with classmates.

Option 6: Comparison of Texts for Different Audiences

ASSIGNMENT: Write an essay that analyzes two or more pieces of the student's own writing produced for different audiences, purposes, and genres. Analyze the writer's own choices in adapting content, form, and style based on the audience, purpose, and genre of the text.

PURPOSES: A writing assignment based on the student's own writing helps them think about their own rhetorical choices and make connections between rhetorical concepts from first-year writing and the texts they write for different parts of their lives.

STRATEGIES FOR TEACHING RHETORICAL AWARENESS AND ADAPTABILITY

First-year writing courses that are centered on rhetorical awareness and adaptability need to provide students with extensive informal, low-stakes experiences with identifying, analyzing, and discussing rhetorical features of texts. Students benefit from frequent, carefully structured activities that help them practice, discuss, and reflect on strategies for developing rhetorical awareness. The following examples illustrate ways to translate disciplinary concepts about writing into learning activities with reading assignments and research sources.

Strategy 1: *Design activities to help students identify and analyze rhetorical features of a text.* To develop rhetorical knowledge through critical reading, students need intensive, ongoing support in identifying and analyzing features of a text. The *Framework for Success in Postsecondary Writing* (Council of Writing Program Administrators, National Council of Teachers of English, and the National Writing Project 2011) provides an overview of the rhetorical concepts instructors might cover through activities that help college students develop rhetorical knowledge:

- Write and analyze a variety of types of texts to identify
- The audiences and purposes for which they are intended
- The key choices of content, organization, evidence, and language use made by their author(s)
- The relationships among these key choices and the ways the text(s) appeals or speaks to different audiences.

Instructors can help students develop language for discussing rhetorical features of a text and then identify and analyze accompanying rhetorical strategies through activities described in table 5.3.

Strategy 2: *Teach and model varied critical reading strategies.* Students also need consistent practice with using different critical reading strategies that help them adapt the way they read to different literacy situations, especially if they are inexperienced readers who had limited opportunities to develop such strategies in their prior educational experiences. Here are some examples of teaching practices that help students develop a range of critical reading strategies:

- Model for students the strategies experienced readers use through discussion questions that prompt them to vary the way they analyze a text (for example, identifying claims and supporting evidence, connecting supporting evidence to a thesis, evaluating evidence in relation to an audience and a purpose, interpreting figurative language).
- Provide frequent opportunities for students to synthesize (bring together) concepts from more than one text and from different parts of the course.
- Assign a low-stakes in-class writing prompt (or online discussion activity) that asks students to write a paragraph about an assigned

Table 5.3. Learning activities for helping students identify the rhetorical features of a text

Direct instruction	Create a short reading guide for each assignment that includes background information to help students identify the context. Model how to identify rhetorical features of different types of texts (e.g., website, news article, opinion piece, research reports in different disciplines). Write discussion prompts that start with asking students to identify the context, author's background or expertise, audience, purpose, and main point(s). Examine and discuss different examples of how writers structure arguments based on the audience and purpose of a text, using assigned readings.
Group discussion activities	After modeling how to identify rhetorical features, have students practice identifying audiences and purposes with assigned texts and independently located sources that they use for writing and explain the basis for their judgments. Make a brief discussion about the basic features of a text a routine part of every small and large group reading discussion. Select two or more pieces that report on the same research for different audiences (for example, a scholarly article and a news report about the findings of the research). Have students analyze differences in the structure, content, and word choice of the two texts. Have students analyze and discuss examples of published writing and student texts that demonstrate how to analyze and evaluate a text.
Low-stakes writing	Assign in-class writing that prompts students to identify and discuss one strategy a writer uses to support and develop an argument for a particular audience and purpose. Then use students' responses as the starting point for in-class discussions about the text or workshop activities for an analysis assignment.

   text that practices a different type of critical reading (analysis, interpretation, evaluation, synthesis). Start with basic prompts about easier texts that focus on reading comprehension and analyzing a main point. Later in the course, move on to more complicated tasks (for example, critically analyzing the claims of a text or identifying and analyzing an example of a genre convention).
- Throughout a longer research project, ask students to report on, write about, and discuss their lines of inquiry and learning from the sources they read. In the later part of a course, focus in-class writing and discussion activities on independently selected sources students find for their research projects.

Chapter 7, "Reading and Writing Are Interconnected Activities," discusses additional teaching practices for helping students develop flexible reading strategies.

Strategy 3: *Design activities to help students explore conventions and strategies for varying writing contexts.* Table 5.4 provides examples of activities that help students develop an awareness of how writers adapt their writing strategies for different contexts and genres.

Table 5.4. Learning activities for teaching rhetorical awareness

Direct instruction and whole class discussion	Analyze and discuss the syllabus to explain and illustrate what it shows about expectations for college-level writing and reading. Discuss examples of writing prompts from different fields of study to discuss and analyze different disciplinary writing conventions. Examine and discuss the features of different research articles that demonstrate genre conventions, ways of establishing knowledge, and ways of communicating in a field of study.
Group discussion activities	Analyze writing assignment instructions for the course to explore what they show about conventions for first-year writing and instructor expectations. Ask students to share and discuss assignment instructions from other courses they are taking to analyze what they show about disciplinary literacy. Analyze and discuss differences between informal and formal online writing based on students' own experiences with online and digital writing. Ask students to examine a writing studies text (a short text written by experts for experts or students) to identify and discuss the rhetorical features that illustrate the norms, values, and language of writing studies as a discipline. Have students analyze audience and purpose in a shared research article and then apply that learning to discussing sources they find for a writing project.
Low-stakes writing	Ask students to analyze a recent message they've written for a real audience (e.g., a text message, social media posting, work message, email to a professor). Have them identify the choices they made about content and style based on the context for their message. Then ask students to share and compare what they have written. Ask students to write about how they adapt their literacy strategies for a course they are currently taking.

Strategy 4: *Help students develop meta-cognitive awareness through reflection on their rhetorical choices.* Reflective work can be a particularly effective way to help students consider the rhetorical choices they make as readers and writers. Table 5.5 shows examples of learning activities that help students reflect on their own rhetorical choices.

ASSESSING RHETORICAL LEARNING

Assessing first-year writers' rhetorical awareness and adaptability requires instructors to monitor students' collective and individual progress across a course. Assessment of rhetorical learning takes place in both informal moments (class discussions, quick in-class writing or discussion postings, or process work) as well as through formal graded writing tasks. The following teaching practices can help instructors incorporate ongoing assessment of first-year writers' rhetorical knowledge into a writing course.

Create opportunities for students to demonstrate rhetorical knowledge. Provide varied types of informal and formal assessments. Assessing a

Table 5.5. Learning activities for reflecting on rhetorical choices

Learning Activities	Teaching Strategies
Author's notes to introduce writing projects	Have students write a brief note to introduce each major writing project for the course that explains the choices they made as a writer.
Requests for feedback	Ask students to write a formal request for feedback for each draft of their writing projects with different questions for each audience (classmates, the professor, and, potentially, writing center consultants or a co-requisite support course instructor).
Analysis of disciplinary literacy choices	Develop discussion activities or low-stakes writing assignments that encourage students to analyze the writing they produce for different audiences and purposes for their current college courses and major fields of study (or trade for technical college students). Have students bring examples of their own writing from varied contexts to class or share them online.
Analysis of writing for non-academic purposes	Assign a low-stakes writing activity (for example, in-class writing or an online discussion) that asks students to analyze and discuss how they adapted their writing strategies for a literacy task outside of school, using examples from one or more pieces of their own writing written for a particular context.
Genre conventions analysis	Create an activity that asks students to discuss the choices they make as writers in relation to genre conventions for a specific context (for example, another course or their workplace writing), including if and why they choose not to follow those conventions.

student's development of rhetorical adaptability requires asking students to read and write in a wide range of contexts and for multiple purposes and audiences. By definition, rhetorical adaptability means making rhetorical choices and changing reading and writing strategies for different literacy tasks. For that reason, assessing students' growing rhetorical knowledge and abilities to adapt their reading and writing to different rhetorical situations can't be taken care of in a single rhetorical analysis assignment. Instead, instructors can holistically assess students' abilities to apply rhetorical strategies across multiple reading and writing contexts. This can include short in-class opportunities to demonstrate analysis, end-of-class "exit tickets," or one-minute papers in which students briefly analyze the audience and purpose of a text.

Assess how students use rhetorical strategies as readers. Assessing rhetorical awareness in reading requires students to engage with (a) multiple types of readings in different genres written for different audiences and purposes and (b) multiple opportunities to write about and discuss texts across an entire semester. Instructors need to monitor how students demonstrate rhetorical adaptability in how they use texts in their formal writing assignments—both how they write about reading and how they demonstrate varied analysis strategies and types of thinking about texts.

Instructors can also do formative assessments of students' rhetorical awareness as readers through low-stakes in-class writing, online discussion activities, and in-class discussions that require them to discuss rhetorical features of texts and practice different critical reading strategies (e.g., analysis, synthesis, evaluation, interpretation).

Ask students to reflect on their rhetorical choices. Some parts of assessing students' rhetorical awareness can only take place when instructors directly ask students to discuss their rhetorical choices as readers and writers. Assessing rhetorical awareness includes providing students with an opportunity to reflect on and demonstrate their rhetorical choices. For example, instructors might ask them to discuss or write about their selection and use of sources, how they adapted the structure of a text to genre conventions, or how feedback has informed their choices about revision. Options for reflection include informal in-class writing, reflective discussion activities, author's notes to accompany a polished draft of a formal assignment, portfolio cover letters, peer review reflections, or other types of self-assessment writing.

PROVIDING EFFECTIVE FEEDBACK

Developing rhetorical knowledge, awareness, and adaptability at the college level typically requires students to have authentic experiences with writing for readers. For this reason, structured opportunities for feedback are an essential part of designing a first-year writing course to support student learning. Feedback from a single instructor is insufficient for helping students adapt their writing to the needs of varied readers, which is why activities that focus on peer feedback help students learn about how to write for multiple readers. We recommend four strategies for using reader feedback as a tool for supporting students' development as rhetorically flexible readers and writers.

Provide structured opportunities for feedback and multiple attempts to adapt students' reading and writing strategies to the demands of a college writing course. Instructors need to have realistic expectations about what even experienced college writers can successfully demonstrate within a single semester. Students need multiple opportunities to practice adapting their writing to different rhetorical situations, but they do not need to completely master new genres or show a solid understanding of complex writing purposes to demonstrate learning and literacy development. This development happens over time and throughout a college degree (and beyond).

Use peer review as an opportunity for providing authentic audience feedback. Peer review workshops are a structured opportunity for student writers to receive feedback from an authentic audience that is different from an instructor. Instructors need to recognize that peer feedback is different from instructor feedback, and they can encourage students to provide comments based on their varied and unique experiences as readers rather than expecting students to provide the same types of feedback the instructor would give.

Frame peer review workshops in terms of rhetorical learning. When students read and respond to peer writing, they receive practice in developing the ability to think about how to respond to the rhetorical choices of other writers. Instructors can help students understand that much of their learning from peer review activities will come from their experiences as readers and the rhetorical knowledge they will draw from to read other students' work and provide effective feedback that meets the individual needs of other writers within the context of a project and their purposes for writing. Peer review provides an important layer of learning in helping first-year writers develop rhetorical awareness—especially when an instructor creates a classroom culture that focuses on developing a community of writers who share and respond to each other's texts as authentic readers.

Base feedback and grading criteria on realistic expectations of students' rhetorical knowledge. Rhetorical knowledge and accompanying literacy strategies develop slowly over time throughout a student's postsecondary educational experiences. Context, audience, purpose, and genre are complex meta-concepts; it usually takes feedback and guidance (and multiple attempts) for students to understand these concepts, identify them in texts they read, discuss them articulately, connect them to their own literacy experiences, and use them effectively in their own writing. Instructors need to expect that most students will have a limited but emerging understanding of rhetorical concepts in a first-year writing course, and they will continue to develop rhetorical awareness in subsequent college courses.

Teaching students about rhetorical awareness and adaptability provides instructors with an excellent opportunity to reflect on the rhetorical strategies they use as educators, their own teaching practices, and the extent to which they do (or do not) adapt their course design and teaching to the varied learning needs of students in flexible ways. The following reflection questions can help instructors assess how they teach rhetorical awareness and adaptability in a writing course. In particular, they draw from concepts in this chapter to help instructors think through whether their teaching practices support students who haven't had experience with thinking about rhetorical awareness or

APPLYING AND CONNECTING

Student Perspectives: Transfer of Knowledge

In a published research study on college students' transitions between a first-semester writing course and a second-semester writing course, Holly and Joanne noted that "when moving into the more advanced writing course, students struggled to translate their English 101 learning into rhetorical flexibility—that is, the ability to make appropriate choices for (and determine the contours, shape, and demands of) new writing assignments when the purpose, audience, and, subsequently, structural and stylistic conventions had changed" (Hassel and Giordano 2009, 28). Students also experienced challenges with source-based writing that required college reading strategies. One student in the study explained her approach to addressing audience writing: "This is a big one, I use this. I figure out what point I am trying to get a cross [*sic*] with this paper. I work it out from there usually . . . basically base it on either the students or the teacher, it helps a little but not that much" (32).

> *Reflecting on Student Perspectives*
> - How would you help a student like the one quoted above develop a more complex understanding of audience?
> - What strategies might you use to emphasize the relationship among audience, purpose, genre, and situation?
> - What barriers do you see students typically encountering to their ability to think like a writer about audience and purpose?
> - What barriers do instructors themselves create with assignments that seem to have no authentic purpose or audience?

Student Perspectives: Reflection on Progress

The following student writing excerpts are from a research project on assessing students' placement into writing and reading courses in English 102: Composition II. The first student research study participant wrote this cover letter:

> To begin, I feel I am strong with my choice of words and the viscosity or how well my paper flows. I need to work on my mechanics, mainly my comma use as well as spelling. Spelling is not very obvious thankfully. This is due to spell check. Commas became an issue as evident in my second larger paper. Overall I felt I usually had a good intro and nice well rounded body paragraphs but lacked when it came to MLA and mechanics.

My goals at midterm were to gain a better understanding of MLA. I felt I gained a little bit of understanding but not much as i [*sic*] had hoped. I plan to continue to work on this in the future whenever I have to use MLA documentation in another class. Extrapolating that, I will apply the concepts and convention of this style of writing to my future classes as well.

In conclusion, I would consider myself a strong college writer that has to work on his mechanics and occasionally slow down and think when he writers. All in all, this class has given me good incite [*sic*] into my own style of writing.

A second student in English 101: Composition 1, a first-year first-semester writing course, wrote the following as part of a larger portfolio cover letter:

> The piece that I had the most trouble with is definitely the fourth essay: Re-Seeing Community. I had a lot of trouble with this because I've never seen anything like it before. The easy [*sic*] required me to explore a community and just simply talk about it. No thesis, no comparison, and nowhere to go. The topic was easy because I really loved the place that I grew up, but I ran into a problem coming up with sources because I needed to reference a book, and no books that were relevant to what I was trying to say had ever been published about Westby. A second major problem that I ran into was the structure of the writing. I had no idea how to simply talk about a community. The only way I survived this writing was by taking the structure of one of the chapter's [*sic*] in *Population 485* [a nonfiction book read by the class] and mirroring Perry's organization. In this chapter, he ran through town and dialogued about every building that he passed, which is kind of what I did in my essay.
>
> On the other end of the spectrum I find it interesting that Essay Three: Comparative Analysis was one of the assignments that I thought was very well written with a lot of good detail and not much fluff, but you [the instructor] found it to be inadequate. In this essay I wrote with as much political correctness as I could, and I got all the solid arguments and supporting statistics that I could found [*sic*] but somehow you found glitches. However, it gave me an awareness of how much work it is to write [a] paper that is controversial and yet tries to be sensitive to the thoughts and feelings of others. Every word has to be chosen with care and not be offensive if the paper is to be successful in persuading.

Reflecting on Student Perspectives

- What are the different writing, reading, and research needs you see these students expressing?
- Which elements of this threshold concept *writers write for different purposes and audiences, and often in predictable conventions* do you see illustrated more or less effectively in the student reflections?
- What strategies might you use to structure formal opportunities for reflection (like cover letters or author's notes) to surface this threshold concept?

Instructor Perspectives: Teaching Rhetorical Adaptability

In the "First-Year in the Two-Year Project" Joanne and Holly conducted (Giordano and Hassel 2023), one of the participating instructors wrote about the challenges of helping students understand how rhetorical purposes and strategies differ, noting that students tended to fall back on previously learned approaches and struggle to bridge the gap to new genres and purposes:

> Helping my students struggle through academic research and attending the professional development event have left me thinking about how to design assignments that students have a better chance of succeeding at. The assignment sequence that I have used in past composition courses has not worked particularly well for my coreq students, and I want to design all future courses with those students in mind (both because I feel particularly drawn to teaching coreq courses and because I believe this will benefit all students). I am working through a new assignment sequence for next semester that will do more to reinforce key academic writing skills and allow students to transition between units more smoothly. To give a concrete example: my coreq students were able to write successful rhetorical analysis essays, but I noticed that they were still doing rhetorical analysis when we moved on to academic argument and I struggled to get them to adapt to the genre shift. I want these transitions to be smoother next semester (when I will be teaching INRW/1301 [Integrated Reading and Writing] again, along with two sections of dual credit Composition II and a tech writing class).

Instructor Perspectives: Responding, Reading, and Teaching with Purpose

In the 2019 TYCA national survey of English faculty, some respondents described their pedagogical practices as follows:

> The strain of grading essays, which I grade closely, marking every error, is completely invisible to outsiders. Faculty who are not responsible for teaching writing have no idea how much time it takes, and how relentless it is. I spend much time in class working one-on-one with students as well as in my office. It is exhausting. If I did not receive gratification from my students' progress, I would have difficulty continuing to teach under the strain. I would also find it very difficult to teach writing reasonably well if I had more than my load of five classes. It is necessary for me to have a complete break in the summer from the intensity of teaching writing in order to be ready to begin again in the fall. (TYCA workload survey response)
>
> Particularly when I teach our large introductory literature classes (cap size 35) and these students have not necessarily had English 101, I don't assign papers. I have come up with alternatives. I don't have time to teach how to write papers and literature at the same time. I also don't have time to grade that many papers. So if I assign a paper, it's highly structured and I use a grading rubric. (TYCA workload respondent)

S. J. Williamson, a former high school teacher and PhD student, explained her evolving philosophy on moving from secondary to postsecondary writing classrooms as follows:

> When I taught high school, I felt like a puppet lecturer just mimicking whatever strict lessons and texts the people in power at the school district and state wanted me to teach. Best practices were standard, not optional. My creativity felt drained. Much like my own students, I didn't want falsely advertised one-size-fits-all approaches to writing or teaching writing. My first thoughts when transitioning from the high school English classroom to the first-year composition courses I teach at the college level are centered around freedom and empowerment for both myself as instructor and my students as writers. Sure, I still had some basic requirements involving assessment, textbooks, and professionality, but those requirements guided me rather than restricting me. I no longer had to teach texts themselves, assign grammar quizzes, or write essay paragraphs with the whole class copying my model and hoping the lesson would somehow help them write an essay on their own eventually. Instead, I felt empowered to structure the first-year composition classroom around what I believe is the most important part of writing: a toolbox of writing skills students could learn about, experiment with, and use for any type of writing assignment.
>
> I like to focus on the connection between writing and introspection. There are so many techniques and tools for brainstorms, outlines, organization, revision, and reflection. My students don't need to be an expert in all of them to succeed both in the class and outside in the real world; they just need a safe space to experiment with different techniques and tools in order to find out what works for them as writers and whatever genres, purposes, or rhetorical situations they need to address. I am no longer judge of how many rules my students follow or strict enforcer of how every single second must be spent. In the college classroom, I am a curator of useful knowledge, tips, and tricks. I am a facilitator for students to talk through their ideas, struggles, and successes with during the writing process. I am a model for what a great writing process might look like when one tries various ideas until they find their own unique path. I don't have to be something I'm not in order to teach writing. Both my students and I can be ourselves while we wrestle with our writing processes. We can be different and still get to where we need to be.
>
> In addition to students writing for themselves during their process, they also must learn to write for others. This is where I've seen so many of my students shine. Despite the different majors, experiences, and career paths of my students, they all have the capability to lean into their unique experiences as they write. They know things I can't teach them: their values, goals, dreams, and realities. They can write to address real needs, and that writing doesn't have to look like the stereotypical 5-paragraph essay they've been taught to write in high school. Depending on the needs of their readers, purposes, and rhetorical situations, they can write blog posts, PowerPoint presentations, advertisements, posters, TikTok reels, letters, different types of articles, narratives, and pamphlets. Providing students with the vocabu-

lary, tools, and techniques to create these different texts allows them to focus more on how and why one should create real-world texts instead of getting caught up solely in rules that dictate what one must do. Students must learn to think critically for themselves and make their own decisions during the writing process, making sure to balance what works for them and what would be best for their readers. Though this is a challenge at first for many students who long to be prescribed a one-size-fits-all answer to their academic concerns, most students eventually learn the essential skill of consideration for themselves as writers and their audience as readers.

Reflecting on Instructor Perspectives
- What relationships do you see among the three instructor perspective examples in relation to the threshold concept *writers write for different purposes and audiences, and often in predictable conventions*?
- What material conditions make it challenging for instructors to structure courses that help students develop their rhetorical knowledge and adaptability? What constraints or cultures influence the potential for instructors and students to work toward this threshold concept? What strategies would you use to balance the workload realities of writing and reading-intensive courses, student learning, and instructor labor?
- What past practices have you used that you want to change, abandon, or reimagine?

Program or Disciplinary Perspectives: Constraints and Flexibility

Writing programs or institutions often have specific guidelines, either developed by the department or imposed by another entity such as a general education program, statewide guideline, or transfer articulation. Consider how some, any, or all of the following kinds of constraints taken from a sample of program requirements (available on the web) might influence your pedagogical options.

- "By the end of the writing sequence, students should be able to write thesis-driven argument papers. 'Argument' in this context is broadly defined to mean making a claim with which reasonable people could disagree and supporting that claim with appropriate evidence. To meet this goal, instructors are expected to structure assignments so that students have ample practice constructing this type of essay." (University of Louisiana at Lafayette)
- "English Composition II is a three-credit, general education course that continues the emphasis of Composition I on expository/analytic writing, with a greater focus on critical thinking and writing in response to the class readings of short stories, poetry, and drama. Students will learn to evaluate and respond to the ideas that they encounter within the selections. The course will aim to develop

students' writing skills, essential for the production of persuasive, well-supported essays. A research paper is required for this course. The prerequisite in this course is WRT-101: Composition I." (Bergen Community College, New Jersey)

- "Students produce three major writing projects, each of which: meaningfully engages with 2–3 sources; is preceded by a Critical Engagement Assignment that focuses on summarizing, analyzing, and synthesizing the selected sources for that project" (Rowan University, Composition I) and "Students produce at least two major writing projects included in the final portfolio: Each should make a particular kind of argument (definition argument, evaluation, proposal, etc.), following genre conventions, to advance inquiry into a specific student-selected topic; Each should meaningfully engage with at least 2–4 credible sources found through research; One of the major writing projects should be a non-academic genre: a research-based composition that is not a conventional scholarly essay and follows the conventions of a genre intended for a non-scholarly audience" (Spelman College, Georgia)

- Capstone portfolio: "An academic argument or critical essay written during your time at Spelman. Although this essay does not have to be argumentative, a critical essay will still have a discernible thesis that takes a clear position, with strong topic sentences in each paragraph that provide evidence and support for that thesis. A critical essay will not inform (explain something), narrate (tell a story), or be reflective (recall a personal experience). Though these genres might be a part of the essay, the focus of the essay should be a critical or argumentative position. This essay may or may not include research; however, if you do include sources, you must properly document the use of those sources. The essay must be 1,000 words or more." (Spelman College, Georgia)

- "ENGL 1201 College English I and ENGL 1201–0160 are First Year Writing Courses; the main subject of coursework consists of the writing and reading processes of expository and persuasive rhetoric/argument.

  - Students are required to write between three to five papers (fifteen–twenty pages of formal writing).
  - TAs and TFs must assign at least four papers.
  - At least ONE paper, the research paper and the last of the semester, 5–6 pages.

- In addition to strong ideas and organization, these papers should also demonstrate the students' understanding of sound grammar, mechanics, and vocabulary. Prewriting and rewriting techniques are stressed as necessary to all papers; thus the importance of gathering information, organizing, clarifying, shaping, drafting, and revising is emphasized. ENGL 1201 requires students to write generally shorter, well-developed papers, though the last paper must be a somewhat longer researched essay." (Seton Hall University, New Jersey)

- "ENGL110XM—College Composition I with Corequisite (4-2-5): As the cornerstone of College Composition I, students will conduct intensive semester-long research on a topic culminating in an appropriately formatted and documented 10–12 page persuasive research paper. The course emphasizes writing as a process that undergoes various stages toward completion and engages a variety of rhetorical approaches. This process-writing method gives students the tools that underlie effective academic writing and ensures adherence to the conventions of standard written English. College Composition I—Corequisite is designed for students who need practice in foundational skills while simultaneously engaging college-level reading, writing, and research skills. Weekly lab sessions will reinforce skills and topics directly related to the lecture and assignments. Prerequisites: Placement into or completion of ENGL095M." (Manchester Community College, New Hampshire)

Reflecting on Program and Curricular Guidelines
- The kinds, type, and focus of writing tasks can be significantly proscribed by a department or course catalog. Use some of the sample course descriptions provided to brainstorm how you might provide students with the maximum number of opportunities to write for a variety of audiences, purposes, and situations while still aligning your course with the expectations of the institution.
- What do these examples illustrate about how first-year writers need to adapt their writing not only to differences between high school and college but also to the requirements of a particular writing program?
- How might expectations for particular kinds of writing tasks, number of pages, or hours of labor differently shape students' opportunities to develop the concept *writers write for different purposes and audiences, and often in predictable conventions*?

QUESTIONS FOR REFLECTION AND DISCUSSION: WRITERS WRITE FOR DIFFERENT PURPOSES AND AUDIENCES, AND OFTEN IN GENRES WITH PREDICTABLE CONVENTIONS

- To what extent is rhetorical awareness at the center of the course? What overall changes to the course might help students develop the rhetorical knowledge and awareness required for adapting their reading and writing strategies to varied and unique literacy contexts?
- What can I expect students to know about rhetorical knowledge when they start my first-year writing course? Is the language I use for discussing rhetorical features of texts and related rhetorical concepts appropriate for the student populations in my institution? How might I change my approach to explaining and discussing concepts that build rhetorical knowledge to reflect the needs of my students?

- How effective are the assigned readings in helping students develop rhetorical awareness about context, audience, purpose, and genre? To what extent do the assigned readings support students' abilities to adapt their reading and writing strategies to different types of texts?
- To what extent do the assigned readings and accompanying writing assignments help students practice a variety of different critical reading strategies and ways to write about texts (for example, reporting on information, analyzing arguments, evaluating evidence, analyzing writing strategies, interpreting data, interpreting figurative language)?
- Do I provide students with ongoing and repeated experiences of identifying, discussing, and analyzing the rhetorical features of texts and authors' writing strategies in addition to discussing the ideas and arguments in a text? Do I give students enough practice with identifying and analyzing rhetorical strategies before I expect them to demonstrate proficiency with analyzing a text through a formal, graded writing assignment?
- To what extent do my classroom or online learning activities help students practice and adapt their reading and writing strategies to different types of literacy tasks? Do assigned learning activities focus on a range of literacy strategies, not just those that might apply to an English course?
- To what extent do my writing assignments provide students with opportunities to make rhetorical choices? Do students have enough flexibility to make their own choices about content, form, and style as they adapt their writing to a particular genre and purpose?
- Do students have sufficient opportunity to practice writing for different audiences, purposes, and genres and with varying expectations for formality, form, content, and style? What changes to informal and formal writing activities might help students think about and practice how to adapt their writing to the demands of varying rhetorical situations?
- Do I provide structured opportunities for students to analyze and discuss their own rhetorical choices as readers and writers in their literate lives (for example, for the first-year writing class, other courses, their workplaces, and other contexts)? What changes might I make to the course to help students make connections between abstract rhetorical concepts taught in the course and their own literacy experiences?

6
WRITING PROCESSES ARE INDIVIDUALIZED, REQUIRE READERS, AND REQUIRE REVISION

This chapter provides an overview of the threshold concept writing processes are individualized, require readers, and require revision. We explain why learning how to understand, develop, and engage in a multi-stage writing process for different rhetorical situations is a critical concept for college students. We give an overview of scholarship and disciplinary statements related to writing processes, and we also outline concepts that help students learn about how to adapt writing processes for different writing contexts. The chapter also provides a variety of teaching ideas for helping first-year college students develop flexible writing process strategies.

THE IMPORTANCE OF TEACHING ABOUT WRITING PROCESSES

One of the most important concepts for supporting inexperienced first-year writers is that *writing processes are individualized, require readers, and require revision*. Understanding and applying this concept allows college writers to cross a threshold from being novices to becoming more experienced (see Sommers and Saltz 2004). This concept also opens pathways for students to become flexible writers across academic disciplines, in their workplaces, and in other parts of their literate lives. Effective writing course design and instruction provide significant learning experiences for students that help them first develop an awareness of their own individual writing processes and then learn how to adapt their process strategies to varying rhetorical situations. However, many students have had multiple educational experiences that taught them to value grades and trained them to focus on the final versions of texts they produce. This shift away from process to writing products is logical because grades have a real-life value and can both open and close educational and career pathways for college students. Grades represent a finality in the work of a writing project, emphasize an end point beyond which writing can no longer be improved, and signal that learning is over. When combined with negative instructor comments, grades may

https://doi.org/10.7330/9781646425372.c006

also teach some students (particularly those at open-access and community colleges) that they are not or cannot become good writers. Writing courses that help students develop flexible, individualized processes can strengthen their abilities as writers, undo negative thinking about writing, and expand their understanding of how writers work.

In our experiences as researchers and writing teachers, we have found that many students have unrealistic expectations about the amount of work, number of drafts, use of feedback, and in general what it might take to produce a piece of writing they consider to be effective (see Phillips et al. 2019). Some students wrongly assume that "good writing" is only produced by "good writers," a group to which they do not belong—writers who effortlessly produce organized, readable, well-researched prose upon demand. Collin Brooke and Allison Carr (2015) identify the importance of messy writing processes with the concept "Failure Can Be an Important Part of Writing Development." Students, they argue, "must have the opportunity to try, to fail, and to learn from those failures as a means of intellectual growth" (63). Writing process work is a key way for students to learn that challenges and failures in writing processes are an unavoidable (and normal) part of developing a piece of writing and growing as a writer. Effective college writing instruction helps students learn from messy and unpredictable processes of drafting, recognizing problems, discarding, rewriting, learning from feedback, and making additional changes.

However, it can be difficult to teach students about writing processes without unintentionally defaulting to a prescriptive view of a uniform or linear process. Some traditional writing textbooks focus on defining writing processes as a sequence of "steps" of composing a researched thesis-driven essay (see Rose 1981). While these steps are helpful for writing novices to define a writing process in general, they may be prohibitive for students who have tried similar processes before and been unsuccessful as well as for students who attempt to apply the same process to every writing situation. They also do not teach students the critical skill of adapting writing processes to meet different writing contexts. Instructors can support students in learning that *writing processes are individualized, require readers, and require revision* by incorporating this concept and the practice of writing process into teaching, learning activities, feedback, writing assessment, and student reflection. Learning and applying strategies for flexible writing processes with scaffolded support from an instructor opens a pathway to postsecondary literacy development, especially for students who have anxiety about writing or whose writing has been treated disrespectfully by readers or teachers.

Knowledge about flexible writing processes is empowering for first-year college students when they recognize that their writing can be messy and that small steps lead toward completion of a larger project.

DISCIPLINARY RESEARCH ABOUT INDIVIDUALIZED WRITING PROCESSES

As a discipline, writing studies has a strong foundation of theory about writing processes through decades of research on literacy development. Some of the earliest and most influential work about processes and literacy development emerged in the late 1960s through the early 1980s, including Ken Macrorie (1968), Donald M. Murray (1968), Janet Emig (1971), Peter Elbow (1973), Sondra Perl (1979), Nancy Sommers (1980), and Linda Flower and John R. Hayes (1981). Although empirical research on literacy development has a longer history (particularly focused on young writers), each of the landmark studies from these scholars contributed to the growing understanding of not just how people acquire literacy but of how they continue their development, particularly as they adapt to new writing and reading contexts.

That early work has come to serve as the foundation for much of what we know about literacy development in college and beyond. Sommers (1980), for example, established knowledge about the role of attention to process and definitions of process activities as pedagogically important. Perl (1979), likewise, used empirical methods that gathered multiple products from writers' efforts. Perl analyzed the composing moves made by the writers participating in her project. From those data, she was able to derive conclusions about characteristics of writing and writers ranging from the time spent and strategies used during prewriting, the behaviors of writers during composition of sentences, when and how frequently editing occurs, to the kinds of editing operations writers selected (322). Emig (1971) used a multi-method approach (e.g., recording students' composing processes, examining their writing products). Although her work has been re-evaluated for its implications and conclusions (see Voss 1983), it nonetheless traces how composing processes work by breaking them down for the compositional moves made by writers throughout the process of moving from invention to drafting and beyond.

The importance of this research to the threshold concept *writing processes are individualized, require readers, and require revision* is that it systematized the effort to draw conclusions about how composing happens, what student writers in particular do as they approach a writing task, and what we can learn about supporting students' literacy development.

Subsequent writing studies work has built on this foundation, for example, the Teaching for Transfer Curriculum (see Andrus, Mitchler, and Tinberg 2019; Tinberg 2015b; Yancey 2019), large-scale writing projects like the Stanford Study of Writing (Stanford n.d.), and Nancy Sommers and Laura Saltz's (2004) research on novice writers. The rich body of scholarship about writing processes is an integral part of writing studies as a field, and first-year writing instructors can use their knowledge of and experience with processes to help students understand that *writing processes are individualized, require readers, and require revision* and apply that concept to their own writing.

WHAT INSTRUCTORS NEED TO KNOW ABOUT TEACHING WRITING PROCESSES

Bridging the gap between disciplinary knowledge and student experiences requires instructors to support students in developing individual writing processes they are able to adapt for different situations. The National Council of Teachers of English's (NCTE) "Professional Knowledge for the Teaching of Writing" (2016) acknowledges that students often have to unlearn misconceptions of the writing process before they can understand the important elements of developing and revising a text: "Understanding what writers do, however, involves both thinking about what texts look like when they are finished as well as thinking about what strategies writers might employ to produce those texts." A strategic approach to understanding, using, and adapting writing processes can be difficult for novice college writers to learn, especially when flexible rhetorical processes are new to students or are counter to what they sometimes have already learned about writing. In many academic disciplines, having to do an assignment or text over again means you failed—you did it wrong and have to do it over, correctly. This mental model does not productively map onto writing as a mode of learning or communicating but can be difficult for student writers to move away from.

Students' preoccupation with a final written product can become an obstacle to learning, especially if they have not yet developed process strategies to help them produce polished writing that meets the (sometimes unrealistic) standards for writing they have learned through educational experiences. As Davida Charney (2002, 95) notes, "Some scholars argue that generalizations about writing processes are too far removed from real-world practice, inevitably turn into rigid rules, or create paralyzing self-consciousness." Introducing students to the many overlapping and intertwined strategies and processes that contribute to the final product can help students take on smaller, incremental, manageable tasks that are less overwhelming individually and support students as they learn to understand, apply, and adapt writing processes.

Disciplinary statements and research about writing processes emphasize the importance of practice and feedback in the development of an adaptable and effective writing process. For example, the Conference on College Composition and Communication's (CCCC) "Principles for the Postsecondary Teaching of Writing" (2015) describes the role of feedback in helping students learn about writing processes: "Writers need time and feedback as they develop successful processes for analyzing audience expectations, creating ideas, conducting research, generating text, and revising and editing." Likewise, NCTE's "Professional Knowledge for the Teaching of Writing" (2016) explains that development of an understanding of the writing process takes place "through extended practice over years, of a repertory of routines, skills, strategies, and practices, for generating, revising, and editing different kinds of texts." In other words, students must first learn what writing processes are composed of, how they function, and how processes adapt for different writing tasks before they can understand and adjust their own writing processes.

Students also need support in developing flexible writing processes that change with different situations. The *Framework for Success in Postsecondary Writing* explains that "[the] ability to employ flexible writing processes is important as students encounter different types of writing tasks that require them to work through the various stages independently to produce final, polished texts" (Council of Writing Program Administrators, National Council of Teachers of English, and the National Writing Project 2011). Students cannot gain such experience when they are not encouraged to revise throughout a course or when they are allowed to revise only one or two pieces of writing. Effective writing course design provides students with multiple varied experiences with process activities to help them learn how to adapt their writing process strategies to different rhetorical situations. Carefully planned writing process activities and opportunities for revision are especially important for students who have had limited experience with learning about and applying process strategies.

WHAT STUDENTS NEED TO KNOW ABOUT INDIVIDUALIZED WRITING PROCESSES

First-year writing instructors can help students learn and apply the threshold concept *writing processes are individualized, require readers, and require revision* by teaching students to critically reflect on their own writing processes, especially how they adapt their writing strategies to different projects and academic purposes. Disciplinary texts discuss the importance of meta-cognition, reflection, and self-assessment in students' understanding of their individual writing processes. NCTE's "Professional Knowledge for the Teaching of Writing" (2016) discusses the importance of developing "reflective abilities and meta-awareness about writing. The procedural knowledge developed through reflective practice helps writers most when they encounter difficulty, or when they are in the middle of creating a piece of writing." Likewise, the *Framework* identifies meta-cognition as a habit of mind that helps students identify and apply their learning from one writing project to the next (Council of Writing Program Administrators, National Council of Teachers of English, and the National Writing Project 2011). When students are asked to reflect on and self-assess their processes, they can more easily build on their knowledge with each project. The iterative, recursive, and reflective nature of writing processes is intrinsic to writing course design, instruction, and assessment.

When students develop strategies for making purposeful choices about how to adapt their writing processes (and related reading and research strategies) for different literacy tasks in a first-year writing course, they develop valuable skills that have the potential to transfer to other contexts. For many inexperienced college writers, learning how to adapt their writing processes to different rhetorical situations and their own needs as writers can be more important for their literacy development than producing a polished final draft of an assignment. Developing flexible and reflective writing process strategies provides students with a foundation for growing, learning, and adapting as they continue to progress in their postsecondary education and apply learning about writing to future professions, current workplaces, and other literacy tasks outside of school.

In addition to learning about their own individualized writing strategies, first-year students also need structured experiences to help them develop strategies for interacting with and learning from a community of other writers. Disciplinary research shows that the dialogic communities created as part of the writing process are one of the ways writers work out how to improve their drafts. Charles Bazerman and Howard Tinberg (2015, 61) discuss the importance of the relationship between writers and readers, emphasizing how important it is for writers to both read text from the perspective of a reader and have an open mind to value the responses of readers who are less attached to the ownership of the writing because they are interacting primarily with the words on the page. In first-year writing courses, these dialogic interactions can come from one-on-one conferences and other types of instructor feedback. They can also take place in the form of formal peer review activities or less formal writing workshops, which help writers become critical readers of their own and their peers' work (see Phillips and Ahrenhoerster 2009; Stallings and Formo 2014).

Students also need to learn that writing processes are rarely discrete linear demarcations of progress. They are recursive, overlapping, frequently messy, and sometimes chaotic experiences. Novice college writers need to learn that unpredictable writing processes are a normal experience even for what they perceive to be straightforward academic writing tasks. Students need to know that it's normal (and not a sign of ineffective writing) for writers to compose a draft and find that they need more research, that the structure of the piece needs to be revised, or that some ideas need to be separated or combined. Students also need to recognize that their positions on a writing project can shift and change in response to finding further research or receiving feedback. They also need to know that the time spent on sentence-level revision can vary for different projects, especially when they write about complex ideas linked to logic, evidence, and explanation that often require sentence structures that are less familiar to and often infrequently used by novice writers. Our experience is that many first-year writers don't fully understand the recursive nature of writing because their prior learning experiences (especially outside of English courses) have emphasized a finished, polished, and graded project. Instructors play an important role in "normalizing" the way processes work through their course design and feedback processes.

STRATEGIES FOR TEACHING WRITING PROCESS IN WRITING COURSES

Students learn about the writing process by practicing different elements of brainstorming, drafting, research, feedback, revision, and editing for multiple writing assignments in different genres throughout a course. The more opportunities they have to learn about and practice different strategies and approaches, the more they can learn how to adapt writing process activities to their own needs and different rhetorical situations (see Emig 1971; Perl 1979). Students need structured opportunities to learn how each part of a writing process contributes to the development of a text and how different rhetorical tasks require different writing processes. Students also need instructor feedback throughout their time spent on a project so they can critically reflect on their writing process activities and how they are shaping and developing their writing (see Sommers and Saltz 2004).

Instructors can work toward creating inclusive writing courses that support literacy development for all writers by designing multiple classroom or online activities or both that help students learn about and apply varied strategies for adapting writing processes to their own literacy needs. Students who have had limited experiences with identifying effective strategies for planning and implementing complex writing projects need instruction and learning activities that guide them through writing challenges and teach them to break larger projects into more manageable process stages or steps. Almost all first-year writers (regardless of their educational backgrounds and prior experiences) need structured activities that help them learn how to adapt process work to varying rhetorical situations. Successful college learning requires students to develop the ability to change their process strategies for research and writing projects based on varying disciplinary literacy conventions and the demands of different courses. Some students also need support in learning how to make adjustments to an in-progress project in response to unexpected challenges, unfamiliar tasks, and time constraints. The teaching strategies in this section offer first-year writing instructors ideas for how to help students understand that *writing processes are individualized, require readers, and require revision* and then how to apply that knowledge to varied college writing projects both in first-year writing and in other courses.

Strategy 1: *Design purposeful process activities and strategically sequence them across the course.* First-year college students can develop effective research and writing processes through structured opportunities to learn about and practice strategies more experienced writers use to manage complex college writing projects. Structured learning activities also provide students with individualized support in adapting process strategies to the requirements of an academic assignment and their own needs as writers. Table 6.1 provides an example of how to build learning support into the process for a research-based writing project.

Strategy 2: *Facilitate consistent but short process workshops throughout every stage of a writing project.* Most writing instructors know about and use strategies for organizing formal peer review workshops for complete essay drafts. Novice college writers also benefit from multiple smaller workshop activities spread across most or all class periods (or online learning modules) between the time when students receive an

Table 6.1. Examples of process activities for a writing project

Process Work	Examples of Activities	Learning Purpose
Preview the project	Direct instruction to explain the project; online discussion of students' questions about the project and grading criteria; small group discussions of examples from previous class sections	Clarifies assignment instructions for each student; ensures that process work builds on an understanding of assignment requirements and options
Identify topics	In-class free writing; group brainstorming; online discussion of topics; informal background reading activity	Models strategies for generating ideas; helps students learn from each other's strategies for identifying topics
Create a project plan	Formal or informal project plan assignment; in-class or online workshop to share and get feedback on project planning; online instructor feedback or short one-on-one discussions	Creates a structured way for students to plan their research and writing process work; models effective planning strategies; helps students break a large project into manageable stages or steps
Find credible sources	Direct instruction and modeling for using library databases and finding credible online sources; in-class workshop for finding sources through guided instruction; brief reflective writing on research processes	Provides scaffolded support for helping students navigate an individualized research process; shows students that research processes vary for different writers based on the topic and focus of a project
Read and evaluate sources	Direct instruction on strategies for reading research sources, with examples; informal writing activity to evaluate a research source; in-class or online workshop to share evaluations and receive feedback on sources; reflective writing about next steps for finding and using sources	Helps students apply critical reading to a research process; provides scaffolded support for helping students evaluate both sources and their processes for finding research sources
Plan for an essay and organize evidence from sources	Discussion of models for essay planning strategies; essay planning or outlining assignment; in-class or online essay planning workshop	Supports inexperienced writers in organizing complex evidence from sources around a thesis; provides students with feedback on their essay planning strategies
Draft an essay	Informal discussions or quick workshop activities for partial drafts of an essay; brief reflective writing about progress for drafting; formal workshop for a complete or partial draft	Provides students with feedback on work in progress; helps instructors identify students who need extra support with drafting a project; helps students learn about varied strategies and processes that other student writers use
Revise an essay	Modeling for revision strategies using examples of student writing; quick activity to revise part of an essay during class; in-class or online revision workshops; one-on-one instructor conferencing; online discussion about revision strategies using examples from students' writing	Teaches effective strategies for revision; helps students adapt revision strategies to a writing context; gives students individualized support with revision strategies

Continued on next page

Table 6.1—continued

Process Work	Examples of Activities	Learning Purpose
Edit an essay	Discussions based on models for editing; short activity to edit part of a text in class; in-class or online discussions about editing strategies using examples from students' work	Helps students adapt editing strategies to the requirements of an assignment; reinforces learning about individualized editing strategies

assignment and when they complete a draft for peer review. Frequent workshop activities teach students how to develop flexible process strategies based on the requirements for an assignment, work through challenging parts of a project with instructor and peer support, and get to the next stage in their individual writing processes.

Workshop activities also move some of the learning experienced college writers do on their own to a classroom or online learning space where students can receive help in moving a project forward toward completion. Rather than assuming that particular aspects of the writing and research process are easy and available and clear to all, structured opportunities to model and share those practices make them visible and allow students to share successful strategies with each other. Participation in regular writing workshops normalizes the idea that different writers use individualized processes because students have the opportunity to read and discuss a wide variety of work from other student writers in different stages of completion for multiple projects over time.

Instructors can vary the length and purposes of each activity depending on the assignment and point in a semester or term. Tables 6.2–6.4 provide examples of learning activities that help new college students learn about and apply writing process strategies to their own writing, ranging from quick activities to longer workshops.

Strategy 3: *Create strategic, informal opportunities for feedback across a course.* Providing regular and varied feedback on writing process work is an essential part of teaching students that *writing processes are individualized, require readers, and require revision.* Feedback is also a crucial part of supporting students from diverse educational, cultural, and linguistic backgrounds who are inexperienced with identifying and using strategies for navigating new types of writing and research processes. Most instructors are familiar with the practice of providing students with feedback on a complete essay draft that students then revise before submitting it for a grade or including it in a course portfolio or ePortfolio. In addition to formal feedback attached to a completed writing product, students who are

Table 6.2. Examples of quick writing to prepare for workshops (about five minutes)

Activity	Learning Purpose
Write a quick update on progress toward completing the project	Helps students identify their own learning needs for a project for a point in the writing process; provides a way for instructors to offer individualized support
Brainstorm for search terms	Prepares students to look for sources during a library database research workshop
List relevant course readings	Starts students on the process of identifying textual evidence; prepares students for discussions of relevant sources for their individualized projects
Write a request for feedback from peers	Teaches students how to ask for feedback based on a rhetorical situation and to identify their needs for the next stage in a writing process; creates an environment in which students learn to give varying types of feedback
Create a list of questions to discuss in an instructor conference	Helps students develop the ability to assess their own needs in relation to their writing processes and draft texts; sets the stage for a student-centered writing conference
Write questions for readers to answer about essay planning or a draft	Increases students' awareness of the role of readers in providing feedback; helps peers focus feedback on writers' individual needs
Identify a section of the essay that needs more evidence or thesis support	Provides structured support for identifying a manageable revision task; prepares students for discussions of revision strategies based on their own work
Make one change to a sentence to improve clarity	Provides structured support for identifying a manageable editing task; creates a supportive way for students to give each other feedback on sentence-level writing
Revise a thesis statement based on feedback	Moves work for a challenging task into the classroom; helps students learn how thesis statements or main ideas vary based on writers' individualized needs for differing projects

transitioning to college learning benefit from feedback on smaller writing process activities that lead to a completed draft, including support for how they adapt writing processes to their own learning needs in addition to feedback on the texts they write. For some students, instructor feedback is the most important part of helping them learn to adapt their writing strategies and processes to different rhetorical purposes at the college level. However, the process of giving useful feedback can significantly increase instructors' workloads unless they use strategic feedback strategies that meet their own needs in addition to supporting students' progress and learning for a project. By using quick feedback strategies throughout the time line of a writing project, instructors can reduce their workload for formal graded drafts while providing students with feedback when they need it most and while they are still doing learning for the project.

Tables 6.5 and 6.6 for in-person and online teaching, respectively, show examples of strategies for providing frequent feedback on writing

Table 6.3. Examples of short small group workshop activities (about fifteen to twenty minutes)

Activity	Learning Purpose
Share and discuss varying perspectives on an issue	Prepares students for a writing project; helps students identify ways to respond to varied perspectives of different readers
Evaluate and discuss the relevance of a source for an individual writing project	Helps students adapt the way they find sources based on the requirements for an assignment and relevance for their own projects; teaches students about differences in processes for finding relevant sources based on a writer's focus
Evaluate the credibility of evidence that authors use in a source	Provides a structured way for students to practice evaluating the credibility of a source; teaches students to critically evaluate sources as a regular part of writing processes
Discuss ways to narrow and focus an argument or an analysis	Provides students with feedback on the focus of a project before they begin writing; helps students learn about varied strategies for narrowing the focus of an essay or other text based on differing rhetorical situations
Share and revise thesis statements, supporting points, or supporting evidence	Provides students with feedback while they are still drafting an essay; offers students support with completing a challenging part of a project
Work in a small group to revise a paragraph	Helps students practice collaborative writing strategies before applying that learning to a larger project

Table 6.4. Examples of longer workshop activities (more than twenty minutes)

Activity	Learning Purpose
Find sources in a library database through a small group activity combined with individual work time and instructor support	Offers structured support for completing research tasks and finding sources; helps students learn that research processes vary based on the focus of an individual writer's project
Share and discuss an outline, prewriting, or other planning for a writing project	Gives students structured support and feedback for essay planning; teaches students about varied strategies for planning a project
Examine and discuss how multiple sources work together to develop and support a thesis and then plan for revision	Helps students evaluate supporting evidence and identify gaps in that evidence for further research; shows students multiple ways of organizing evidence
Examine and discuss how supporting points and supporting evidence work together to support a thesis	Helps students examine how different parts of their entire essays work together; shows students different ways to support and develop a thesis; gives students focused feedback for revision

process activities that help instructors support students' literacy development while also managing their own workloads.

Another way to provide individualized support while reducing a teaching workload is to schedule instructor conferences during a class period and then work with students one on one during the time

Table 6.5. Informal feedback strategies for in-person teaching

Feedback Strategy	Example of How to Implement Each Strategy
Give quick in-class feedback	Ask students to identify a question or issue for a one-minute mini-conference. While students are completing group work or individual writing tasks, move around the room and meet briefly with each student to answer their questions and give feedback on their process work.
Do a process work check-in with whole class feedback	Ask students to periodically submit their in-process work for a project for complete/incomplete credit. Summarize a few key recommendations for the entire class through a quick discussion and an online handout.
Facilitate a whole class writing workshop	Have students take turns sharing and discussing a small part of their work with the entire class (for example, a thesis statement or thesis support for a paragraph).
Facilitate a small group conference during a peer review workshop	While students are completing peer review activities, spend a scheduled amount of time with each group to provide feedback and support.
Answer questions students write in class or in an online context using Padlet or JamBoard	Ask students to write one question about their projects on a card or sticky note and then add their notes to a whiteboard. Have students group their questions into categories and then answer the most pressing questions.
Assign an informal instructor note activity	Have students write a monthly check-in note to let you know how they are doing and ask questions about their projects. Focus time on responding to students who need extra support.
Offer focused revision feedback	When students have already received feedback on a draft in progress, focus feedback on the final draft entirely on revisions they identify when they submit the assignment.
Hold in-class instructor conferences	During small group work time, offer scheduled instructor conferences for students who are unable to attend a conference outside of class because of scheduling conflicts, work, or caregiver responsibilities.

normally spent on teaching and preparing for class. Conferences can take place in a classroom, in an instructor's office, online through a videoconferencing tool like Zoom, or over the phone. To manage their time, many experienced writing instructors focus on providing effective, individualized feedback during conferences with students, but then they don't offer written comments on the same draft or other work except to support students who need extra help or who can't attend a conference. Using class time for writing conferences is a standard practice for college writing programs but may require approval from a department chair or other supervisor. When conferences take more than one class period, instructors can give students research or writing process activities to do on their own or in small groups to help them work toward completing the current writing project.

Table 6.6. Informal feedback strategies for online teaching

Feedback Strategy	Example of How to Implement Each Strategy
Set up an open discussion board for each project	Create a discussion board that students can use for asking and answering questions about a project and seeking feedback on their process work.
Design an informal activity based on the assignment instructions	When students receive instructions for major assignments, create and facilitate an informal discussion about the instructions and grading criteria.
Give whole class feedback for writing workshops	In peer review workshops for essay planning or complete drafts, identify the most important issues and questions from the workshop and then write a list of feedback recommendations to share with the entire class.
Write selective feedback directly in a discussion board	For online writing workshops that focus on process work, provide selective feedback directly in the discussion board to help students identify models to draw from based on other students' writing.
Create and maintain a feedback template	Create a template of frequently used feedback arranged by assignment type to create consistency in the support students receive. Copy and paste comments from the template and individualize them for each student's project.
Do an informal check-in	Periodically use the messaging or email system within the learning management system (LMS) to send all students a blind-copy message inviting them to reply if they have questions or need help (and to ignore the message if they don't need support).
Assign an informal instructor note activity	Have students write a monthly check-in note to let you know how they are doing and ask questions about their projects. Focus time on responding to students who need extra support. Post overall feedback for the entire class (without identifying students' names) in an announcement or course module.

If institutional policies, time constraints, or other issues prevent an instructor from canceling class for conferences, an instructor can facilitate conferences individually or in small groups during a regular class period while other students complete discussion activities or individual writing and research tasks. Another alternative to formal writing conferences is an open workshop class period without planned activities for times in a course when the workload for a project is intensive for students and the instructor. Students who need help attend class to meet individually with the instructor, talk through their process work, collaborate with each other in small groups, or work independently on their projects. Students who mostly just need time to finish part of a project can work independently outside of class and then write a quick report to the instructor with an update on their process work for a project that is submitted through the LMS or a Google form. Open workshop days help students identify their own needs for a project and then determine how to spend their time. Instructors can adapt both in-class conferencing strategies and open workshop days to online courses that meet synchronously through videoconferencing.

Strategy 4: *Normalize the messiness and uncertainty of drafting and revising.* Writing instructors, especially those who teach at open-admissions campuses, need to help some students understand that college-level writing processes often involve unpredictable challenges and occasional setbacks that require feedback and support. These can range from not knowing how to get started with words on a page to being stymied by using feedback for revision to editing and proofreading for style and citations. Instructors can normalize the unpredictable nature of writing processes by modeling equitable and inclusive responses to students' writing process challenges and by creating a classroom culture that helps students take risks with their process work. The following practices provide examples of teaching strategies that help students work through challenging moments in their progress toward completing a writing project. In addition to supporting the concept that *writing processes are individualized*, these strategies also reinforce the threshold concept *writing can be taught and learned.*

Communicate an approach to writing process activities that reduces anxiety and signals that you are available to help students deal with challenges. Use supportive language that normalizes the idea that different students might be at different stages in a project even with preassigned deadlines. Help students understand that they can come to you for support if they fall behind other students on a project without a grade penalty.

Avoid punishing students for submitting incomplete drafts or bringing unfinished work to in-class workshops. Account for inequities in students' prior learning experiences and current circumstances by assuming that incomplete or missing drafts are connected to challenges with writing process activities or complicated life circumstances rather than a resistance to or disrespect for course policies and the instructor. Instead of lowering grades or making negative comments when students have incomplete or missing drafts, focus on helping them identify barriers to completing an assignment and provide them with strategies for moving a project forward to a finished draft. Give students credit for the process work they submit online even when it's not complete, and encourage them to create a plan for finishing the project. At the same time, when more experienced writers work ahead of the class or bring highly polished work to class, emphasize that students always have more to learn with a writing project. The goal of an effective writing teacher is to help students move forward with their work using a variety of flexible strategies.

Work with students on process activities during class regardless of the work they do (or do not) bring to a workshop. In a student-centered writing workshop, different writers can be at different stages in a process and still give each other feedback on the work they bring to class (even if they only have ideas that aren't yet in writing). Depending on the class period, students who aren't as far along in a process as their peers can work in groups with the rest of the class to provide feedback, learn from other students' work, and get started with the next steps in their project. Students can also do different activities in the same class period to help them move their work forward from one stage of an individualized writing process to another. Sometimes students benefit from meeting in a group with other students who are behind so they can receive direct instruction from their teacher and work together on the same stage in a process. For online writing workshops, encourage students to submit whatever they can complete by a workshop deadline so they can receive feedback from the class and think through their next steps in a project.

Occasionally reserve time during writing workshops for students to work individually on making small changes to their writing based on feedback they received in class. Then follow up with an opportunity for additional feedback from peers either at the end of the class period or at the beginning of the next class. Moving a small amount of revision work to the classroom can help some students identify manageable steps in a revision process.

Make writing process challenges a topic of study for part of the course. Instructors can design in-class and online activities that give students opportunities to reflect on and discuss obstacles, setbacks, and unanticipated changes to writing processes. Here are just a few examples of the many ways an instructor might help students think critically about writing process challenges:

- Assign an informal reflective activity that asks students to write about and then discuss a time when they faced a challenge with completing a project but worked through finishing it.
- Show examples of your own process work, and discuss some of the challenges you had to navigate to complete it.
- Have students analyze and discuss examples of student writing for varying stages of an individualized writing process to illustrate strategies other students used in the past to deal with challenges for the project students are working on in the current course.
- Design an informal writing activity or discussion that helps students describe what they have learned about writing process challenges that they can apply to future writing experiences inside or outside of school or both.

- Ask students to identify and discuss misconceptions about writing process work that they have encountered, then have them critically reflect on how their expanding understanding of individualized writing processes has changed over time.
- At the end of the course, ask students to write advice to the next class about strategies for overcoming challenges with different writing projects in the course and their experiences with writing process activities. Share their advice with the next group of students (after receiving students' permission).

Use methods for assessment and grading that provide time for students to work through challenges for a project. For example, some instructors accept the major writing projects and portfolio work that students can complete by the end of the semester without a grade penalty. Others offer a late work submission deadline for a midterm grade and a second late work deadline for a final grade. Some instructors give students the option to make up missed in-class writing workshops through a writing center visit or instructor conference. Some give students the option to revise any major writing project until the last day of classes. Others accept late work at any point in the course but offer feedback during class or in one-on-one conferences instead of making written comments to manage their own workload for late submissions. Inclusive writing instructors can use varied methods for focusing their assessment practices on what students can learn from challenging writing processes instead of cutting off pathways to course completion through restrictive grading policies that focus on compliance with deadlines.

Strategy 5: *Create structured activities to help students reflect on their writing process work.* Teaching students to reflect on and self-assess their writing process work (from invention to final product) helps them adapt individualized processes to different assignments, trace their learning in a course, and connect their processes to the rhetorical situation of an assigned writing task. Students' reflective work also provides instructors with valuable feedback on course learning activities and helps them identify how to adjust their teaching strategies to support students in completing varied stages of a project. Students' informal and formal writing about their reading, writing, and research processes creates a way for instructors to provide feedback on process strategies (and not just the texts students write). Table 6.7 gives examples of writing activities that help students critically reflect on their writing process work and identify their learning needs for differing points in a project.

Table 6.7. Examples of reflective writing about process work

Writing Activity	Implementation Strategy
Author's notes for draft work	Assign a short note for draft work to help students introduce a piece of writing, discuss their choices as writers, and reflect on their processes for completing the project
Author's notes for final drafts	Have students update their author's notes (or write a new one) for final drafts of a writing project to identify how they revised their work based on reader feedback
Feedback requests for online writing workshops	Ask students to introduce their writing projects and identify the types of feedback that would be most useful for the current stage for their writing project
Workshop prewriting	Give students a few minutes before an in-class writing workshop to write a request for feedback, identify questions to discuss in a peer review workshop, and create a plan for what they would like to accomplish during the workshop
Workshop follow-up writing	After a workshop, give students a few minutes to reflect on their learning from the workshop and create a plan for their next steps in the writing process
Instructor conference plan	Assign an informal activity to help students self-assess their process work for a project and identify the issues they plan to discuss in a one-on-one or group writing conference
Portfolio reflections	Ask students to include an informal or formal reflection to introduce a portfolio (or ePortfolio) that self-assesses their literacy development and discusses their learning from writing process work across the course

ASSESSING STUDENT LEARNING ABOUT WRITING PROCESS

Purposeful process activities provide instructors with an effective way to assess and monitor student learning and literacy development across a first-year writing course. Students' work for and experiences with writing process assignments and related learning activities provide instructors with feedback they can use to make adjustments to teaching and give students individualized learning support to help them successfully complete writing projects. Table 6.8 provides suggestions for designing informal learning activities instructors can use to assess student learning for multi-stage writing processes. The examples describe how a writing process activity can support formative assessment of student learning and literacy development. The examples also show how assessment of short process activities can help an instructor identify how to make adjustments to teaching to support student learning about recursive and flexible writing processes.

Structured in-class and online process activities help instructors reinforce the concept that *writing processes are individualized, require readers, and require revision*. A college-level process approach to writing can be

Table 6.8. Examples of informal activities to assess process work

Process Activity	Assessment Purpose	Potential Responses to Support Learning about Writing Process
Ask students to write informal requests for feedback (e.g., an online submission or an in-class activity before a workshop)	Provides information about students' challenges, goals, needs, and the types of feedback they want to receive to support their learning	Give feedback that reflects students' learning goals; identify patterns of issues to support with clarification, models of writing, and learning activities
Assign process-focused author's notes for draft work	Helps instructors understand students' thinking about processes and experiences with individualized processes for an assignment	Give feedback that helps students move a project forward to completion; learn about students' experiences with processes to inform teaching for subsequent semesters
Check in individually with each student while the class does group work	Identifies students' challenges and learning needs for a project at a specific moment in time; monitors the progress of individual students while reducing workload for out-of-class feedback	Provide quick one-on-one instruction and feedback to help students with process work; use students' own process work to teach them about individualized writing strategies
Ask students to share and discuss their process work with the class through an online discussion board	Gives a quick snapshot of process work for the entire class while also teaching students about varying individualized processes	Use submitted work to identify successful writing strategies; identify patterns of challenges for the entire class
Design a small group activity that asks students to discuss how they apply concepts related to processes to their own work	Assesses students' conceptual learning about processes; monitors how students connect process concepts to their own experiences	Facilitate a discussion to strengthen students' understanding of unclear concepts and synthesize their ideas about individualized processes
Design an in-class or online workshop to help students find and evaluate sources for a writing project	Monitors students' progress with using technology tools to find sources for writing; identifies students' research needs	Provide individual support to help students find credible sources; identify research process issues to discuss with the entire class
Ask students to report informally on the findings of library database research	Assesses students' progress in finding and evaluating credible research sources	Give students feedback on sources before they start writing an essay; support students in finding appropriate sources for an individualized project

unfamiliar to some students, and informal instructor feedback on students' individual processes for a project can help all students (regardless of prior experience) practice writing strategies for types of writing that are new to first-year writers. Instructors can use short process activities to provide students with feedback on writing projects at strategic moments of a course to help them adjust their process work and learning strategies before submitting a final graded draft. Instructors might reflect on this question to guide the way they assess students' progress through process activities: *what is my students' process work telling me about how I can support their learning through adjustments to teaching?* Short learning activities help instructors identify challenges that make it difficult for students to navigate part or all of a writing project and then provide scaffolded support (through either whole class activities or individualized instruction) to help them identify successful individualized strategies for completing a project.

Formative feedback on completed drafts of writing projects can either reinforce or undermine first-year writing instructors' efforts to teach students that *writing processes are individualized, require readers, and require revision.* Some approaches to assessing complete drafts can reinforce final writing products in a way that can become detrimental to student learning over time. For example, when comments on an essay draft focus entirely on sentence-level issues, they don't help students learn about how to use revision to work through bigger picture writing issues like organization, evidence, and analysis. Table 6.9 provides different examples of process-focused feedback for students.

A focus on writing processes has been a dominant strain of scholarship and pedagogical education for several decades. Perhaps because of this ubiquity, instructors may neglect to integrate, name, and instruct students directly about flexible writing processes. The key to the threshold concept *writing processes are individualized, require readers, and require revision* is for instructors and students to recognize that the process for composing, revising, editing, and implementing the multiple other elements of the process of writing is not lockstep or linear. Naming and teaching how processes work (for writing, reading, researching, and thinking) helps students develop the procedural knowledge about their own approach to writing that can help them gain confidence in approaching new tasks and subjects throughout college and beyond.

APPLYING AND CONNECTING

Student Perspectives: Representing Process

In a past research project, Holly and Joanne examined how students' placement profiles aligned with their writing experiences in the composition and reading or learning support courses they completed over several semesters. Review the portfolio cover letter and handwritten revisions submitted by a participating student, Sandy (figures 6.1–6.3).

Table 6.9. Examples of process-focused feedback strategies for a draft

Strategy	Feedback Practices	Purposes
Reduce student anxiety about process work	Don't give letter grades for work in progress Replace grade penalties for incomplete drafts with support for finishing a project	Reinforces that a process approach focuses on learning; disconnects process work from a grade
Use language that encourages revision	Write comments that point to a future draft (e.g., "for the next draft, you might"; "as you revise this draft"; "as you continue to work on this project") Use a supportive tone for feedback on drafts	Reminds students to revise; directs students to options for revision; helps students move a project forward to the next draft
Support writers' individual choices about process work	Ask students to identify the types of feedback that would be most helpful at a particular stage of a draft	Provides individualized feedback; responds to students' process challenges
Provide support for moving a project forward to completion	Give a short to-do list of two or three big picture issues to work on Discuss students' next steps during class or in a writing conference	Gives students focused strategies for revision and other process work; helps students manage their time for a process; helps student complete the most essential parts of an assignment
Distinguish between revision and editing	Focus comments on revision (not sentence correction) Model revision strategies while giving feedback in conferences with students Focus feedback for final drafts on students' revisions	Helps students learn how to respond to feedback with revision; reinforces learning about revision from the course
Support learning from writing center experiences (or from TRIO and other learning assistance programs)	When needed, give one or two targeted suggestions for a writing center session Avoid using language to suggest that the writing center will edit or fix students' work	Helps students work with writing center tutors to move a project forward; helps students' receive support that focuses on the requirements for an assignment
Point forward to subsequent learning	On final drafts, provide suggestions of things to work on for the next project For the last course project, give feedback to support learning in the next course	Reminds students that learning from one project can be applied and adapted to another; helps students connect learning from a project to another context

Reflecting on Student Perspectives

- What kind of thinking do you see taking place in the annotated paper copy of Sandy's essay?
- How does Sandy represent her process in her cover letter? Does it seem aligned or not with the paper copy edits?
- What electronic or pen and paper strategies might you use in your classroom to help students trace and represent their writing and thinking processes?

"Case Study of Myself as a Writer" is the next paper I have included into my portfolio. This piece of writing is something that I have learned from not only the words on the paper but the content of the words. Writing is something that truly fits the description of "practice makes perfect." Paragraphs are the main issue I have in all of my papers. I have not spent a great deal of time on this but I know that after the papers I wrote this semester I will practice even more. My paragraphs are always too long and contain information that can possibly be broken up. From this paper, I have also learned that the format of each paper is really important because I messed up on my margins and it does not look as professional as the correct formatted papers. This paper has also taught me to add more detail to make it more descriptive. This is something I tried to work on all semester and I have been getting better but there is definite room for improvement in this area. I included some process work for this piece of writing. The process work that I have included was two peer review workshops and one process letter. I think that from these I have learned from just the questions that it asks. It makes me think about it for myself and then also from some one else's perspective. Some of the feedback really had an affect on what I wrote in my paper. I also have included a process letter; I believe that this really shows me what I have been doing instead of my just thinking of what I have. Explaining in paper can affect my paper in a positive way because it forces me to think about it deeper. Another reason it is helpful is the feedback

Figure 6.1. Sandy's cover letter explains her revision process for a paper in her first-year writing course.

from the instructor. This tells me what is important to keep within the context and what should be taken out. Which I believe is a very important part of the writing process. The reason I have put so much process work along with this piece is because I believe with this piece I have come a long way from the beginning and the process work is what aided my in this journey.

    The next piece of writing I have included in my portfolio is a paper about

Figure 6.2. Sandy's cover letter explains her revision process for a paper in her first-year writing class.

164　WRITING PROCESSES ARE INDIVIDUALIZED

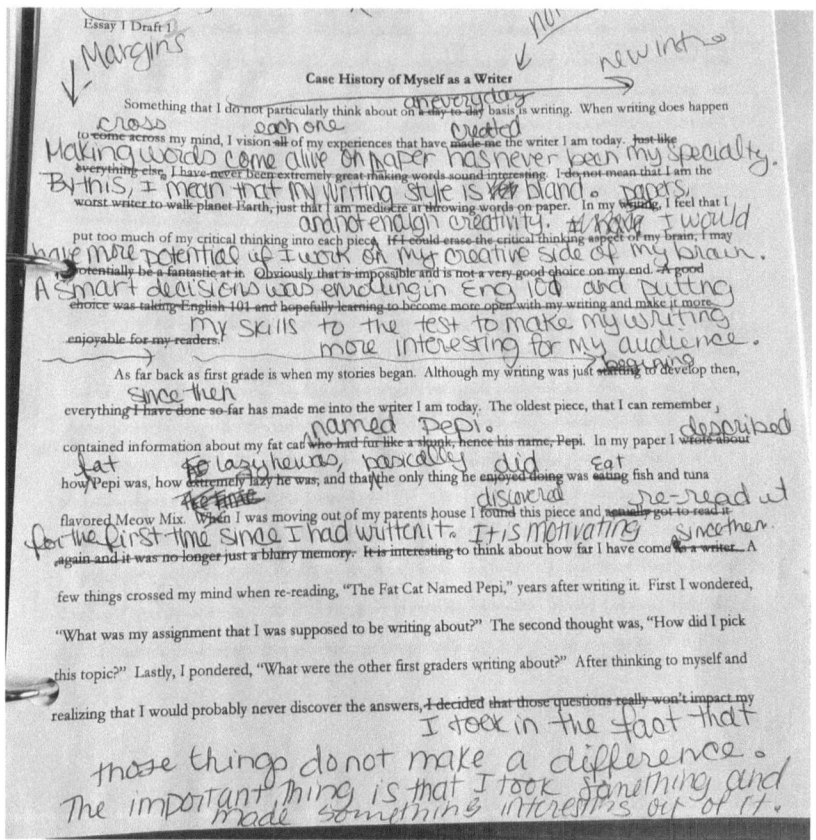

Figure 6.3. Sandy's revision and editing of "A Case Study of Myself as a Writer"

Instructor Perspectives: Navigating Tensions

In response to the Two-Year College English Association Workload Committee (2019) survey, respondents described some of the challenges of their local contexts as well as adjustments they had made to account for workload increases. One instructor, for example, described adjustments to evaluation and process they made to account for increased course caps:

> This semester caps were removed and just ONE of my ENG 111 (first semester writing courses) has 95 students in the class . . . this is not counting my other 5 courses that I teach. I have had to shorten the length of assignments for this class in order to grade papers in a timely manner. Also, I am have not [*sic*] taken up rough drafts for my comments. I only accept final drafts. I do have a professional class tutor in place so that helps a lot. She can't grade papers, but she can give students feedback.

I thought about dropping the number of required essays the class writes but that is set by our department, and we are all supposed to be uniform.

A second respondent described pedagogical, assessment, and policy adjustments made to handle the workload of two-year college faculty members, who typically teach five sections (or fifteen credits) per term: "I no longer respond to students' individual papers; I require students to come to office hours and/or schedule meetings/conferences to get feedback. I require students to use academic success services more, even though there's a limit to the support that peer centers can provide. I engage students in more peer reviewed sessions. I ask students to write fewer essays. I do not grade Daily in-Class or homework assignments (though I do have them submit them for me to see if they are headed in the right direction)."

Reflecting on Instructor Perspectives
- What is possible or prohibited in relation to this threshold concept in your own workload?
- What material conditions support or impede your ability to structure your class practice around the threshold concept *writing processes are individualized, require readers, and require revision*?
- What would your ideal classroom look like that would be completely aligned with honoring and fostering this threshold concept?

Program or Disciplinary Perspectives
In Holly and Joanne's research study "First-Year in the Two-Year" (Giordano and Hassel 2023), one participant adjusting to their new teaching context wondered: "On a more administrative level, I have also been wondering about the scheduling of English courses, the expectations of word and page counts, etc., and the large differentiation between instructors who teach at community colleges. How much consistency is too much/how much variety is too much? How do we ensure enrollment in our courses, successful pass rates, and still maintain adequate academic rigor? How important is it for faculty to norm to each other in the teaching of writing? Reading? Literature?"

Reflecting on Program or Disciplinary Perspectives
- In thinking about your own context, in what ways are writing instructors expected to follow particular policies or guidelines around course content, numbers of words produced, pages written, or writing assignments completed?
- What norming expectations are there in your current context? Do instructors participate in any kind of shared assessment of student

work or professional development activity in which instructors discuss their approaches?
- Is there a writing program coordinator or other leadership person or team who sets the expectations for "what happens in a writing course"?
- Are there state guidelines, institutional outcomes, or other constraints that shape the student experience in a writing course?

QUESTIONS FOR REFLECTION AND DISCUSSION: WRITING PROCESSES ARE INDIVIDUALIZED, REQUIRE READERS, AND REQUIRE REVISION

- To what extent does your current approach to teaching students about writing and research processes help them adapt their process strategies to varied rhetorical situations? How might you adjust your teaching strategies to help students learn that processes vary for different projects and different writers?
- What strategies might you use for helping students break larger projects into manageable, individualized process steps or stages?
- What learning activities might you use to help students successfully complete a multi-stage writing project over time? In your teaching context, what types of process activities would be most useful for helping students develop flexible writing process strategies?
- What teaching strategies do you use for helping students deal with challenges they encounter in the process of completing a writing project? What teaching practices might you use and adapt to your courses to support students who encounter obstacles with writing process activities and with finishing a project?
- How does conceptualizing peer review and instructor feedback as an integral part of the writing process affect how it is taught as part of the student writing process?
- For many reasons, instructor feedback has traditionally been paired with the assessment of student writing. What are the benefits and drawbacks of separating feedback on writing and grading student learning?
- When and how might you integrate strategic feedback practices into your course based on your students' learning needs?

7
READING AND WRITING ARE INTERCONNECTED ACTIVITIES

This chapter explores the threshold concept reading and writing are interconnected activities. We explain why teaching students about reading is essential for first-year writing courses and why instructors need to directly address connections between reading and writing. We give recommendations for teaching students how to adapt their reading strategies to varied literacy tasks. We also describe teaching strategies for helping students develop postsecondary literacy skills by making connections between their experiences as readers and their work as writers.

Reading and writing have always been inseparably connected in the teaching of English at every level of students' literacy development. In "Professional Knowledge for the Teaching of Writing" (2016), the National Council of Teachers of English (NCTE) asserts that a key foundational principle for writing teachers is that "writing and reading are related." Courses that are designed to support students' postsecondary literacy development through connections between reading and writing have been part of the profession of teaching writing for many years (Bartholomae and Petrosky 1986; Laine 2003). However, as Daniel Keller (2013, 25) points out, assigning reading is not the same as teaching reading. Many writing instructors and programs play less attention to reading instruction and student reading development than they do to writing, even though most of the activities in a first-year writing course require students to draw from their experiences as readers.

The initial book on threshold concepts, *Naming What We Know: Threshold Concepts of Writing Studies* (Adler-Kassner and Wardle 2015), didn't include dedicated sections on the connection between reading and writing or discussions of the role of reading in writing studies. However, in the follow-up book, *(Re)Considering What We Know: Learning Thresholds in Writing, Composition, Rhetoric, and Literacy* (Adler-Kassner and Wardle 2019), Patrick Sullivan (2019, 113) proposes that instructors "embrace deep reading as a threshold concept in our discipline" and that they "place deep reading at the heart of meaning-making in the composition classroom." We agree with the idea that deep reading and other ways of approaching critical reading are essential for first-year college students' literacy development. However, our focus in this chapter is on the more foundational but challenging understanding of literacy and the connections between reading texts and writing them, which students need to learn before expanding their thinking about reading and writing in more complex ways.

Understanding the threshold concept *reading and writing are interconnected* is crucial for students' postsecondary literacy development. Identifying the inseparable connections between reading and writing and then applying that knowledge to their own experiences with literacy is a fundamental part of how students become proficient college readers, writers, and learners. Most concepts and activities in a writing course (even those that may seem disconnected from reading) depend on a writer's understanding of texts that stems from their experiences as readers. For example, writing conventions only have meaning within the context of writing for specific audiences and purposes that are driven by the needs of an audience. The National Council of Teachers of English (2016) articulates this principle as follows: "Conventions of finished and edited texts are an important dimension of the relationship between writers and readers." Similarly, to learn the concept that "writing grows out of many purposes," students need experience with reading a variety of texts written for different audiences and purposes (National Council of Teachers of English 2016).

The "CCCC Position Statement on the Role of Reading in College Writing Classrooms" (2021a) outlines the importance of focusing on reading in writing courses, "the need to develop accessible and effective reading pedagogies in college writing classrooms so that students can engage more deeply in all of their courses and develop the reading abilities that will be essential to their success in college, in their careers, and for their participation in a democratic society." This statement assumes that, like instruction in writing, instruction in reading is most ethical and effective when it engages students' diverse experiences, needs, and capacities and when it works from an asset-based (rather than a deficit-based) theory of learning.

RESEARCH ABOUT CONNECTIONS BETWEEN READING AND WRITING

The relationship between reading and writing has had a somewhat fraught history in the discipline of writing studies, in part because the early efforts to define composition and rhetoric as distinct from literary studies seemed to call for an emphasis on composing rather than analyzing texts. Another potential reason stems from the belief that college students (and even high school students) should already know how to read proficiently despite the gaps between their prior learning experiences and expectations for postsecondary reading. Subsequently, full integration of reading scholarship into the preparatory materials and disciplinary publications has not been fully achieved. That being said, associations like the College Reading and Learning Association and, more recently, the Conference on College Composition and Communication (CCCC) have made efforts to make visible the role of reading in postsecondary literacy development. Writing studies scholars from both research universities and open-access institutions have called for an increased focus on reading instruction and support in college writing classrooms (Carillo 2015, 2017; Giordano and Hassel 2019; Horning and Kraemer 2013; Phillips and Giordano 2016; Sullivan, Tinberg, and Blau 2017; Wilner 2020).

Although the connections between reading and writing processes may seem obvious, the role of reading in college writing courses is one that has been under-attended to, with few major texts that prepare college writing instructors providing resources on how specifically to support students as readers and writers. Writing for academic purposes often requires reading and responding to a range of text types, and the kinds of foundational skills students develop in their first-year literacy courses can be critical—especially in preparing students to recognize that reading tasks and text types vary across disciplines in higher education, in the workplace, and in other parts of their literate lives. Further, students begin college with widely varying levels of preparation and types of experiences with reading. The CCCC "Position Statement on the Role of Reading in College Writing Classrooms" (2021a) explains that "reading, then, goes well beyond mere comprehension of words and texts, and instructors need to realize that students may be more or less familiar with different types of reading. Indeed, individual students may be proficient with multiple reading approaches or may struggle with basic comprehension."

Meanwhile, expectations about the kinds of academic and nonacademic literacies students need are increasing. The NCTE statement "Definition of Literacy in a Digital Age" (2019), for example, asserts that "literacy has always been a collection of communicative and sociocultural practices shared among communities. As society and technology change, so does literacy. The world demands that a literate person possess and intentionally apply a wide range of skills, competencies, and dispositions. These literacies are interconnected, dynamic, and malleable." Manifestations and demands of this kind of literacy in the statement range from "participate effectively and critically in a networked world" to "consume, curate, and create actively across contexts" to "examine the rights, responsibilities, and ethical implications of the use and creation of information" (National Council of Teachers of English 2019). It's clear that the demands of literacy today far exceed the commonplace understanding of reading and writing, though literacy continues to be a foundational skill expected in college courses.

Keller (2013, 33, 34) draws from Deborah Brandt's (1995, 2009) work and points out that even though literacy skills have accumulated such that "materials and practices from old and new forms of literacy coexist in society and within the experiences of individuals," college students are often expected to have what Keller calls a "right" kind of literacy, for example, the "expectations and moves of academic writing." As we discuss in the chapters on rhetorical adaptability (chapter 5) and linguistic diversity (chapter 8), those moves and expectations can privilege particular ways of using rhetoric and language.

As the NCTE definition of literacy shows, today's readers and writers are composing in more and more varied contexts than ever before in the history of human literacy. The proliferation of information dissemination electronically and in many modes means people are reading to write and writing about texts in their daily lives as well as in more traditional academic contexts. Keller (2013, 5) describes changes in the use of written texts as "a culture of acceleration" in which "literacy is tied to educational, business, social, and technological contexts that value speed and increasingly enable and promote faster ways of reading and writing." He explains that "literacies can accelerate: appearing, changing, and merging with other literacies, or fading at a faster rate" (7). This means that college writing courses and instructors have responsibilities to support students in interconnected areas of literacy, to develop a flexible set of literacy practices that will allow students to navigate evolving literacy practices and these complex reading and writing contexts. Effective writing instruction (and college teaching in any discipline) now requires instructors to consider how digital reading and online communication shape students' experiences with literacy and learning (Cohn 2021).

At the same time students are using texts in a wider variety of ways, instruction and support for college reading is increasingly being reduced or eliminated outside of writing courses. A national college completion agenda has put pressure on institutions to accelerate students from non-degree-credit developmental English (and sometimes English language–learning) courses and move them into first-year writing either with or without supplemental co-requisite support (Adams, Gearhart, Miller, and Roberts 2009). A parallel reform movement has eliminated standalone reading programs at many institutions, replacing them with integrated reading and writing courses (Doran 2019; Saxon, Martirosyan, and Vick 2016b). Because of changes to developmental education programs, many community college writing instructors are now expected to teach reading strategies in developmental writing courses, and students often arrive in first-year writing without having the intensive support and experience learning about college reading strategies they used to receive in standalone reading courses. For inexperienced readers who are expected to move rapidly through writing course sequences without standalone reading support, teaching reading in writing courses becomes a part of providing them with inclusive and equitable access to a college education.

WHAT INSTRUCTORS NEED TO KNOW ABOUT CONNECTING READING AND WRITING

First-year writing may be the only course in which some students learn about and develop key literacy strategies for postsecondary reading. Students are sometimes expected to use complex literacy skills, but they aren't learning how to develop and apply those skills in other courses. As college writing teachers, it's also important to know that reading and textual analysis skills—without careful consideration and scaffolding—may not transfer to students' other courses or literacy contexts. Small-scale longitudinal research by Annie Del Principe and Rachel Ihara (2017) and Ihara and Del Principe (2016) as well as the National Center on Education and the Economy suggests that students may not be receiving support and instruction for developing sophisticated reading skills in their courses across the curriculum. Ihara and Del Principe (2016, 233) found that students participating in their research projects engaged with reading assignments unevenly and sometimes not at all, while their research typology of reading tasks across the curriculum suggested that students were asked to read in very limited ways ranging from "a supplement to [a] lecture" "reading to complete a task," "listening and taking notes as a text," and more rarely, analyzing or reflecting on texts. Other research by the National Center on Education and the Economy (2013, 26) showed that "only English composition classes reliably assigned more complex texts to students and required students to analyze, reflect on, and evaluate what they have read." This means that (at least for some students) a carefully designed first-year writing course may be the most essential course for laying a foundation for lifelong critical literacy skills and strategies.

One of the primary reasons why first-year writing instructors need to actively teach students about the interrelated connections between reading and writing is that many, if not most, of their writing tasks require them to read, analyze, and write about texts (including shared course readings and research sources). For example, the *Framework for Success in Postsecondary Writing* lists multiple suggested activities for first-year writers that build on the connection between reading and writing, including analyze "a writer's choices," "read texts from multiple points of view," "write about texts for multiple purposes," and "craft written responses to texts that put the writer's ideas in conversation with those in a text" (Council of Writing Program Administrators, National Council of Teachers of English, and the National Writing Project 2011, 6–7). Further, all writing assignments based on written research sources require students to independently find, read, understand, analyze, and write about often challenging texts. To build a solid foundation for postsecondary learning and literacy development, students need to understand that reading and writing are typically not separate activities. As Eric Paulson and Jodi Patrick Holschuh (2018, 36) note, "The primary reason that integrating reading and writing is beneficial is focused more on their shared local, cognitive, and language bases and pedagogical interrelatedness; that is, at its core is the perspective that as modes of language, they are inextricably related."

Providing students with support and instruction related to reading is especially important in first-year writing courses that emphasize independent research because secondary research is a reading activity. Research activities attached to a writing project require students to use complex strategies for integrating reading and writing. First, students need to work independently to find and read credible sources for college writing. Second, college-level research often requires advanced comprehension strategies in scholarly databases with texts written by experts for experts, and students need to adapt to the reading conventions of different disciplines. Library database texts are written in ways that reflect the conventions of those disciplines, and students need support with navigating those differences. Though research (or the strategies college writers need to use to gather sources for academic work) is often conceptualized as a distinct skill from reading, they are in actuality overlapping skill sets.

The Association of College and Research Libraries' (ACRL) "Framework for Information Literacy for Higher Education" (2016) is the standard for information literacy and includes literacies that intersect heavily with the kinds of outcomes first-year writing aims to cultivate. Defining information literacy as "the set of integrated abilities encompassing the reflective discovery of information, the understanding of how information is produced and valued, and the use of information in creating new knowledge and participating ethically in communities of learning," the document establishes knowledge practices and dispositions sophisticated readers develop to navigate the increasingly complex landscape of information. The six frames of the document outline mental paradigms, strategies for inquiry, and content-knowledge about the ways information is created and circulated—many of which depend on students' ability to read many different types of texts for a range of purposes. The ACRL framework illustrates that connections between reading and writing play a complex role in the forms of literacy students need to develop and draw from throughout their literate lives.

WHAT STUDENTS NEED TO DO TO DEVELOP AS COLLEGE READERS

First-year writing students are typically inexperienced with the varied and complex ways they need to use reading as college learners. In *What Is College Reading*, Alice Horning and co-editors (2017, 7) argue that *all* college-level reading should be understood as a "complex, recursive process in which readers actively and critically understand and create meaning through connections to texts." Postsecondary reading requires students to develop new and complex reading strategies. Thomas Bean, Kristen Gregory, and Judith Dunkerly-Bean (2018, 90) characterize the reading skills students need for college success as follows: "to read complex texts independently"; "to read complex texts using strategic tools, such as note-taking"; "to engage in multiple readings of text passages to ensure comprehension"; and "to synthesize information across multiple texts." Most college students will need to learn these skills because college academic reading constitutes a new set of practices and discourses that differ from their experiences with literacy in K–12 education and (especially for returning adult learners) the workplace. Further, college reading assignments vary across and within disciplines and often include dense content and what Bean and coauthors describe as a "substantial concept load" (90).

With these needs in mind, college writing teachers can support students' reading development with instruction and activities that support the complex and varied ways they will use texts as college readers and writers. The following chart shows examples of the wide variety of reading purposes students often encounter in their first college year.

Examples of College Reading Purposes
- Developing background knowledge for a reading, writing, and/or research task
- Skimming a text to identify the main idea or key points
- Scanning a text to look for a specific piece of information
- Reviewing a previously read text to use it for a writing project
- Understanding concepts that lay a foundation for learning about writing and literacy
- Reading and following instructions for learning activities, assignments, and projects
- Analyzing models of student writing to learn about how to complete an assignment and write for a particular academic genre
- Exploring reading, writing, and learning strategies they can apply to academic literacy tasks
- Analyzing a text to identify the strategies writers use to adapt their work to an audience, purpose, and genre
- Evaluating a text as a potential relevant source for a writing project
- Identifying evidence in a text that supports and develops the student's thinking for a writing project
- Identifying specific ideas and examples to cite in a writing project and making related decisions about what to summarize, paraphrase, or quote
- Analyzing and responding to the arguments an author makes
- Assessing the features of a text that establish its credibility for an audience and a purpose
- Analyzing and evaluating research methods authors use in academic texts
- Analyzing research data to draw conclusions about the findings
- Connecting ideas from texts to a student's own experiences with literacy
- Synthesizing ideas from multiple sources
- Reading and responding to the work of other students.

These common reading experiences in first-year writing are different from each other and require varied approaches to both comprehension and critical reading. The diverse ways students need to draw from reading as writers means they need to develop flexible reading strategies. They also need to develop an awareness of how reading strategies for

Table 7.1. Questions for analyzing the features of texts used as sources

Textual Feature	Questions for Analyzing the Text
Purpose	What is the purpose of this text?
Author	Who is the author? What is the author's expertise? What is the author's social and cultural background (if available in the text)?
Audience	Who is the most likely audience for this text?
Context	Where and when was this text published? Is it a print or a digital text? What information surrounding the publication of this text helps readers understand its cultural, social, and historical context?
Genre	What is the type of text? What reading strategies work well for this type of text?
Reading resources	What resources are available in the text to support reading comprehension (e.g., headings, abstract, glossary, charts)?

writing courses are different from the way they read in other types of courses, especially those that focus more on reading for memorization and test taking (Bean, Gregory, and Dunkerly-Bean 2018). Flexible reading strategies are easier for students to develop when they understand the different purposes for reading and when instructors purposefully design their courses to teach students how to adapt their reading for varied academic purposes.

To develop college-level reading comprehension skills and critical reading strategies, students need experience with identifying, analyzing, and evaluating the features of a variety of different types of texts. Carefully reading the basic features of a text (such as genre, audience, and purpose) provides students with clues about how to read and understand it. They also learn how the reading and writing conventions used for college literacy tasks vary across different fields of study. The features of a text also help readers determine its credibility, which is an essential part of finding and using sources for college writing.

Although identifying the basic features of a text seems like a simple task, many college students need to learn or review how to use the features of a text to increase their critical reading strategies, especially with the more challenging texts they will read across multiple fields of study in their first and second college years. Table 7.1 provides some examples of questions students can use in short responses to readings, small group activities, and whole class discussions to analyze the features of texts they will use as sources for college writing:

Students also need structured learning activities that will take them beyond identifying and discussing the basic features of a text to exploring the more complex strategies experienced readers use to adapt the way they read to varying reading tasks and purposes. Table 7.2 gives examples of how to teach students about reading for different situations.

STRATEGIES FOR TEACHING ABOUT CONNECTIONS BETWEEN READING AND WRITING

A first-year writing course can help students develop reading and writing skills simultaneously, but instructors need to intentionally structure a course in ways that support reading development. At some institutions, typical approaches to the design of a writing course privilege writing tasks, assignments, and rhetorical terminology over tasks that do not necessarily encourage students to strengthen comprehension strategies or demonstrate critical reading skills. In designing a course that gives equal support to these interrelated dimensions of literacy, instructors may need to shift their thinking about what writing instruction looks like. This includes thinking carefully about writing assignments that are specifically focused on engagement with texts (and not just citing or referencing sources). In this section, we discuss four basic course design strategies that can help first-year writing instructors create or redesign a course that strengthens students' postsecondary literacy development through activities that help them learn about and practice making connections between reading and writing.

Strategy 1: *Focus assignments and activities on learning about literacy.* One of the easiest ways to help students connect reading and writing is to focus course readings, learning activities, and writing assignments on topics related to literacy. In our own courses and the program we designed at our previous two-year institution (Phillips and Giordano 2016), we assign texts about reading, writing, and literacy, which we've found from our research helps students begin to learn about key issues for first-year writing while also giving them an opportunity to make connections between texts and their own literacy experiences and development both inside and outside of school. Although this approach is similar to the Writing about Writing movement (Wardle and Downs 2020), it includes texts not just about writing but also about reading, linguistic diversity, information literacy, digital reading, and other forms of literacy—which helps students make connections among readings, key concepts for first-year writing, and their own literate lives. Rather than focusing on the work of writing studies scholars, a literacy-focused first-year writing course can also draw from authors from diverse personal, professional, and academic backgrounds to explore issues related to reading and writing that students can connect to their own learning.

Table 7.2. Adapting to different reading purposes

Reading Situation Variable	Examples of What Students Need to Know about a Text	Examples of Questions to Help College Readers Analyze Texts	Examples of Learning Activities
Purpose for reading	Experienced readers adapt their reading strategies based on academic and personal reasons for reading a text.	Why am I reading this text? What are the academic purposes for reading it? What is my own purpose for reading the text? Is it different from the instructor's reasons for assigning it?	Reflective writing on the strategies students use for different reading purposes Direct instruction or class discussions of the varied purposes for reading in first-year writing
Related academic tasks	For college courses, assignments and other learning activities often determine the reading strategies students need to use.	Will I use this text for an assignment or a learning activity? If so, how might I adapt my reading strategies based on how I will use it in the course?	Reflection on or discussion of differences between reading for first-year writing and reading for different courses Direct instruction and small group discussions on how to approach reading tasks based on the directions for related assignments
Genre	Understanding the genre for a text provides reading clues that help readers figure out how to read it.	What features of the text help establish its genre? What are the conventions of that genre? How do those conventions help me understand the text?	Whole class discussions, small group activities, and responses to reading that require students to analyze a wide variety of genres across an entire course
Disciplinary reading conventions	Each field of study has unique reading conventions, and those conventions shape the strategies experienced readers use to understand and analyze a text.	What do experienced readers do with texts in this course and in the other courses I am taking? How do I adapt my reading strategies for different courses? What reading strategies work well for first-year writing?	Short written responses, whole class discussions, and small group discussion activities focusing on the reading conventions and strategies students use across all of their courses, with attention to differences between those disciplines and first-year writing
Text complexity	Experienced readers adapt their reading strategies and reading rate (speed) based on the complexity of a text.	How long is the text? How long are the sentences and paragraphs? What is the vocabulary level for this text? What level of experience with reading is required for understanding this text?	Direct instruction on how college texts have different levels of complexity Discussions of how to adapt reading strategies and reading rate based on the complexity of a text

Continued on next page

Table 7.2—continued

Reading Situation Variable	Examples of What Students Need to Know about a Text	Examples of Questions to Help College Readers Analyze Texts	Examples of Learning Activities
Prior knowledge	A reader's prior knowledge of a topic is an important part of understanding and remembering reading.	What do I already know about the topic? How will my prior knowledge impact my understanding of the text? Do I need to do background reading of easier texts before reading this text?	Reflective writing or self-assessment activity focusing on students' prior understanding of a topic Class activities reviewing and discussing knowledge from previous related texts
Personal difficulty level	The factors that make a text difficult are complex and unique to each individual reader. Adapting reading strategies to challenging situations requires personal choices.	Do I understand what I am reading? If not, why not? What strategies might help me increase my understanding of the text? Is the reading strategy I am using working for me? If not, what strategies might work better for my reading purpose?	Reflective or self-assessment writing Direct instruction on strategies for monitoring reading comprehension

A writing about literacy approach to first-year writing also helps students explore and write about how their own individual and diverse social, cultural, linguistic, and educational backgrounds shape their experiences with literacy. Potential texts about literacy include those that have traditionally appeared in first-year writing textbooks, such as Amy Tan's "Mother Tongue" (2006) and Gloria Evangelina Anzaldúa's "How to Tame a Wild Tongue." But they might also include texts from a variety of nonfiction genres that explore a range of literacy topics—for example, strategies for online reading, college students' experiences with reading and writing, recent research on reading or writing, experiences of first-generation college students, students' rights to their own language, linguistic diversity in the local community, and personal literacy practices.

Strategy 2: *Design writing assignments to help students develop a wide range of skills for drawing from their learning as readers.* While it may seem obvious that source-based writing assignments help students understand that reading and writing are interconnected activities, not all assignments that use texts support students' development as postsecondary readers—especially when they are not encouraged or permitted to explore their own critical reading strategies and individual thinking about texts. Examples of assignments that potentially limit students' opportunities to develop as postsecondary readers include summaries that don't require any analysis or individual response to the text, learning activities that misapply strategies for literary study to reading other types of texts, rhetorical analysis assignments that focus on features of a text that the instructor (and not the student) identifies, quizzes on factual information from readings, discussion activities that focus on closed-ended questions about texts (especially when students don't have the opportunity to ask their own questions), and writing assignments that are about single interpretations of a text without giving students a chance to explore their own insights. These common types of learning activities in writing courses don't provide students with opportunities to explore their own thinking about texts and make connections between texts and their work as writers.

In contrast, a more effective approach to integrating texts into first-year writing is to create flexible and carefully sequenced learning activities that help students draw from and build on their own literacy strengths, experiences with reading, and thinking about texts. The following examples illustrate ways to structure a first-year writing course around increasingly more complex source-based writing projects. Each of these writing activities is designed to help students (a) make connections between their own experiences with reading and writing, (b) practice using reading in a writing project, or (c) both. Assignments that integrate reading and writing also provide evidence of learning that helps instructors trace students' postsecondary literacy development and identify their needs as readers as well as writers.

The following types of writing projects help students learn that reading and writing are interconnected activities while also developing their abilities to complete increasingly more challenging postsecondary literacy tasks:

1. First-week reflection on reading and writing
2. Formal writing project focused on shared course discussion texts
3. Second formal writing project that analyzes a text
4. Third formal writing project based on independently located research sources
5. Concluding reflective project to bring together learning from the course.

First-Week Activity: Reflecting on Reading and Writing

An early-semester activity that focuses on both reading and writing provides instructors and their students with a starting point for tracing

Table 7.3. Reflective assignments for supporting reading and writing connections

Options	Description
Informal literacy narrative	A short essay (or other type of writing) that discusses and reflects on the students' prior experiences with reading and writing (including how their educational, linguistic, cultural, social, and racial backgrounds shape their thinking about literacy)
Introductory self-assessment	A short learning activity that helps self-assess their prior experiences with reading and writing, sometimes in connection with the learning goals of a first-year writing course
Diagnostic essay	A low-stakes (non-graded) in-class or online activity that asks students to write an informal essay that uses evidence from the first reading assignment to support their ideas
Informal response to a text	A learning activity in which students respond to the first reading assignment in the course

students' literacy development across a course. A carefully designed reflective learning activity at the beginning of the course also provides an opportunity for instructors to get a sense of where students are as readers and writers, their thinking and attitudes about literacy, and their prior experiences with reading and writing. Students can also begin to learn about how their own experiences with reading and writing are interconnected and how their work as writers often depends on their work as readers. Table 7.3 describes a few different options for early-semester reflective assignments that help students begin to make connections between reading and writing.

First Formal Project: Writing about Shared Course Texts

The first project in a course that focuses on connections between reading and writing typically asks students to write an essay or other formal text based on shared class discussion texts with or without informal research (for example, interviews or online reading). In the early days of first-year writing, students benefit from learning how to use texts as evidence to support their ideas before engaging in more complex reading tasks that require them to analyze writing strategies, interpret texts, and write from independently located research sources. By using the texts students read and discuss in class, instructors can monitor students' reading comprehension and development as readers, model for students how to incorporate texts into writing projects, and anticipate and respond to students' learning needs for both reading and writing. Students can learn about strategies for writing from sources by using texts they are familiar with, and they can learn from the perspectives other students have about the texts they have read.

Table 7.4. Designing a writing project based on assigned course texts

Options	Description
Text-based argument	An essay that uses shared class discussion texts (chosen by the student) to support and develop an argument
Literacy study	A project that uses course readings about literacy and informal primary research (for example, interviews or surveys) to explore the literacy practices of a cultural, social, educational, and/or workplace community
College learning and literacy project	A project that uses course readings about college reading and writing (with or without informal interviews) to explore a literacy topic connected to a student's educational goals

These early assignments that focus on writing about reading typically work best when students have a range of related course texts to choose from rather than a required set of a few readings selected by the instructor so they can practice identifying texts and evidence based on their individual needs as writers and the focus of their own writing projects. This means that instructors need to purposefully select the texts students read at the beginning of the semester with a focus on related readings that use evidence, present compelling arguments, and invite inquiry. Table 7.4 describes three different approaches to an early-semester writing project that focuses on shared class discussion texts.

Second Formal Project: Analyzing a Text

One frequent option for a source-based writing course is an assignment that focuses on analyzing a text, which can strengthen students' critical reading strategies and help them learn how to move from summarizing ideas from sources to other forms of writing about reading. However, it's important to assign an analysis assignment later in a course after students have had time to practice understanding, discussing, and writing about texts in a more basic and foundational way. Analysis assignments are most effective when instructors devote substantial class time to helping students think through how reading and writing strategies that focus on analysis are different from the strategies used for reading and writing about texts in an informational or argumentative way. Instructors can plan ahead for an analysis assignment by assigning texts earlier in the semester that provide interesting opportunities for students to think about and analyze the strategies writers use to communicate with readers based on the audience and purpose of a text. Students benefit from being able to select their own texts from among a collection of course readings and choose the

Table 7.5. Designing a writing project that analyzes rhetorical features of a text

Options	Description
Analysis of an author's writing strategies	An essay that analyzes the writing strategies an author uses to support and develop a text for an audience and a purpose
Analysis and evaluation of evidence an author uses	An essay that analyzes and evaluates the credibility and relevance of evidence used by an author in support of an argument
Synthesis	An essay that analyzes and synthesizes the arguments three or more authors make about a complex issue and compares the authors' arguments to the students' thinking about the issue

features of a text to focus on based on their own experiences and reactions as readers.

Table 7.5 lists common types of analysis assignments based on course texts. Chapter 5, "Writers Write for Different Purposes and Audiences," gives additional examples of writing projects that help students analyze the rhetorical features of reading assignments and other written texts.

Third Formal Project: Writing about Independent Research

One of the most common projects for first-year writing is a research project based on students' own library database, online research, or both. This type of assignment works well in a course that focuses on connections between reading and writing because research is a reading activity. However, instructors need to create time in a first-year writing course to help students read, respond to, evaluate, and discuss the texts they find for their research projects. At this point in the course, the reading assignments in first-year writing can focus entirely on the texts students find for their writing projects. In-class or online discussion activities can then focus on helping students use effective strategies for reading research sources, evaluate and discuss the credibility and relevance of the texts they find, share what they learned from their research, and discuss ways to draw from their reading as they work toward developing an essay or other text. Instructors don't need to assign additional readings or assignments. Rather, they can focus on helping each student develop their projects and understand the texts they have selected from their research.

When research projects focus on literacy, they help students develop confidence in the subject matter for first-year writing as well as their ability to understand research texts. The research projects themselves can become opportunities for students to explore self-selected topics about

Table 7.6. Designing a research-based literacy project

Options	Description
Literacy research project	A project that uses sources to explore a self-selected topic related to reading, writing, digital communication, or other forms of literacy
Further exploration of topic based on reading or previous writing	A project in which students conduct further research on a topic based on a previous essay, class discussion texts, or both
Literacy community project	A project that uses secondary sources, personal experience, and potentially informal primary research to explore the literacy practices of cultural, linguistic, or social community the student identifies with

literacy that meet their own educational, linguistic, or personal literacy goals. Table 7.6 gives examples of literacy-based research projects.

Concluding Project: Reflecting on Reading and Writing Development

A final reflective assignment can help students bring together their learning from across the course, reflect on their experiences with reading and writing, trace their own literacy development across the course, and think ahead to how they might apply their learning from first-year writing to future literacy experiences both inside and outside of school. The final project is much more substantial than the start-of-semester reflection and can normally replace a final exam for the course, especially at institutions that require a finals week learning activity. The evidence for each of these activities can come from the students' own writing, their experiences with reading and writing, course texts, research, and course outcomes or their personal learning goals. Table 7.7 gives examples of end-of-semester reflective activities that help students make final connections between their experiences as writers and as readers.

Strategy 3: *Provide low-stakes opportunities for writing about reading and reflecting on literacy.* Regular (as frequently as every class period) nongraded or complete/incomplete reflective work and writing about reading with varying purposes helps students explore and practice multiple strategies for using texts for postsecondary learning. Literacy-rich but low-stakes activities contribute to significant learning and can prepare students for major writing projects. Sometimes in-class activities (like quizzes or short written responses) focus too much on testing whether a student read a text (or understood what the instructor wants them to know about a text) instead of supporting actual learning and students' literacy development. By shifting away from coursework that focuses on

Table 7.7. Designing an end-of-course reflective assignment

Options	Purposes
Portfolio with a cover letter	A reflection to introduce a portfolio that discusses what each piece of work shows about the student as a college reader and writer
ePortfolio page with a reflection	A collection of work on an ePortfolio page that includes an overall reflection on the student's development as a reader and writer, short reflections to introduce each piece of work, or both
Reflection on development as a college reader and writer	An essay or multimedia project that traces the student's development as a reader and a writer across the semester, including in other courses
Reflection on learning outcomes	An essay that self-assesses the student's literacy development in relation to course outcomes or specific learning goals for first-year college reading and writing
Reflection on applying learning to future literacy experiences	An essay or multimedia project that reflects on learning from the course and explains how the student will apply that learning to future experiences with reading and writing both inside and outside of school

reading compliance (i.e., whether the student did the reading) to varied and increasingly complex learning activities that explore different ways of using reading for writing, instructors can help strengthen students' reading comprehension and help them practice multiple ways to use texts in their own writing. At the same time, low-stakes writing about reading can prepare students for discussion activities, encourage them to complete reading assignments, and make their reading assignments more relevant to their work as writers.

The following list gives examples of different ways an instructor might develop prompts for low-stakes writing activities followed by related direct instruction and small group discussions to help students develop as college readers:

- Articulating what students do and don't understand about the text
- Working toward critical analysis by moving from comprehension to articulating thinking about authors' ideas
- Identifying the features of a text that establish its credibility
- Identifying main points (or arguments) and key components of a text
- Analyzing how an author adapts writing strategies to an audience and a purpose
- Practicing strategies for evaluating a text
- Generating ideas for writing assignments
- Identifying how they will use a text in a writing assignment (quotes, examples, ideas)
- Connecting ideas from two texts
- Connecting the text to their own literacy experiences

- Encouraging students to write their own discussion questions that focus on critically analyzing an assignment
- Identifying how a text fits into a larger discussion about literacy issues from the course.

Low-stakes writing about texts and reflections on students' experiences with literacy can become a regular part of active learning in a first-year college writing classroom. Table 7.8 provides a basic example of how to incorporate writing about reading directly into an in-person writing or synchronous (real-time) virtual class period.

Instructors can use a similar approach in online courses by carefully structuring weekly learning modules based on activities that help students bring together their reading and writing assignments. Table 7.9 provides an overview of how to structure an online learning module that strengthens connections between reading and writing.

Strategy 4: *Provide varied opportunities for students to reflect on their experiences as readers.* One of the most important and practical ways first-year writing instructors can help students make connections between reading and writing is to develop activities that ask them to explore their own experiences with literacy. Although many writing courses and programs require students to complete reflective work about their experiences as writers, fewer directly encourage students to think about and discuss their experiences with reading, including how reading shapes their work as writers. The following list gives examples of learning activities that help students reflect on and discuss their experiences as both readers and writers:

- Assignments that help students set reading goals and priorities for the course
- Written reflections or discussion journals about students' experiences with literacy
- Writing assignments and discussion activities that encourage students to connect texts to their own literacy practices outside of school or their work in other courses
- Activities that ask students to explore their literacy development across all the courses they are currently taking
- Group discussions that encourage students to explore their experiences with reading assigned texts
- Group activities that ask students to share how they are using assigned texts and reading from research in their current writing projects (or in revision for previous projects)
- Written or oral responses about students' experiences with reading and responding to each other's texts during in-class or online writing workshops

Table 7.8. Example of a class session that integrates reading and writing

Beginning of class: Whole class introductory meeting	Follow up on students' issues and questions from the previous class period; ask students to report on their writing process activities since that class period and their questions about take-home reading activities.
Activity 1: Individual writing about reading	Ask students to write informal, short, open-book, open-note responses to a structured prompt that encourages them to explore literacy strategies while also giving them flexibility to think through their ideas about the current reading assignment, multiple texts from across the course, or their own independent research.
Activity 2: Whole class learning	Design a short mini-lecture or whole class discussion on the reading assignment and literacy strategies students are working on at the current moment in the course.
Activity 3: Small group work	Assign one or more small group activities that draw from the in-class writing about reading and help students pull together ideas from the whole class discussion or mini-lecture. Give students a structured responsibility or task they will report back on to the entire class.
Activity 4: Large group synthesis and review	Lead a large group discussion that creates an opportunity for students to bring together their learning from the class and readings by reporting on and discussing their learning from the small group work.
Wrap-up and learning preview	Preview the next reading assignment (including its purpose in the course) and upcoming activities for the current writing project.

Table 7.9. Example of an online course module that integrates reading and writing

Module overview	Include an introduction to the module and learning outcomes, suggested schedule or homework pacing guide, and a module to do the list of required and suggested activities
Reading strategies learning	Create one or more module learning pages that describe a reading strategy, which might include definitions, short "how-tos," a video, and links to online resources
Reading assignment	Include a brief introduction to the text, an overview of how students will use the text in the course, the title and author with an online link (or page numbers for a textbook), and analysis or reflection questions that help students practice the module reading strategies
Writing strategies learning	Provide one or more learning pages that discuss writing strategies for the module with key terms, examples, videos, and links to online resources
Discussion	Facilitate a structured online discussion that helps students analyze the reading assignment (and often previously assigned texts) while also practicing writing strategies from the module and reviewing strategies from previous modules
Writing process activity	Assign an independent writing activity or writing workshop discussion that helps students connect learning from the module to their current writing projects

- Portfolio or ePortfolio reflections that prompt students to trace, reflect on, and evaluate their experiences with both reading and writing in the course.

A selection of these activities used across a course can help students apply their knowledge about reading to their own experiences as readers and their work as writers while also helping them trace their own literacy development as college learners.

First-year college students need multiple, varied experiences with reading, short learning activities, and formal source-based writing assignments to develop an understanding that *reading and writing are interconnected* and to then apply that knowledge to their own teaching. The reading-intensive approach to teaching first-year writing we have described in this chapter provides students with a foundation for literacy development in other English courses, other disciplines, and their literate lives outside of school. Part of reaching all writers in an inclusive, student-centered writing course means supporting students' growth as readers in addition to their writing.

APPLYING AND CONNECTING

Student Perspectives: Writers as Readers

In a non-degree-credit academic reading support course, students in a research project on placement assessment completed a first-week self-assessment. One student, Moua, wrote:

> As a reader, I think that I am only at like a freshman level [of high school] because I haven't really read an entire book since my freshman year. Reason why is because I don't really have anyone but my friends to talk to and ask questions about school readings. I never really had an [sic] friends in my reading classes to help me understand what I actually read. Also, I have become lay [sic] due to my lack of work in school.
>
> None of my siblings ever really liked the idea of school and so they never really paid attention to school too but I want to be different and so this is why I wanted ot [sic] learn more and extend my knowledge so I can teach others about how and what life is about. Tell others of the hardship that I encountered and the fun of learning things that you're interested in. I believe that with his [sic] class I can learn how to become a better reader and advance to [a] more challenging class, but most important to help me become a better reader and understand the readings I read.

Reflecting on Student Perspectives
- What are some ways you as an instructor might start to engage a student like Moua who self-assesses as an unmotivated reader but hopes to pursue a college degree?

- What classroom strategies might you use to support developing or struggling readers whose prior experiences may not be well-aligned with college reading expectations?
- What strategies could you provide to readers like Moua who seek opportunities to connect with other readers about texts but lack an immediately available way to do so?

Instructor Perspectives: Curricular Questions

In the "First-Year in the Two-Year" project (Giordano and Hassel 2023), instructors were assigned to teach either standalone reading courses (non-degree credit) or sections of integrated reading and writing courses in which reading outcomes were a component equal to writing-related outcomes for the course. One participant shared their experiences with these courses: "Although we have an ENGL 1301 textbook, it is almost useless. I ended up using it for the readings and creating Reading practice materials (and maybe reader response paragraphs assignments) from them. Because of the way ENGL 1301 is mandatorily paired with INRW 0399, the unspoken idea is to really make INRW 0399 an extension of ENGL 1301 so that the work assigned in ENGL 1301 can be fine-tuned in INRW 0399. As such, no textbook has been adopted for INRW 0399. The instructors do not have to use the ENGL 1301 textbook; teachers can use OER materials." In the TYCA Workload Committee (2019) survey, a respondent spoke to the process of implementing reading-writing–connected goals into the curriculum: "One of the biggest changes I've made in my approach to teaching is that now nearly half of my course is about reading—an Integrated Reading and Writing model is fantastic, but I'm not a reading instructor by education, so it has been a self-taught process. Three years in, and I'm making progress, but there's so much more I (we) could be doing for these students."

Reflecting on Instructor Perspectives

- What background and experience do you have in encouraging students to make connections between their reading and writing practices? What learning gaps do you need to work on through further study to develop strategies for teaching students that reading and writing are interconnected?
- What are the distinctions between reading for specific purposes as a writer and reading for analyzing literature, analyzing a text rhetorically, or reading for information?
- What challenges have you had as a reader in using sources and making connections between your reading and writing practices?

Program or Disciplinary Perspectives: Building a Reading-Aware Curriculum

The "CCCC Position Statement on the Role of Reading in College Writing Classrooms" (2021a) offers four principles and accompanying practices to support reading and writing connections. The four principles are:

- Principle 1: Teach Reading Comprehension
- Principle 2: Teach Reading Approaches That Move beyond Basic Comprehension
- Principle 3: Foster Mindful Reading to Encourage Students to Think Metacognitively about Their Reading in Preparation for a Variety of Reading in Different Contexts
- Principle 4: Teach Students How to Read Texts Closely and Focus on Significant Details and Patterns.

The report "Improving College Success for Students in Corequisite Reading" (Ran, Bickerstaff, and Edgecombe 2022, 8), in one of several findings, concluded that "students who did not pass co-requisite reading and its college-level pairing also failed almost all other courses they enrolled in that term; the majority of these students dropped out from college by the end of year one."

Reflecting on Program or Disciplinary Perspectives
- Considering the large impact reading skills have on students' success rates in college, what role can and does reading play in your college writing course? Your curriculum? Your program?
- What challenges or successes do you anticipate emerging from scaffolding reading skills in a college writing course?
- What activities in a single class activity or writing task can you imagine being of use to students at your institution?

QUESTIONS FOR REFLECTION AND DISCUSSION: READING AND WRITING ARE INTERCONNECTED ACTIVITIES

- What are common barriers students experienced when navigating assigned readings or independently located sources? How might you scaffold instruction to help students more effectively work with texts?
- Reflecting on the selection of assigned readings you used for your course, think about whether they should be adjusted in terms of content, difficulty, focus, or genre. How effectively did they help students develop as readers? Which were most successful in engaging students as readers? Which may need to be updated for new student populations or new course emphases?
- What strategies do you use for sequencing when and how to use reading assignments in your course? What changes might you make

to your course schedule and pacing to help students transition from more basic reading and writing tasks to increasingly more challenging and complex literacy tasks? What types of scaffolded support might you provide to help students use increasingly more complex reading tasks?

- To what extent do the major writing projects in the course help students strengthen and develop critical reading strategies? What changes to the design of writing assignments might help students learn how to effectively use sources as writers while also supporting their development as college readers?
- What types of instructional support do you provide to help students successfully understand and use the written sources they incorporate into their writing projects (both course readings and independent research)? How might you develop or revise in-class and online learning activities to help students adapt their reading strategies to meet the demands of different writing tasks? How might you use learning activities to help students make connections between their experiences as readers and their work as writers?

8
WRITERS MAKE CHOICES ABOUT LANGUAGE WITHIN CULTURAL AND SOCIAL SITUATIONS

> *This chapter provides an overview of the threshold concept writers make choices about language within cultural and social situations. We situate this threshold concept within scholarship on linguistic choices and linguistic diversity in higher education. We discuss related concepts that help instructors and their students recognize misconceptions about language and resist linguistic bias. The chapter provides teaching strategies for increasing students' literacy development through a focus on writers' language choices within cultural and social situations.*

Language, rhetoric, and writing are interrelated pieces of a communicative and composing context. Though interconnected, each has a pedagogical role within the context of a college writing course (although there is significant institutional variation in the focus and outcomes of first-year writing programs). As we have discussed throughout this book, writing instruction involves a complex set of skills, content knowledge, and dispositions. One of the most pervasive barriers to and debates about writing pedagogy involves preparing instructors to support writers from diverse linguistic backgrounds, especially how to teach and help students practice writing for diverse audiences, purposes, and genres while simultaneously valuing the linguistic resources and differences students bring to their classrooms.

The threshold concept *writers make choices about language within cultural and social situations* is an essential foundational concept for helping students develop the literacy skills and ways of thinking needed for participation in an increasingly global world. Teaching this concept in first-year writing helps students achieve many of the outcomes outlined in the National Council of Teachers of English's (NCTE) "Definition of Literacy in a Digital Age" (2019), including:

- Participate effectively and critically in a networked world
- Build and sustain intentional global and cross-cultural connections and relationships with others to pose and solve problems collaboratively and strengthen independent thought
- Promote culturally sustaining communication and recognize the bias and privilege present in the interactions
- Determine how and to what extent texts and tools amplify one's own and others' narratives as well as counter unproductive narratives
- Recognize and honor the multilingual literacy identities and culture experiences individuals bring to learning environments and provide opportunities to promote, amplify, and encourage these different variations of language (e.g., dialect, jargon, register).

This NCTE statement illustrates how definitions of literacy continue to expand and the fact that students' individual and communal literacy needs exist beyond a college writing classroom and extend not only into their communities but into a multicultural, multilingual, and multiliterate connected world. As the NCTE (2019) position statement explains: "Literacy has always been a collection of communicative and sociocultural practices shared among communities. As society and technology change, so does literacy. The world demands that a literate person possess and intentionally apply a wide range of skills, competencies, and dispositions." Although no single writing class can address all of students' needs, a set of values can be embraced in a writing class that recognizes and actively discusses this expansive view of literacy that recognizes students' literate worlds outside of the academic setting.

While the threshold concept *writers make choices about language within cultural and social situations* may seem clear, its internalization and understanding can vary for both teachers and writers because beliefs and assumptions about language are situated within cultural communities, institutions, and individual identities. For example, the teaching staff in most college writing programs is predominantly white, as indicated in a 2019 report from the National Center for Educational Statistics, with about 75 percent of college faculty identifying as white (Davis and Fry 2019). The same national study shows that college students are twice as likely as faculty to be Black (6% of faculty versus 12.5% of students) and four times as likely as faculty to be Hispanic (5% of faculty versus 20% of students). In some states, these numbers are even less aligned.

This is noteworthy because instructors' own racial, cultural, and linguistic experiences shape their approaches to thinking about language and teaching students about writing. Both instructors and students can often bring traditional ideas about correctness and usage to the writing classroom, even though much of the established research in the fields of Teaching English to Speakers of Other Languages (TESOL), translingualism, World Englishes, and writing studies has made clear that the use of prescriptive grammatical instruction and emphasis in writing classrooms is out of step with research about how language works. Further, an intersectional understanding of literacy and language acknowledges that multiple overlapping identity categories influence the cultural and social situatedness of any individual writer and speaker. In this chapter, we provide an overview of considerations for writing teachers about the language choices writers make and the contexts in which they make them.

For the purposes of this chapter, we draw from these definitions of linguistic diversity, which is a term that describes at least two different concepts:

1. Communication situations are linguistically diverse in communities, environments, and situations in which people speak more than one language or more than one variety of the same language.
2. The United States and the world itself are linguistically diverse because people communicate through a wide variety of languages.

In a college writing classroom or online learning environment, linguistic diversity can simply mean that students' diverse linguistic and cultural backgrounds shape their experiences with reading, writing, communication, and learning—and their interactions with each other.

RESEARCH ABOUT LANGUAGE CHOICES AND TEACHING WRITING

A deep dive into the history of composition, rhetoric, and writing instruction in the traditions of English will reveal that the roots of writing instruction in English (and accompanying ideas about language) are rooted in British and Scottish universities of the eighteenth, nineteenth, and twentieth centuries, with American writing instruction emerging in elite private universities at the end of the nineteenth century and in the early twentieth century. As historical accounts from Winifred Bryan Horner (1990), Wallace Douglas (1976), and John Brereton (1995) document, very early formal literacy instruction focused on elocution and the traditions of classical rhetoric, with an emphasis on written literacy as it intersected with training for the ministry. As colleges and universities expanded and new populations of (white, male) students studied there, the content of literacy-focused courses (particularly in the early Scottish universities) evolved from logic, Latin grammar, and elocution to focus on the early twentieth-century rhetorical instruction emphasized in US universities—as

Horner (1990, 331) notes, "modes of discourse . . . delineated as narration, description, exposition, argument, and poetry." With their origins in Anglophone countries, translated to the United States, today's writing courses still bear vestiges of this history—including the emphasis on product, on communication through a hegemonic language standard and its accompanying sense of "correctness," and on a narrow set of discursive choices and purposes.

To meet the learning needs of the increasingly diverse student populations in the multicultural and multi-linguistic college writing classroom, instructors need to be familiar with the tremendous research foundation in the last seven decades from writing studies and related fields, including TESOL, cultural rhetorics, linguistics, and sociolinguistics. Scholars like Geneva Smitherman (1986), Jackie Jones Royster (1996), and Elaine Richardson (2003) for example, produced landmark texts on African American language that have informed how writing instruction responds to and builds from the language traditions of African American students. In 2006, Paul Kei Matsuda called for writing scholars to recognize the "myth of linguistic homogeneity" in composition classrooms, and that same year, Suresh Cangarajah (2006) argued for the "place of World Englishes in composition."

Disciplinary statements also provide college writing instructors with principles that provide a foundation for redesigning writing classrooms to support the choices students make based on their linguistic, cultural, and social experiences—including the Conference on College Composition and Communication's (CCCC) "This Ain't Another Statement! This Is a DEMAND for Black Linguistic Justice" (2020), the "CCCC Statement on White Language Supremacy" (2021c), and the College Reading and Learning Association's "Meeting the Needs of Linguistically Diverse Students at the College Level" (de Kleine and Lawton 2015). The CCCC "Statement on Second Language Writing and Multilingual Writers" (2001) describes the definition and learning needs of multilingual writers, calling for a recognition of the tremendous diversity of those whose needs as writing students include "international visa holders, refugees, permanent residents, and undocumented immigrants, as well as naturalized and native-born citizens of the United States and Canada," and recognizing that "multilingual writers can have a wide range of literacies in their first languages, from being unable to read or write to having completed graduate degrees in that language."

The point here is not just to direct readers to resources that have shaped our established disciplinary practices in college writing classrooms but also to note that the specific needs of an instructor, program, or institution are shaped by the literacy needs of the student communities served by that institution. In other words, there is no "one size fits all" set of recommendations about rhetoric, writing, and language instruction. Instructors must learn and understand the needs of the students in their courses, programs, and communities to prepare themselves to be effective teachers of those writing students. For example, Staci Perryman-Clark, David E. Kirkland, and Austin Jackson (2014, 39) assert that "teachers should stress the difference between the spoken forms of American English and EAE [Edited American English] because a clear understanding will enable both teachers and students to focus their attention on essential items," a viewpoint that is complicated by other scholarship on, for example, code switching and code meshing (see Young and Martinez 2011). In this book, we emphasize the practical needs of the diverse student populations that come to our classrooms for the purpose of pursuing their educational, career, and literacy goals and outline the kinds of teaching strategies that will best help those students fulfill those goals.

WHAT INSTRUCTORS NEED TO KNOW ABOUT LANGUAGE CHOICES AND DIVERSITY

As writing instructors, we are already familiar with the ways people make language choices that meet the needs of cultural and social situations, whether spoken or written. Learning and teaching this concept is, however, a lifelong journey, one that evolves and grows as individual communicators encounter new spoken and written contexts that compel them to adjust their assumptions about language and culture while also calling upon their own linguistic and rhetorical resources to successfully navigate varied communication situations.

College writing teachers have varied strengths, linguistic backgrounds, training, and teaching experiences that frame their approaches to the way they teach students about language and how they treat linguistic differences in their courses. Although some first-year writing instructors have extensive graduate training and professional development to help them teach and support writers from diverse linguistic and cultural backgrounds, many instructors need to develop knowledge about language with related teaching skills and strategies slowly over time in their own college classrooms or online learning environments. Some instructors (especially at community colleges) are teaching college writing courses in high schools, prisons, community centers, or workplaces. The context one teaches in, the communities one works in, and the resources one brings to the classroom should be at the forefront of an instructor's pedagogical and assessment approaches to addressing the social and cultural contexts for teaching students about language. Ongoing critical self-assessment of one's own teaching practices and assumptions about student learning within cultural and social contexts is an essential practice of effective college writing instruction.

The following seven concepts can provide first-year writing instructors with a basic starting point for learning about and reflecting on their own assumptions about students' linguistic strengths and the varied ways writers make choices about language within cultural and social situations.

1. *Students' have widely diverse linguistic and cultural experiences that shape the strengths they bring to college writing and their assumptions about their own work as writers.* In any writing course, students are at varying points in their journey toward understanding the social and cultural experiences that shape the way they use language—some with less and some with greater linguistic flexibility than instructors themselves might bring to the classroom. Multilingual students who regularly navigate new communication contexts bring substantial resources and strengths to college from their cultural and linguistic backgrounds—even when those strengths are not recognized or valued by their instructors. Students who speak and write a version of English that is different from the version taught and valued in most public schools and higher education classrooms also have substantial and rich linguistic strengths to draw from as college writers. Examples include students who speak African American English, one of the many Indigenous varieties of English, Cajun Vernacular English, Hawaiian Pidgin, Chicano English, Yeshiva English, and Appalachian English. Similarly, students from rural and working-class communities may use English in ways college instructors don't recognize or respect as part of their social and cultural identities. Some students have an awareness of how their own cultural and social identities shape the way they use written and spoken English, while most are only just beginning to understand the role of culture, education, and life experiences in determining how they think about and use language. Writing teachers have a responsibility to help students build on the multiple resources of their linguistic backgrounds while simultaneously learning new strategies and tools.

2. *Effective writing teachers and programs align teaching and assessment practices with the literacy and learning needs of students who speak, write, and learn in English in widely diverse ways.* Historically, institutions of higher

learning have perpetuated notions that linguistic diversity is a deficit instead of a strength. It can be common for students in the United States to assume that an unmarked and unaccented variety of English is the norm—even if it is a reflection of local and regional linguistic hegemony. In fact, non-native speakers of English constitute a much larger group than native speakers of different varieties of American English. Globally bilingual or multilingual speakers of English are the norm and not the exception (Lippi-Green 2012). Students who grew up speaking a language other than English at home or who spoke more than one language from childhood have extraordinarily diverse trajectories from their early days of learning English to their arrival in a college writing course.

At some institutions, most multilingual students are international students who systematically learned English as a foreign language in other countries over many years. Some learned English through a mix of educational experiences and communicative practice. Others were required to use English as the language for learning in school while speaking another language at home. For example, at community colleges, speakers of World Englishes are a significant and growing population. As the College Reading and Learning Association's white paper notes, "These students hail from countries where a standardized variety of English is (one of) the official language(s), for education and other purposes, and where other non-mainstream varieties of English are usually also used. These countries include mostly former British colonies such as India, Pakistan, Ghana, and Nigeria" (de Kleine and Lawton 2015, 6). They also note that there can be tremendous range in World English–speaking students' oral and written fluency. For example, students with refugee or immigrant backgrounds may have exceptional oral fluency in English with less developed written literacy skills. The reverse can be true of international students at selective four-year institutions who may have extensive formal literacy instruction in written English with limited opportunities to practice listening and speaking. Likewise, the norms of academic edited English may be more or less familiar to students based on their linguistic, cultural, and educational experiences. Students can be proficient in oral and written literacy in English while having limited prior formal educational schooling to prepare them for a transition to the expectations of college writing. In inclusive college writing courses, instructors adapt their teaching practices to account for both the linguistically diverse communities their institution serves and individual differences in the ways students have learned and practiced English.

3. *Effective and inclusive instructors of college writing recognize that students' language backgrounds intersect with other aspects of their social, cultural, and racial identities in ways that reinforce social privileges and discrimination.* Multilingual writers may experience linguistic bias in higher education on the basis of accented or World Englishes while simultaneously experiencing discrimination that is racist. Likewise, some white students from non-prestige (often rural) language dialects experience bias on the basis of their use of a low-status variety of English that does not comport with usage norms for varieties of English valued by college instructors even when they simultaneously benefit from white privilege. Gendered communication styles can influence student participation in classrooms and perceptions about their writing. Some students experience intersectional inequities in college courses based on their race, language background, social class, gender identities, age, disabilities, and other parts of their social and cultural identities.

Well-prepared, inclusive writing instructors recognize that any single axis of identity is an inadequate or incomplete framework for designing instruction. However, that does not mean that students' race, class, language, backgrounds, or other components of their identities do not influence their literacy backgrounds. Some teacher-scholars have emphasized particular aspects of an individual writer's identity (for example, language or race) to draw conclusions about pedagogical or assessment practices that serve students. For example, Asao Inoue (2015, 26) focuses on race as a category of identity and unpacks its influence in college writing courses, aiming to pull out the role of race as it intersects with language difference/diversity: "Race is often marked through language. In short, those who identify primarily as African-American, or Latino/a, or Asian-Pacific American often are the multilingual students or the linguistically different in schools." Rosina Lippi-Green (2012) makes a similar observation in describing results from a study in which student listeners attributed a spoken accent to an Asian speaker and not a white speaker, even when the same recorded audio was played alongside video of each speaker. Other scholars have focused on racio-linguistics to explore the role of language in shaping identity, including the influence language has on ideas about race and also the ways ideas about race shape language (Alim, Rickford, and Ball 2016).

Esther Milu (2021, 437) complicates assumptions that race and language can be collapsed, turning the attention of teacher-scholars to the ways composition pedagogy must develop "effective and unified antiracist strategies that counter Eurocentric linguistic hegemony, white supremacy, racism, and violence toward all Black people in the US contexts and global contexts." She concludes that we (as scholars of language, writing, and rhetoric) need to have "complex conversations about what *really* constitutes Black language" (437, original emphasis), speaking to the importance of an intersectional recognition that considers multiple categories of identity. Scholars like Vershawn Ashanti Young (2009, 71–72) have argued for code meshing rather than code switching (or the idea that speakers of "nonstandard" dialects of American English should compartmentalize their different linguistic resources depending on context—home or school), asserting that literacy educators "teach how the semantics and rhetoric of AAE [African American English] are compatible/combinable with features of standard English. This way the rhetorical force of students' written work and oral fluency will come from a combination of the two—not from translating one from the other." Effective writing instructors treat students as whole students with diverse literacy backgrounds and respond to the self-identified learning needs students bring with them to college while also recognizing that intersectional bias and discrimination can alter the conditions for learning and literacy development for some students across their educational experiences.

4. *Culturally and linguistically responsive writing classrooms affirm students' own linguistic identities and strengths while also teaching them to respect the diverse linguistic and cultural backgrounds of other students and writers.* The "CCCC Statement on Second Language Writing and Multilingual Writers" (2001) explains that campuses are "fundamentally multilingual spaces, in which students and faculty bring to the acts of writing and communication a rich array of linguistic and cultural resources that enrich academic life and should be valued and supported." Given the multilingual nature of higher education and globally connected twenty-first-century communication, competent teaching in writing courses requires instructors to provide a learning environment that supports and sustains students' linguistic and cultural backgrounds. The NCTE statement "Understanding and Teaching Writing: Guiding Principles" (2018b) emphasizes this point with the following principle: "Writers bring multiliteracies, and they bring cultural and linguistic assets to whatever they do." The statement also highlights why exploring cultural and linguistic strengths is an important part of learning about writing: "Because writing is linked to identity, writers represent different ideologies, values, and identities. Thus, writers' cultures and languages influence their writing. Recognizing that students are language users with multiple literacies will help the writing instructor engage students

in writing" (National Council of Teachers of English 2018b). Because students' languages, cultures, and experiences are an inextricable part of who they are as writers, teaching students to recognize and build on their linguistic and cultural strengths should be at the center of every college writing course—not just a component included only in courses designed for multilingual writers.

5. *Instructors' own assumptions about students and language can create linguistic bias and discrimination, with real-life consequences for students.* Teaching for equity, access, inclusion, and justice means that instructors continually engage in reflective thinking about their own biases and assumptions regarding language, literacy, and writing. College writing instructors need to think about the intersectional nature of racism, classism, linguistic bias, ableism, and other forms of discrimination—not just in terms of abstract concepts for social justice but within the context of the literate lives of their own students. Working toward educational equity means directly taking action to reduce bias and discrimination for our own students. Sonya L. Armstrong (2020, 64) describes the importance of situating educational equity within the realities of our own classrooms and teaching experiences: "For me, equity is about teaching the culturally and linguistically diverse students who actually sit with us, not the students others assume are there. It's about the opportunity to transition successfully to higher education. It's about learners' rights to theoretically sound and evidence-based curriculum developed by expert educators. It's about honoring learners' existing languages, literacies, and numeracies, but still ensuring they have access to power discourses in academic contexts."

Writing instructors need to develop the ability to critically reflect on how their own cultural and educational experiences have shaped their assumptions and misconceptions about the ways students can and should use written language. As gatekeepers over a course that is almost universally required for a postsecondary degree, first-year writing instructors also need to continually assess how their own related teaching and assessment practices can perpetuate inequities for students from diverse linguistic backgrounds by creating obstacles to learning, completing the course, maintaining eligibility for financial aid, remaining in good academic standing and having the ability to return for a subsequent semester, making progress toward a degree, and developing a sense of belonging in college.

6. *Competent college writing instructors actively teach students to undo and resist misconceptions about language that perpetuate linguistic discrimination.* For decades, disciplinary statements have affirmed an approach

to teaching writing that both respects students' linguistic backgrounds and dispels myths about idealized uses of language and correctness (Conference on College Composition and Communication 1974, 1998, 2001, 2020, 2021c; de Kleine and Lawton 2015; Suh, Williams, and Owens 2021). The 1974 statement "Students' Right to Their Own Language," adopted by the Conference on College Composition and Communication and updated regularly since its adoption, has sought to lay out the key principles and research that should inform literacy instruction. The document offers instructors a key invitation:

> English teachers at all levels, from kindergarten through college, must uncover and examine some of the assumptions on which our teaching has rested. Many of us have taught as though there existed somewhere a single American "standard English" which could be isolated, identified, and accurately defined. We need to know whether "standard English" is or is not in some sense a myth. We have ignored, many of us, the distinction between speech and writing and have taught the language as though the talk in any region, even the talk of speakers with prestige and power, were [sic] identical to edited written English. (Conference on College Composition and Communication 1974)

What "Students' Right to Their Own Language" has long invited readers to do is to not just learn about how language and writing work but to identify how their own practices in the classroom (which they inherited from their own education) create, reinforce, and perpetuate linguistic bias as well as unsupported myths about how language works.

Although most national guidelines and research do not emphasize a particular kind of grammatical correctness as a core outcome of college writing courses, many students will still find their writing edited and corrected, with attention to surface error outpacing the attention to rhetorical, content, and genre considerations. For example, the "WPA Outcomes Statement for First-Year Composition" (Council of Writing Program Administrators 2014), which is sometimes criticized for taking an overly restrictive position on teaching writing, emphasizes higher-order and substantive dimensions of writing in college—including critical thinking, reading, composition, processes, and rhetorical knowledge. The learning outcomes in the conventions category emphasize knowledge *about* linguistics and conventions—in other words, language choices rather than compliance with a standard version of English. The NCTE statement "Understanding and Teaching Writing" (2018b) places an even greater emphasis on teaching students about their own choices as writers within cultural and rhetorical contexts.

7. *Writing instructors perpetuate inequities when they assess student learning based on misconceptions about language or criteria that differ from what they teach and emphasize in the course.* When writing teachers assess students' writing based on idealized misconceptions about language, they reinforce educational opportunity gaps and make it difficult for students to develop the ability to make flexible choices about their writing. Assessing first-year student writing on compliance with idealized standards of English is especially problematic and inequitable when student work is evaluated and graded on criteria for grammar, punctuation, and style that students never learned or practiced in a writing course. A sentence correction approach to grading privileges students from some linguistic, cultural, and educational backgrounds and disadvantages others while also disconnecting writing assessment from course learning. Grading based on misconceptions about error or on ideals that most first-year writers can't achieve can interfere with the important learning first-year writers need to do, which requires them to take risks, explore their own agency as adult learners, and engage in messy processes as they work toward creating polished writing. New and developing instructors can reflect on their own ideas about literacy and schooling to surface assumptions they may be bringing to the college writing classroom (see Brewer 2020; Brewer and diGennaro 2022).

In preparing materials and designing instruction, writing teachers can ask themselves important questions about how class time (or online learning) is spent, what is emphasized, and what students will actually be assessed on. It is common to spend time on critical reading, research, and writing in a college writing classroom but it is also common for instructors to struggle to actually assess those components of student work and default to correcting rather than assessing. We encourage current and future writing teachers to engage in a rigorous self-examination of how internalized beliefs about language and correctness may interfere with their ability to fairly and justly assess and support students' literacy development. Without competent attention to and implementation of this set of outcomes, writing teachers can be knowingly or unknowingly reinforcing discrimination and bias against a wide range of students while also creating barriers to their retention and degree attainment.

WHAT STUDENTS NEED TO KNOW ABOUT LINGUISTIC DIVERSITY AND STANDARDS

The following concepts can help instructors teach students that *writers make choices about language within cultural and social situations* while also teaching them to resist linguistic bias and ideas about correctness that don't reflect how speakers and writers actually use language.

Concepts for Teaching Students about Linguistic Diversity and Language Choices

1. The United States (and other countries where English is the dominant language) are and always have been linguistically diverse.
2. Standard English is a socially constructed ideal and not a reality.
3. Many beliefs about language correctness are misconceptions.
4. Some ways of using language can be biased and discriminate against individuals or communities.

Concept 1: *The United States (and other countries where English is the dominant language) are and always have been linguistically diverse.* English is the dominant language of the United States, but it is not the only language spoken by Americans. Some natural-born US citizens speak a language other than English at home. However, because of the ways they have been enculturated to think about English, some students have the misconception that speaking another language indicates that someone was born in another country, that all members of society should speak English, or that not speaking English is un-American.

However, linguistic diversity has existed in the United States throughout all of known history. Linguistic diversity includes Indigenous languages that Native Americans spoke (and continue to speak) before the arrival of Europeans, and the Europeans who colonized the Americas spoke different languages. Communities of immigrants in many areas of the country have traditionally used and continue to use other languages at home and in their local communities. Likewise, there are many varieties of English spoken throughout the United States, from non-prestige dialects of English common in rural communities to what April Baker-Bell (2020) calls Black Language. Many speakers of these varieties of English experience linguistic bias and discrimination (sometimes called language discrimination or linguicism), the unfair treatment of an individual or group based on the language(s) they speak or the variety of English they use.

Concept 2: *Standard English is a socially constructed ideal and not a reality.* Standard American English (sometimes abbreviated SAE) is the dominant version of English that is typically taught in schools in the United States and used for professional purposes in most workplaces. Teaching SAE in K–12 education and in college reinforces and establishes it as a standard even though it doesn't reflect the realities of how English speakers use spoken and written English. Unaccented

Standard American English is an idealized version of language that does not actually exist anywhere; as Lippi-Green (2012, 55) writes, "linguists consider the idea of a spoken standardized language to be a hypothetical construct." Lippi-Green explains that "the standard language ideology (SLI) is a bias toward an abstracted, idealized, homogenous spoken language which is imposed and maintained by dominant block institutions and which names as its model the written language, but which is drawn primarily from the spoken language of the upper middle class" (67).

Ultimately, Standard American English reflects a preference that is constructed and reinforced as a form of what Terrence Wiley calls "linguistic hegemony" (quoted in Baker-Bell 2020, 15). Paul Kai Matsuda (2006) identifies this hegemony as a myth that perpetuates misconceptions about college writers. Although English instruction in higher education should consistently cultivate this critical stance of linguistic hegemony, many secondary and postsecondary writing instructors (especially those who are proficient in privileged varieties of English and the conventions/rules of SAE) can find it difficult to divest themselves of this assumption. College writing instructors need to directly teach students about the gap between idealized standards of English and the lived literacy experiences of students and their communities.

Concept 3: *Many beliefs about language correctness are misconceptions.* Correctness is the idea that language (e.g., grammar, usage, words, sentence structure) can or should adhere to rules, follow conventions, and meet social expectations for writing at the sentence level. Many students come to college thinking about proficiency in writing as the absence of error (narrowly defined), which creates misconceptions about what writing is and about their own work as writers. Instructors can actively combat students' misconceptions that writing and literacy are largely focused on the absence of error and "fixing" mistakes and instead emphasize the situated nature of language within various literacy contexts.

If students and instructors focus on errors, mistakes, and correctness, this approach to writing not only reinforces linguistic privilege but also limits the amount of time and effort students may be willing to put into the other dimensions of writing—for example, rhetorical knowledge, critical reading, evidence, voice, clarity, processes, and their own choices as writers. Research by Andrea Lunsford and Karen Lunsford (2008, which replicated a 1986 study) showed that students in the middle of the first decade of the 2000s, when their study was conducted, did not make more errors than they had two decades earlier. In fact, students wrote longer texts, wrote in different genres, and had different errors than they did in the mid-1980s. Lunsford and Lunsford conclude that "student writers today are tackling the kind of issues that require inquiry and investigation as well as reflection and . . . students are writing more than ever before" (792). This is to say that an emphasis on error that reinforces students' idea that there is a standard language ideology can reduce the amount of time and effort they spend on the more substantive dimension of writing required for proficient college literacy activities. Our own decades of experience have shown us how often students who are preoccupied with correctness can resist revision and editing, in part because once they are secure in the correctness of their sentences, they hesitate to introduce new errors by revising large parts of their text. We've frequently taught community college students who have negative views of themselves as writers because instructors in their prior educational experiences have assessed their work for correctness based on idealistic and inflexible standards that are neither clear to students nor consistent across courses.

Students need explicit instruction accompanied by instructors' supportive assessment and feedback behaviors to move beyond a deficit approach to thinking about correctness in their own writing and in the work of others. Understanding this threshold concept is critical to demonstrating and committing to other threshold concepts for first-year writing because beliefs that writing is about error-free prose can supersede learning about writing and developing college literacy strategies in other areas. There is an opportunity cost associated with attention to grammar (which is a radically misused term) and punctuation over other areas of writing instruction and practice.

The following list provides examples of other concepts that help students learn to resist misconceptions related to language correctness and to think critically about how their own language choices are situated within social and cultural contexts:

- Beliefs about correctness and language are cultural. Like other parts of culture, ideas about mistakes and error are situated within specific contexts, vary among social groups, and change over time.
- Beliefs and assumptions about correctness, mistakes, and error are socially constructed aspects of language usage. They are ideas that are meaningless unless they are connected to a specific rhetorical situation.
- Ideas about language correctness have historically been used by people with the social, cultural, political, and financial power to discriminate against individuals and groups in education, in the workplace, and in communities—and they continue to be used as tools for discrimination and maintaining social power.

- In college courses, correctness can be used in ways that purposefully or unintentionally (depending on the context) marginalize student writers, silence their voices, and create barriers to learning. Even when first-year writing courses support students' linguistic differences and writing choices, they can experience barriers to learning in other courses when instructors reinforce unrealistic language standards.
- All writers make mistakes (even in contexts where what is and isn't a clearly defined mistake). Like other aspects of correctness, error-free written language is an unattainable and unnecessary ideal that doesn't reflect the lived experiences of any writer.
- Experienced writers make choices about correctness and adapt their use of language based on the audience, purpose, and context of a situation. Writers' choices are inextricably connected to their cultural, social, linguistic, and educational experiences.

Instructors can incorporate these and other concepts about language correctness into class discussions, reading assignments, and learning activities to help students develop confidence in their own choices as writers and flexibility in how they think about the work of other writers. Many students also benefit from opportunities to reflect on, discuss, and write about the challenges they have experienced in the past because of misconceptions about language correctness.

Concept 4: *Some ways of using language can be biased and discriminate against individuals or communities.* Students need to be able to identify when and how they experience bias and discrimination because of the way they use language based on their linguistic, cultural, racial, and social identities. But they also need to learn about how their own choices as writers can reinforce linguistic bias, maintain inequities, or create a sense of exclusion for readers. Biased use of language includes word choice that is sexist, racist, ableist, heterosexist, and ethnocentric. It can also include the way writers approach content, use examples and evidence, and structure their arguments in ways that perpetuate stereotypes, create microaggressions, and exclude people based on aspects of their identities. Writers should use inclusive language not just because it is an ethically better choice (to include rather than exclude) but because it is more rhetorically effective. Readers who feel alienated by or have negative reactions to a writer's language choices are unlikely to respond positively to the writer's intended message or goals.

Most major professional organizations offer guidance for inclusive language—for example, using language or terms that are preferred by the groups they describe, using "person-first" versus "identity-first" language when discussion people with disabilities, avoiding verbs that are gender-biased ("man the table" versus "staff the table"), and using inclusive pronouns ("they" versus "her/his"). For example, the American Psychological Association (2022) offers a thorough and detailed discussion of "Bias-Free Language" for discussing multiple identity categories as well as history, general principles, and research participation. First-year writers need direct instruction and practice to learn how to be careful and precise about the language they use. The writing course itself as well as the instructional materials should model practices for using inclusive language. Students also need a supportive learning environment to help them undo prior learning and reflect on when and how their own cultural and educational experiences have taught them to use language in ways that both include and exclude others.

STRATEGIES FOR TEACHING STUDENTS ABOUT LANGUAGE CHOICES

Many first-year students have misconceptions and anxieties about language choices that stem from their own educational, cultural, and linguistic experiences. Students need both time and focused practice to unlearn beliefs and assumptions about language, normalize diverse linguistic experiences, recognize and resist linguistic bias, and develop confidence in making language choices within social and cultural contexts. The process of new learning about language choices typically takes place over years of academic and social experiences in college (and not just in first-year writing). For that reason, writing instructors need to use varied teaching practices across an entire course to give students time to learn about, reflect on, and engage in practical learning activities to develop and apply a growing understanding that *writers make choices about language within cultural and social situations.* The following strategies can help instructors incorporate this threshold concept into the design of a first-year writing course.

Strategy 1: *Focus on a rhetorical approach to teaching grammar, usage, and style.* A rhetorical approach to teaching grammar in a writing course emphasizes the strategic and purposeful choices writers make about language for specific situations. Students learn about and practice strategies for making choices about language and sentence structure within the context of their own writing for varied audiences and purposes (in contrast to approaches to teaching that emphasize grammar exercises or rigid sentence correction). Laura R. Micciche (2004, 716) explains that "rhetorical grammar analysis encourages students to view writing as a material social practice in which meaning is actively made, rather than passively relayed or effortlessly produced. The study of rhetorical grammar can demonstrate to students that language does purposeful, consequential work in the world—work that can be learned and applied." Teaching students to view their own language choices through a rhetorical lens both strengthens their literacy development and affirms their linguistic identities.

A focus on rhetorical approaches to teaching grammar and style (Blaauw-Hara 2006; Micciche 2004; Moe 2018a, 2018b) includes:

- Discuss and model the different kinds of language contexts, registers, and situations in which writers make purposeful choices, including academic vocabulary, sentence structure, stylistic choices, and tone.
- Design in-class activities and assignments that analyze the effects of different grammatical and stylistic choices both with published texts and with students' own writing.
- Model and work on language analysis and related reading strategies as a class.
- Encourage students to analyze the effects of different linguistic and syntactical choices in their own writing.
- Ask students to reflect on and write about or discuss their language choices, especially in connection to how their cultural and linguistic identities influence those decisions about language.
- Use examples and students' own writing to discuss and analyze how and why writers make deliberate choices to ignore or actively resist idealized language standards.

Our experience at two-year colleges has been that many first-year students believe the goals of an English course are focused on sentence-level correction; therefore, instructors who use a rhetorical approach to teaching grammar need to provide students with a clear overview of why a focus on linguistic choices within cultural and social contexts will strengthen their literacy development and work as writers in ways that can't be achieved through skill and drill grammar exercises.

Strategy 2: *Empower students to resist linguistic bias and discrimination.* Students need direct instruction and opportunities for critical reflection to develop the ability to counteract the linguistic bias many of them experience in their daily lives in higher education. Regardless of the student population, first-year writing courses are important spaces where instructors can use pedagogies that invite college writing students to recognize and critically examine bias, including both inequities they have experienced and their own unexamined linguistic biases. Examples of teaching strategies that provide students with a basic foundation for resisting linguistic bias and discrimination include:

- Inviting students to analyze writing assignments or past assessment practices they have encountered in their educational experiences (see Slinkard and Gevers 2020 for other pedagogical approaches)
- Using direct instruction to identify and discuss linguistic bias in higher education
- Assigning and discussing position statements about students' rights to their own language
- Assigning and discussing examples of linguistic discrimination from videos, readings, and current news articles
- Designing learning activities or writing assignments with accompanying readings that ask students to reflect on their own experiences with language, power, and critical literacy.

Empowering students to identify and resist linguistic bias is a process that happens slowly over the course of their college experiences. However, first-year writing courses can provide students with a starting point for developing knowledge and strategies that will prepare them for subsequent learning experiences both in college courses and in their communities.

Strategy 3: *Normalize linguistic diversity.* Normalizing linguistic diversity in writing classrooms means intentionally designing instructional practices in a way that creates a true community of writers. Writing instructors can cultivate this kind of environment in multiple ways. Read, for example, Christopher Leary's (2019) discussion of using class anthologies made up of daily writings, which invite students to collect, trade, and assemble student writing samples into personal class anthologies—including texts that are written in languages other than English.

The College Reading and Learning Association's white paper "Meeting the Needs of Linguistically Diverse Students at the College Level" (de Kleine and Lawton 2015) offers a series of evidence-based recommended strategies for supporting and building on the strengths of linguistically diverse students, including building critical language awareness (see Leonard 2021), scaffolding the development of academic language (versus social language), and using culturally responsive and multicultural course content to engage students (see de Kleine and Lawton 2015). Instructors can integrate such approaches into their classrooms by creating learning activities that help students reflect on, write about, and discuss their own language backgrounds and explore how intersectional parts of their linguistic, social, racial, and cultural identities have shaped their experiences with and thinking about literacy.

Table 8.1. Strategies for designing courses about linguistic diversity

Strategy	Examples
Readings about equity, inclusion, and language	Assign and discuss texts about a variety of different issues related to linguistic diversity, bias, discrimination, equity, and inclusion.
Readings that represent students' languages and cultures	Assign, analyze, and discuss texts by authors with varied cultural and language backgrounds, especially those from the communities your writing program serves.
Narrative or reflective essay	Design a formal or informal writing assignment that provides students with an opportunity to reflect on how the language(s) they use and their cultural backgrounds shape their experiences as readers and writers.
Source-based writing assignment	Create an assignment that asks students to explore a self-selected issue related to equity, inclusion, and language by analyzing and responding to shared course readings.
Research essay	Assign a writing project that asks students to use primary and secondary research to investigate an issue related to language and culture.
Research tasks	Encourage students to do research in readings in all the languages they speak; provide them with opportunities to share their findings with other students.

Strategy 4: *Design courses around linguistic diversity.* Pedagogical choices can be accompanied by course content decisions. Many instructors assign and discuss texts that focus on issues related to inclusive language, linguistic diversity, and language choices—including authors from the linguistic and cultural student communities a writing program serves (see Looker 2016). In doing so, instructors can design learning activities that create opportunities for students to directly analyze and discuss information about linguistic, cultural, and racial diversity in the United States. For example, students might analyze and discuss research data about language groups in the United States or in the local community while learning how to use and write about empirical research in their work as college writers. Students can read and discuss articles about language and power while learning how to read and analyze scholarly articles. Instructors can teach students how to use tools in library databases to find and read articles in multiple languages.

Table 8.1 offers specific suggestions for designing courses that focus on linguistic diversity to support the threshold concept *writers make choices about language within cultural and social situations.*

Strategy 5: *Create learning conditions that support students in using and maintaining their multiple languages.* Culturally sustaining teaching practices help students maintain and support their cultural and linguistic identities (Alim and Paris 2017). A linguistically and culturally sustaining writing course helps students make and maintain connections among learning in the course, their languages, and their cultural communities. Writing instructors can create inclusive courses that normalize and encourage the use of multiple languages and varieties of English. The following teaching practices provide some examples of the many ways instructors can apply culturally and linguistically sustaining teaching practices to a college writing course:

- Include a linguistic diversity and inclusivity statement for a syllabus or course orientation that affirms students' linguistic identities and lays a foundation for eliminating linguistic bias in the classroom or online community.
- Write course policies and instructions that explicitly encourage students to draw from all of their languages and linguistic resources for course learning activities.
- Encourage students to share and discuss examples of their literacy practices in their linguistic and cultural communities, including their writing in languages other than English.
- Create learning activities that help students compare and contrast rhetorical strategies, educational norms, and writing conventions from their own and others' cultural and language backgrounds.
- Support students in using multiple languages for planning, prewriting, and drafting.
- Model how to use language tools of library databases, translation tools, and other course learning technologies.
- Support and encourage students in doing secondary research in all of their languages for reading.
- Provide structured opportunities for students to share their learning from reading and research.

Instructors who want to learn more about issues related to using multiple languages as a resource and related rhetorical strategies can read about translingual literacy and related disciplinary debates about teaching (Atkinson et al. 2015; Canagarajah 2015; Horner, Lu, Royster, and Trimbur 2011; Lu and Horner 2013; Matsuda 2014). However, instructors don't need to use a translingual approach to designing writing courses to create opportunities for helping students draw from their linguistic strengths and use all their languages for learning about writing.

Strategy 6: *Use a student-driven approach to assessing learning outcomes that focuses on students' own goals as writers and learners.* Although most departments or programs that offer first-year writing courses have their own outcomes for the course (some of which may be set by a state- or system-level body and required for accreditation), instructors often have flexibility within an individual course to use pedagogical approaches and even grading practices that center learning on students' own

Table 8.2. Designing writing courses based on students' goals

Strategy	Examples
Individual learning plans	Have students create individualized plans for identifying and working toward achieving their own language and literacy goals.
Ongoing reflection	Provide structured opportunities for students to return to and revise both their goals and their plans as they learn more about reading, writing, and literacy.
Individualized feedback	Encourage students to write requests for feedback or author's notes to articulate their individualized goals for a writing project and identify the types of feedback they would like to receive from the instructor and the class to achieve their goals.
Structured conversations	Offer one-on-one conferences or small group activities that create time and space for students to identify and discuss their priorities for learning and language development.
Summative reflection	Conclude the course with a reflection assignment that helps students self-assess their literacy development in relation to their own goals, including how they revised or adapted their goals over time in response to their learning about literacy and language.

goals for learning and literacy development. Examples of strategies for designing writing courses based on students' own goals for literacy and language include those depicted in table 8.2.

Within the framework of a writing course structured around students' own learning goals, instructors can provide students with multiple strategies for choice and negotiation about topics or tools that will be emphasized in class and in the learning activities they complete to develop their personal language and writing goals. This may include online tools, writing center workshops or consultations, or learning management system–based activities that happen through in-class, synchronous, virtual, or asynchronous online instruction.

ASSESSING STUDENT LEARNING TO REDUCE LINGUISTIC BIAS AND SUPPORT LANGUAGE CHOICES

The concept *writers make choices about language within cultural and social situations* and its accompanying principles are not easy to teach, learn, or assess. Writing teachers need to recognize that shifting the ways students think about their own language or the language of others is an ongoing process that will take time beyond one or more writing courses and beyond a college degree. The following principles can help instructors develop inclusive assessment practices that reduce linguistic bias while supporting students' literacy development and learning about language choices.

Principle 1: *Equitable and inclusive assessment is aligned with the learning goals of a course.* Arguably the most fundamental principle of effective college learning assessment is that it evaluates the knowledge and skills students have learned, practiced, and developed in relation to the purpose and goals of a course. Assessment practices (and related grading methods) are inherently inequitable when they emphasize standards that differ from the teaching and learning that happens in a course. For example, if students spend most of their time in a writing course learning about and practicing rhetorical strategies and writing processes, then assessments that prioritize grammar or citation style are misaligned with student learning, teaching, and the purpose of the course. Even when an instructor directly teaches students about grammar and usage, it isn't (and shouldn't be) the primary focus of a college writing course, which means it's not equitable to make it a focus of assessment and grading.

Principle 2: *Grading isn't the same as learning assessment.* Although grading is a teaching activity that is closely connected to and often part of the process of assessing student learning for final writing products, assigning a value to student work through a grade is different from authentic assessment, which should support student learning and inform teaching practices. This principle is easy to overlook when instructors take an approach to grading that focuses on identifying and marking sentence-level errors in student writing. Effective assessment evaluates students' learning and literacy development and progress across a course for the purpose of providing them with feedback to help students learn and instructors improve teaching.

Principle 3: *Correcting and marking errors isn't assessment and doesn't provide students with effective feedback.* Some instructors respond to student work by marking or correcting errors in the text. One especially rigid example of marking texts is when instructors use a numbering or symbol system to mark student writing and then require students to look up corresponding information in a grading guide or textbook. Understanding corrections and marking requires knowledge of what the marks on the page mean, with corresponding skill in translating that knowledge to revision and editing. Inclusive assessment leads to feedback that supports students in making rhetorical choices about revision and applying learning to subsequent writing projects.

Principle 4: *Effective assessment and grading practices in writing courses reflect and reinforce the concepts about writing and literacy that students learn in the course.* It's both unethical and counterproductive to teach students that writing choices are situated within cultural and social situations and then assess student learning using methods that are disconnected from the social context of the students' own work and the context of the classroom or online course community. Assessment, grading, and feedback practices communicate messages to students about what is and isn't important in a course—and where and how they should focus their time and attention.

Principle 5: *Incorporate assessment, feedback, and support for individualized language choices into many different learning activities across a course.* Ensure that students have multiple opportunities throughout a planning, drafting, revising, and editing process to make choices at the linguistic or syntactic level that will best fulfill the goals of both an assignment and the course as well as their own personal writing goals. Support students' linguistic choices by assessing their growth over time instead of focusing on individual achievement of perceived correctness standards on a final written product. Provide feedback that supports the goals students have developed for themselves and the types of feedback they request to help them achieve those goals.

INTERSECTIONS WITH OTHER THRESHOLD CONCEPTS

Because learning about writing and college literacy development are intrinsically connected to language choices, instructors need to weave the threshold concept *writers make choices about language within cultural and social situations* throughout an entire course and connect it to the other threshold concepts through direct instruction, assignments, learning activities, and feedback. Supporting students' language choices and sustaining their linguistic identities are essential parts of helping them understand that *writing can be taught and learned.* Students have difficulty believing they are capable of tremendous growth and learning as writers if instruction and assessment practices reinforce idealized and unattainable standards for language correctness. When writing courses disrespect and devalue students' linguistic, cultural, and racial backgrounds and identities, students have difficulty drawing from their languages and cultural experiences to help them learn and develop as writers.

Similarly, students can't fully understand and apply knowledge about the threshold concept *writers write for different purposes and audiences* until they develop healthy and empowering beliefs about their own language choices and feel supported in making those choices. They also can't effectively adapt their writing strategies to different purposes and audiences without understanding how their own uses of all the languages they speak are rooted in cultural and social situations across a lifetime of multiliterate experiences with communication.

Likewise, learning and applying the threshold concept *writing processes are individualized, require readers, and require revision* provides students with a foundation for taking risks with language choices through opportunities for feedback and revision. Developing flexible writing processes and adapting those processes to varying situations strengthens students' abilities to situate their language choices within cultural and social contexts. Seeking and receiving feedback from instructors and students in a classroom or virtual community in which students' linguistic backgrounds and strengths are valued helps them unlearn misconceptions about language correctness and helps them learn that their own individualized writing processes are grounded in their linguistic and cultural experiences.

Finally, learning that *reading and writing are interconnected activities* is inherently linked to an understanding of how *writers make choices about language within cultural and social situations.* Proficient college-level reading comprehension and critical reading requires students to identify and analyze the social and cultural contexts in which other writers make choices about language. Students' thinking about and learning from texts expands when they learn to value the multilingual literacy identities and culture experiences of other writers (including other students). Connecting these two threshold concepts can also help students recognize that their own experiences with writing are linked to their experiences with reading and learning within the context of their linguistic and cultural identities. The concept *writers make choices about language within cultural and social situations* is truly an essential threshold for first-year writing because it opens new pathways to learning and literacy development that students can draw from in all areas of their literate lives.

APPLYING AND CONNECTING
Student Perspectives: Making Words Match Intention

Joanne and Holly conducted a study that traced how students with academic backgrounds that did not start them in degree-credit coursework experienced their first two years of college writing (Giordano and Hassel 2016). Read these students' reflective writing in the context of this threshold concept.

Student 1: Reflective Paragraph[1]

The specific aspects I plan to reach seek assistance is on paragraph grammars. My English teachers from High school would always tell me I have a good paper, I just need to make my paragraphs more clear. I think this is my number one think I need to improve in both the critical response and position paper and my other English appears in the upcoming future. Sometimes when I read my papers over, i just sometimes have to laugh at my mistakes because sometimes it just don't make sense completely. To decrease the mistake of funky grammar misuse, I will be sure to reread my papers. Don't worry, I'll reread this paper as well.

Student 2: Month-One Self-Evaluation

At this point during the semester, I feel that some of the challenges that I have ith reading are difficulty with vocabulary and comprehension of what I am reading. For example, when I read the book *The Immortal Life of Henrietta Lacks,* there were some parts that had scientific words which it made the whole paragraph more difficult to understand. Also, it took me a while to read a chapter because there were many words that I didn't know. I usually use an online dictionary for an explanation that is easier to understand. My strength as a college reader is annotating while reading. When I read a short chapter from *The Immortal Life of Henrietta Lacks,* I usually write two or three sentences at the front of the chapter to remind me what the chapter is about. I like to make a connection to my personal experiences when I read some parts in the book. For example, I understood how Deborah felt that her mother's cells seemed important to the scientists than her mother did personally. For the next essay I can use that as supporting evidence.

As a college writer, I feel that when I write essays that relate to my personal experiences, my essays re stronger. For example, in my essay "The Benefits of Writing," I wrote where I am as a writer and made connection between each paragraph which helped the essay to flow more smoothly. Some of the areas where I'm challenged in writing are grammar, tense, and clarity. Sometime, I have unique ideas but I don't how to write them in English. In this course we only have a short time to write in class responses and that is difficult for me. I usually take a lot of time to think about it. Another example is that the Hmong language doesn't contain different tense like English. For me that is still the hardest part to distinguish when I write. Sometimes my sentences don't make sense because I write them as I would say them in Hmong.

---

1. Student writing appears as written.

Student 3: From a "Case Study of Myself as a Writer" Assignment

As I sat at my computer desk thinking of what to write for my scholarship essay, I twiddled my thumbs and twirl in my chair, much the same as I'm doing now. I hated to write, but I knew that it was important to get this done, so I did what I do best; I wrote it quick, simple, and to the point. I didn't bother making it real fancy and dressing it up with pretty words, since I hoped that the people reading it were after the real meaning.

In my essay I wrote not only about accomplishments, but also the struggles that I have faced. During my freshman year of High School my father was arrested for growing and selling drugs. When he went to jail my brother, Ben, became my guardian and he developed a drinking problem. I have known what it is like to be extremely poor and I know what it's like to not have enough food to eat. I do not use it as an excuse and I don't use it for pity; it's only a fact that I needed them to understand. Despite my upbringing, I managed to graduated High School with a 4.1 GPA, joined many school activities, and was well liked by my peers. I expressed in my essay that if I were to be awarded this scholarship, it would help out the cost of my schooling greatly. It was my hope to one day save species from extinction and if I were to achieve that, then I would prove to everyone that I am more than where I come from. It would prove that it doesn't matter who you parents were or how much money you had, the only thing that matters is here and now.

Reflecting on Student Perspectives
- What kinds of thinking do you see these student writers doing in relation to the threshold concept *writers make choices about language within cultural and social situations*?
- What other ways would you want these writers to grapple with this threshold concept if you were their instructor?
- What teaching strategies might you use to help these students achieve the literacy goals they identify in their reflections?

Instructor Perspectives: Different Programs and Resources

In Holly and Joanne's research study "First-Year in the Two-Year" (Giordano and Hassel 2023), a participating instructor at a two-year college in the US Midwest reflected on her background teaching ESL (English as a second language) courses and how she saw opportunities to apply some of that previous experience to a new and different context: "I feel like I have been drawing heavily from my experience in ESL and remedial English instruction with my developmental Reading and Writing courses, and my undergraduate program in my ENG 101.

The developmental courses I am teaching need more explicit instruction than my mainstream courses, and I have noticed that some of the strategies from my ESL coursework—differentiation, drawing attention to language forms, explicit modeling and comprehension checks—are necessary in this new context as well."

Reflecting on Instructor Perspectives
- What previous experiences have you had with linguistically and culturally diverse student writers?
- What past experiences have you had with teaching writing or language in contexts different from your current one?
- What practices might be relevant across those contexts, and which may not be productively translated to a new setting?

Program or Disciplinary Perspectives

In "First-Year in the Two-Year" (Giordano and Hassel 2023), one of the participating instructors wrote about her experiences teaching a co-requisite course (a degree-credit support course that blended academic reading instruction with writing instruction):

> In the co-requisite "Integrated Reading and Writing" course I'm teaching, nearly half of the students are L2 students, many of whom moved to the US very recently. This is the population I feel least prepared to work with, as I've never received any specific training for teaching L2 students. The situation is especially tricky because many of these students are very skillful language users who happen to be new to the English language; they really do not need a co-requisite course as much as they need an L2-specific section of composition (which my institution does not offer at this campus). I've asked for specific professional development opportunities to help me work with L2 students, but evidently these opportunities are not currently available. I can certainly do my own research in this area, but it would be nice if the college offered more systematic training given the significant population of international students at my school

Reflecting on Program or Disciplinary Perspectives

Consider the student populations at your school and how or whether the program resources you have are aligned with students' needs. Some food for thought:

- How are students placed into writing or reading courses?
- How is linguistic diversity accounted for?
- What training or background do instructors in your program have for working with multilingual students?

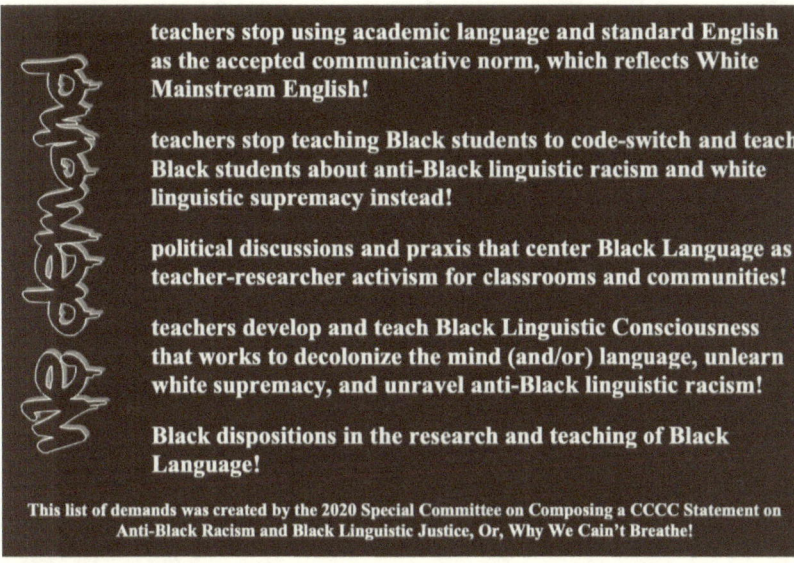

Figure 8.1. From "This Ain't Another Statement! This Is a DEMAND for Black Linguistic Justice" (CCCC 2020).

- What methods are available in your context to identify students' academic and linguistic needs?
- What curricular options might be developed or revised to meet students' linguistic and academic needs?

Disciplinary Perspectives

Consider the list of demands that appear in the Conference on College Composition and Communication's "This Ain't Another Statement! This Is a DEMAND for Black Linguistic Justice" (2020) (figure 8.1).

We Demand
  Teachers stop using academic language and standard English as the accepted communicative norm, which reflects White Mainstream English!
  Teachers stop teaching Black students to code-switch and teach Black students about anti-Black linguistic racism and white linguistic supremacy instead!
  Political discussions and praxis that center Black Language as teacher-research activism for classrooms and communities!
  Teachers develop and teach Black Linguistic Consciousness that works to decolonize the mind (and/or) language, unlearn white supremacy, and unravel anti-Black linguistic racism!
  Black dispositions in the research and teaching of Black Language!

This list of demands was created by the 2020 Special Committee on Composing a CCCC Statement on Anti-Black Racism and Black Linguistic Justice, Or, Why We Cain't Breathe!

Reflecting on Disciplinary Perspectives
- In what ways is your classroom or program aligned with these demands?
- What adjustments could or should you make to respond to these demands?
- What institutional, programmatic, or personal barriers might prevent response?
- Which students are included or left out by changes that respond to the demands?

QUESTIONS FOR REFLECTION AND DISCUSSION: WRITERS MAKE CHOICES ABOUT LANGUAGE WITHIN CULTURAL AND SOCIAL SITUATIONS

- To what extent do your teaching strategies help students understand and value linguistic diversity as a key component of developing and strengthening strategies for communication and literacy?
- To what extent do your teaching strategies and classroom or online interactions support or create barriers to learning for students whose language backgrounds are different from the dominant culture(s) of the community in which you teach? What adjustments to your teaching might help you create culturally and linguistically sustaining classrooms or online learning spaces?
- Have you focused your assessment values and strategies on the literacy development students have demonstrated throughout the assignment sequence? Are you aligning your assessment criteria with the areas of emphasis and focus of the course instruction?
- In thinking about your overall course experience, reflect on what areas students struggled with or what aspects of students' learning accomplishments were and were not captured by the assessment measures you used. For example, if you assigned a portfolio or used a rubric to assess students' achievement of the course outcomes, can you revise the guidelines or the criteria and refine them in ways that reflect what you've noticed?
- What can you conclude about supporting students' linguistic development from the requests for feedback or reflective writing students have completed in your course? As you review portfolios or final writing projects, what do you notice across the student work as a whole? Are there patterns students identify that can help you revise and rethink the way you approach grammar, style, linguistic choices, and rhetorical effect?

9
CONCLUSION
Continuing to Develop as a College Writing Teacher

This concluding chapter discusses current developments in and potential future directions for writing studies research and their implications for first-year writing. We explain how ongoing learning about teaching and developing pedagogical adaptability are essential strategies for building a sustainable career as a writing teacher.

There is a broad array of approaches to teaching college writing, driven by classroom research, theory, and experience. In this book, our aim is to equip college writing teachers with a foundation of principles for teaching first-year writing, recognizing that each instructor brings their own perspectives, experiences, and professional expertise to their courses. We hope that *Reaching All Writers* offers a foundation readers can use and adapt to their own teaching contexts. Instructors can develop and strengthen pedagogical adaptability with ongoing reflection and professional learning.

In this closing chapter, we chart what future development in the field of writing studies might look like, as well as how the roles and responsibilities of college writing instructors evolve over time. Likewise, we make recommendations for readers who hope to continue their professional learning—their development of pedagogical adaptability—throughout their careers. Our goal for this book is to create a guide for teaching first-year writing that helps instructors develop strategies for supporting postsecondary literacy development for students from diverse educational, cultural, social, racial, and linguistic communities—in other words, *all* writers.

PEDAGOGICAL IMPLICATIONS OF FUTURE WRITING STUDIES RESEARCH

As the information landscape becomes more complex, new areas of research and scholarship within the field of writing, rhetoric, and composition studies call on instructors to adapt their practices. Likewise, changes at the state and national levels around placement, curriculum, assessment, professional development, and secondary-postsecondary pipelines place demands on writing teachers to pivot quickly, build relationships, and respond to changing student populations. New areas of research add to disciplinary knowledge of inclusive and equitable writing pedagogies that meet the needs of a broad range of students, including attention to neurodiversity (Smilges 2021), universal design for learning (Tobin and Behling 2018), a focus on identity and circulating rhetorics of difference in writing classrooms (Kerschbaum 2014), and trauma-informed pedagogy (Tayles 2021). Research on critical language awareness (Leonard 2021; Shapiro 2022), antiracist pedagogies (Baker-Bell 2020), translingualism (Horner, Lu, Royster, and Trimbur 2011), and multilingual writing pedagogies (Canagarajah 2006; Matsuda 2006) likewise call on all writing teachers to continually update their own learning and teaching strategies to meet the needs of the increasingly linguistically, racially, and socially diverse students in higher education. Such developments also reflect the reality that most speakers of English are speakers of other languages and that global Englishes are a new norm for many institutions.

While online writing instruction has been an area of scholarly work and a common teaching and learning context, the Covid-19 global pandemic called on nearly every college writing teacher to quickly develop at least some technological proficiency to be able to participate in remote emergency instruction. Although leaders of the National Council for Online Education (2022) have directly observed that "Emergency Remote Instruction Is Not Quality Online Learning," initial exposure to technology-enhanced instruction and the accompanying levels of flexibility and independent learning it requires will inevitably continue to inform the way colleges and their faculty plan their learning environments in the future. The increasing use of online environments for academic learning—and the increasingly digital sites of communication everyday writers participate in—seems also likely to demand the design of curricula, pedagogy, and assessment that build students' capacities for composing digitally and multimodally.

Expanding scholarly arguments about the nature of reading, literacy, and meaning making will press writing teachers to think expansively about the literacies that happen in their classrooms. J. Logan Smilges (2021, 106), for example, writes that "reading is to be understood in its colloquial sense—that act of making meaning out of letter-symbols on a page. Literacy/ies, on the other hand, is to be understood more broadly, referring to all meaning-making practices. Literacy includes reading but is not limited to it." Accompanying this scholarly trend are the institutional and legislative mandates to eliminate what used to be structured as standalone courses focused on helping new college students develop college reading skills. Elimination of standalone reading courses in states like California, Florida, and Texas means that instructors previously credentialed only to teach reading are now cross-training as writing teachers while writing teachers will find more pressure to address skill building in reading to prepare students for college literacy demands. No doubt, too, the research and scholarship on how students transfer learning from one course to another, one year to another, or one setting to another writing context will continue. Early research on transfer from Linda Adler-Kassner (2012), Anne Beaufort (2007), Mary Jo Reiff and Anis Bawarshi (2011), Dana Lynn Driscoll and Jennifer Wells (2012), Kathleen Blake Yancey, Liane Robertson, and Kara Taczak (2014), and others along with recent longitudinal research (Smith, Girdharry, and Gallagher 2021) suggests that writing teachers will be expected to think prospectively and intentionally about teaching practices that support students as they encounter new writing tasks. At the same time, we are pressed to consider how and whether writing courses must be solely the province of academic writing. Scholars like Rosanne Carlo (2020) challenge us to think beyond utilitarian composing knowledge to meet the full needs of students' literacy journeys.

Most writing instructors train in graduate school to teach college writing, but increasingly, college composition is being offered in high school settings by high school teachers credentialed to teach for university credit. Such instructors bring extensive pedagogical experience but perhaps less background knowledge in the composition research and theory that formal coursework provides. Furthermore, there is no reason to think that dual credit or concurrent enrollment writing courses will not be a core part of many instructors' course loads in the future. As the September 2020 issue of *Teaching English in the Two-Year College* ("Dual Credit Programs" 2020) and Kristine Hansen and Christine R. Farris's edited collection *College Credit for Writing in High School* (2010) reveal, dual credit composition requires careful thinking about staffing, logistics, preparation, accountability for teachers and students, and support from writing programs. Dual credit courses can be taught in various ways: by high school teachers credentialed by a local college or university to teach a university-credit course in a high school (sometimes concurrently stacked with "non-college" curricula), with high school students traveling to a campus for or enrolling in online versions of college-level writing courses, or with college instructors teaching college courses on-site at a high school. These collaborative endeavors require instructors to think not only about their own courses but also about how they might teach in such spaces, mentor high school teachers as part of a dual credit program, and teach students who have earned first-year writing credits before arriving on a college campus.

ONGOING LEARNING AS A STRATEGY FOR PEDAGOGICAL ADAPTABILITY

As the most universally required and offered college course in the United States, first-year writing is simultaneously ubiquitous and specific to local contexts. Every successive new teaching setting requires an assessment of what is new, what is different, and which teaching practices support student learning. Pedagogical adaptability for inclusive teaching requires combining both old and new resources with the ability to be flexible, discarding practices that do not serve a current teaching context and replacing them with strategies and content that do serve that context.

Pedagogically adaptable writing instructors engage in ongoing learning. Accessible resources to support learning about teaching have flourished in the last two decades. There is a growing number of book series, journals, social media, and digital resources for ongoing professional development in teaching that stretch beyond scholarly journal articles and graduate coursework. Journals on the scholarship of teaching and learning, as well as societies like the International Society for the Scholarship of Teaching and Learning and its journal, *Teaching and Learning Inquiry*, produce cross-disciplinary research. Publishers like West Virginia University Press and Stylus specialize in books that focus on research-based teaching practices. Similarly, publishers like Utah State University Press and the WAC Clearinghouse have growing collections that highlight teaching in writing studies. Virtual opportunities for national and regional conference attendance make professional engagement more affordable than ever, while digital credentialing and badges provide professional development opportunities for instructors beyond graduate coursework. Many colleges and universities have teaching and learning centers that provide instructors with pedagogical resources, workshops, online courses, speaker series, and individual consultations.

The Covid-19 global pandemic revealed just how suddenly instructors can be called upon to adjust their course modality and teaching strategies, sometimes through emergency remote instruction or sometimes through a planned effort to offer ways for a student to access and participate virtually in a course. As instructors progress through their careers, identifying and using institutional or professional opportunities can help them adapt their teaching to new technologies or teaching modalities while also helping students learn in virtual environments. Larger institutions may have dedicated campus e-learning or technology programs or both that provide one-on-one support, training guides, and workshops. Instructors at less well-resourced institutions may need to go beyond the institution to professional groups like the Online Learning Consortium, Every Learner Everywhere, the Global Society of Online Literacy Educators, the Conference on College Composition and Communication's Online Writing Instruction standing group, and online learning special interest groups in other professional organizations.

In addition to engaging in individual professional development for teaching, instructors also need to situate their ongoing learning within their local institutional contexts. Instructors who trained at large universities with significant research and graduate program services may be surprised to learn that smaller institutions may not offer the kinds of resources that were standard at those institutions. Instructors cannot assume that faculty development offices, teaching and learning centers, faculty mentoring, and other structured programs will be part of their new work contexts. Instructors may need to take initiative to identify peer mentors, seek out senior faculty for support, and create opportunities that build on the professional experience and expertise of colleagues (such as reading groups of faculty learning communities). As the coauthors of this book can attest, a critical mass of colleagues can be an instructor's most valuable resource.

Other kinds of self-initiated learning can be specific to a new context, institution, or student population. Assessing the educational, linguistic, cultural, and social needs of a new student population can be challenging, particularly when instructors have unexamined assumptions about what it means to be "college ready" or what the contextual benchmarks are for college writers. All campuses are required by accreditors to provide transparent information to prospective students and other stakeholders. Many institutions provide short reports about student demographics, majors, admissions, and graduation rates through a campus website (for example, a "Fast Facts" page). Reports about student success and retention in writing courses (often by demographic groups) are often available from a writing program coordinator or department chair.

More specific and helpful information can be found by asking students about their experiences, background, and goals. Start-of-term introduction letters, student surveys, or mid-course check-ins can be useful tools for instructors to get a sense of how well their pedagogical and curricular approaches are aligning with the needs of the students in their courses. Increasingly, campuses are using fine-grained data tools like Navigate or campus-specific dashboards, which faculty and advisers can use to track student engagement in their courses, meetings with advisers, progress toward a degree, and other indicators down to the student and course levels.

Another way to support self-initiated learning is through reflective practice, which is the willingness and ability to regularly evaluate our approaches and whether they serve our pedagogical goals and the needs of the classroom. Developing this skill is essential to sustain a professional career in college writing. Throughout this book, we offer many opportunities for reflective activities, including the "Questions for Reflection" section at the end of each chapter. These reflective activities are intended to provide support for the recursive labor of reflective practice.

REACHING ALL WRITERS: PEDAGOGICAL ADAPTABILITY AND CAREER SUSTAINABILITY

Throughout a career as a writing teacher, changes are inevitable. Whether the changes are institutional, programmatic, curricular, demographic, disciplinary, economic, personal, or political, they impact the responsibilities, contexts, or abilities of writing teachers. These changes require an ongoing process of reflection to ensure that the goal of "reaching all writers" is achievable and possible in the writing classroom. A teaching career is very different from a teaching moment or a training period, and prospective thinking is one way to practice imagining how a commitment to the teaching of writing may look at different points in time.

New and changing courses require instructors to adapt their practices to different ways of teaching and supporting students. Even instructors who remain in the same writing or literacy education program for many years can expect to change as the realities of their institutions evolve over time. A need for change can come from curricular revisions within a department or program, from revisions to general education or associate degree requirements at an institution or in a statewide system, and from mandates imposed by legislation and statewide reform efforts. We have found ourselves in nearly all of these circumstances, trying to adapt to an unexpected change for reasons often outside our control. We have continually asked ourselves, what do we need to do in this moment and in these circumstances to be an effective, equitable, and inclusive writing teacher?

Institutions change through increases or decreases in demographic groups in a local community (for example, through immigrant resettlement or changes in the K–12 population). Student populations also change because of new recruitment practices or new institutional programs that attract particular types of students. To sustain a career as a teacher of writing, instructors need to prepare for and adapt to inevitable adjustments as their writing programs evolve to meet the needs of new student communities. Open-admission and community college campuses are more likely to experience demographic shifts, in part because their missions focus on serving local communities. Understanding the local landscape and cultivating pedagogical adaptability can make programmatic shifts less challenging and more rewarding.

Even when an instructor commits to a career at a single institution, pedagogical adaptability includes anticipating that at different stages of one's career, priorities can change. For example, during a time of heavy service responsibilities or of intense caregiving, writing instructors can and should examine their pedagogical priorities and consider how to adjust their teaching approaches to maintain a balanced workload while meeting both their students' and their own needs. Sometimes, managing a teaching-intensive workload with other responsibilities means getting rid of unnecessary teaching tasks that do not meaningfully contribute to students' development and opportunities to show learning. Working papers by the Two-Year College English Association's Workload Issues Committee offer some insight into workload management strategies (Giordano and Wegner 2020), the labor of assessment (Hassel and Klausman 2020), and the emotional labor of open-access writing teaching (Hassel, Sullivan, and Wegner 2020), as well as into how to account for all the demands on one's time in a teaching-intensive faculty role.

Another important consideration in planning for workload sustainability and reflective practice is recognizing that many college writing instructors work in suboptimal material conditions. Perhaps they are poorly compensated, have a heavy teaching load, teach students who have significant academic needs, or have an unstable employment situation. It is important for writing instructors to be aware of the (im)balance between the rewards of the classroom and the material realities of a career in teaching college writing. Faculty and writing instructors with relative agency may be able to exert influence on material improvements in the teaching and learning conditions for students and teachers at their institutions. Engaging in "teacher-scholar-activism" (see Sullivan 2015) can leverage resources such as a faculty or college-wide senate, a faculty association, or a union to improve overall working conditions for teachers (and, therefore, learning conditions for students). Furthermore, the identity and positionalities of faculty can shape the way they experience the institutional space; changes to structures, policies, or processes can make the environment more equitable and inclusive for people with diverse experiences, backgrounds, and needs.

In other words, reaching all writers means making a commitment to the success of all students, their literacy development, and their retention in higher education—or at least creating conditions so success is as possible as the cultural and social circumstances of a teaching context allow. Reaching all writers means thinking carefully about how to remove barriers for students and instructors in the writing classroom and online learning environments. First-year writing courses are central to equity in higher education both because they are required for degree completion and they help students develop literacy skills that serve as a foundation for further college coursework and the rest of their literate lives.

REFERENCES

Adams, Peter, Sarah Gearhart, Robert Miller, and Anne Roberts. 2009. "The Accelerated Learning Program: Throwing Open the Gates." *Journal of Basic Writing* 28.2. https://files.eric.ed.gov/fulltext/EJ877255.pdf.

Adler-Kassner, Linda. 2012. "The Companies We Keep *or* the Companies We Would Like to Keep: Strategies and Tactics in Challenging Times." *Writing Program Administration* 36: 119–140.

Adler-Kassner, Linda, Isabel Baca, and Jim Fredricksen. 2014. *Understanding and Teaching Writing: Guiding Principles*. Urbana, IL: National Council of Teachers of English.

Adler-Kassner, Linda, John Majewski, and Damian Koshnick. 2012. "The Value of Troublesome Knowledge: Transfer and Threshold Concepts in Writing and History." *Composition Forum* 26. http://compositionforum.com/issue/26/troublesome-knowledge-threshold.php.

Adler-Kassner, Linda, and Elizabeth Wardle, eds. 2015. *Naming What We Know: Threshold Concepts of Writing Studies*. Logan: Utah State University Press.

Adler-Kassner, Linda, and Elizabeth Wardle, eds. 2019. *(Re)Considering What We Know: Learning Thresholds in Writing, Composition, Rhetoric, and Literacy*. Logan: Utah State University Press.

Alim, H. Samy, and Django Paris, eds. 2017. *Culturally Sustaining Pedagogies: Teaching and Learning for Justice in a Changing World*. New York: Teachers College Press.

Alim, H. Samy, John R. Rickford, and Arnetha F. Ball. 2016. *Raciolinguistics: How Language Shapes Our Ideas about Race*. Oxford: Oxford University Press.

Ambrose, Susan A., Michael W. Bridges, Michele DiPietro, Marsha C. Lovett, and Marie K. Norman. 2010. *How Learning Works: 7 Research-Based Principles for Smart Teaching*. San Francisco: Jossey-Bass.

American Association of Community Colleges. 2022. "Fast Facts." https://www.aacc.nche.edu/research-trends/fast-facts/.

American College Health Association. 2021. "National College Health Assessment Reference Group Executive Summary." https://www.acha.org/documents/ncha/NCHA-III_FALL_2021_REFERENCE_GROUP_EXECUTIVE_SUMMARY.pdf.

American Psychological Association. 2022. "Bias-Free Language." https://apastyle.apa.org/style-grammar-guidelines/bias-free-language.

Andelora, Jeff. 2005. "The Teacher/Scholar: Reconstructing Our Professional Identity in Two-Year Colleges." *Teaching English in the Two-Year College* 32.3: 307–322.

Andrus, Sonja, Sharon Mitchler, and Howard Tinberg. 2019. "Teaching for Writing Transfer: A Practical Guide for Teachers." *Teaching English in the Two-Year College* 47.1: 76–89.

Angelo, Thomas A., and K. Patricia Cross. 1993. *Classroom Assessment Techniques: A Handbook for College Teachers*. San Francisco: Jossey-Bass.

Anson, Chris. 2016. "The Pop Warner Chronicles: A Case Study in Contextual Adaptation and the Transfer of Writing Ability." *College Composition and Communication* 67.4: 518–549.

Anzaldúa, Gloria Evangelina. 2021. "How to Tame a Wild Tongue." In *Borderlands = La Frontera: The New Mestiza*, edited by Ricardo F. Vivancos Pérez and Norma E. Cantú, 53–64. San Francisco: Aunt Lute Books.

Armstrong, Sonya L. 2020. "What's Been Keeping Me Awake at Night: The Future(?) of 'the Field.'" *Journal of College Reading and Learning* 50.2: 56–69. DOI: 10.1080/1079 0195.2020.1750849.

Association of College and Research Libraries. 2016. "Framework for Information Literacy for Higher Education." https://www.ala.org/acrl/sites/ala.org.acrl/files/content /issues/infolit/Framework_ILHE.pdf.

Atkinson, Dwight, Deborah Crusan, Paul Kei Matsuda, Christina Ortmeier-Hooper, Todd Ruecker, Steve Simpson, and Christine Tardy. 2015. "Clarifying the Relationship between L2 Writing and Translingual Writing: An Open Letter to Writing Studies Editors and Organization Leaders." *College English* 77.4: 383–386.

Bailey, Thomas R., Shanna Smith Jaggers, and Davis Jenkins. 2015. *Redesigning America's Community Colleges: A Clearer Path to Student Success*. Cambridge, MA: Harvard University Press.

Bain, Ken. 2004. *What the Best College Teachers Do*. Cambridge, MA: Harvard University Press.

Baker-Bell, April. 2020. *Linguistic Justice: Black Language, Literacy, Identity, and Pedagogy*. Oxfordshire, UK: Routledge.

Bandura, Albert. 1997. *Self-Efficacy: The Exercise of Control*. New York: W. H. Freeman.

Barkley, Elizabeth, and Claire Howell Major. 2016. *Learning Assessment Techniques: A Handbook for College Faculty*. San Francisco: Jossey-Bass.

Barnett, Elisabeth, Elizabeth Kopko, Dan Cullinan, and Clive R. Belfield. 2020. "Who Should Take College-Level Courses? Impact Findings from an Evaluation of a Multiple Measures Assessment Strategy." Center for the Analysis of Postsecondary Readiness. https://ccrc.tc.columbia.edu/media/k2/attachments/multiple-measures-assessment -impact-findings.pdf.

Barnett, Pamela E. 2013. "Unpacking Teachers' Invisible Knapsacks: Social Identity and Privilege in Higher Education." *Liberal Education* 99.3: 30–37.

Barradell, Sarah, and Tai Peseta. 2014. "Promise and Challenge of Identifying Threshold Concepts: A Cautionary Account of Using Transactional Curriculum Inquiry." *Journal of Further and Higher Education* 40.2: 262–275.

Bartholomae, David, and Anthony Petrosky. 1986. *Facts, Artifacts, and Counter Facts: Theory and Method for a Reading and Writing Course*. Portsmouth, NH: Boynton/Cook.

Bauer, Lauren, Kristen Broady, Wendy Edelberg, and Jimmy O'Donnell. 2020. "Ten Facts about COVID-19 and the U.S. Economy." Brookings Institution. https://www.brookings .edu/wp-content/uploads/2020/09/FutureShutdowns_Facts_LO_Final.pdf.

Bawarshi, Anis. 2003. *Genre and the Invention of the Writer: Reconsidering the Place of Invention in Composition*. Logan: Utah State University Press.

Bawarshi, Anis, and Mary Jo Reiff. 2010. *Genre: An Introduction to History, Theory, Research, and Pedagogy*. Fort Collins, CO, and Anderson, SC: WAC Clearinghouse and Parlor Press. https://wac.colostate.edu/books/referenceguides/bawarshi-reiff/.

Bazerman, Charles. 2009. "The Problem of Writing Knowledge." In *The Norton Book of Composition Studies*, edited by Susan Miller, 502–514. New York: Norton.

Bazerman, Charles. 2015. "Writing Speaks to Situations through Recognizable Forms." In *Naming What We Know: Threshold Concepts of Writing Studies*, edited by Linda Adler-Kassner and Elizabeth Wardle, 35–37. Logan: Utah State University Press.

Bazerman, Charles, and Howard Tinberg. 2015. "Text Is an Object Outside of Oneself That Can Be Improved and Developed." In *Naming What We Know: Threshold Concepts of Writing Studies*, edited by Linda Adler-Kassner and Elizabeth Wardle, 61–62. Logan: Utah State University Press.

Bean, Thomas, Kristen Gregory, and Judith Dunkerly-Bean. 2018. "Disciplinary Reading." In *Handbook of College Reading and Study Strategy Research*, ed. Rona Flippo and Thomas W. Bean, 89–97. Oxfordshire, UK: Routledge.

Beaufort, Anne. 2007. *College Writing and Beyond: A New Framework for University Writing Instruction*. Logan: Utah State University Press.

Behling, Kirsten T., and Thomas J. Tobin. 2018. *Reach Everyone, Teach Everyone: Universal Design for Learning in Higher Education.* Morgantown: West Virginia University Press.

Bensimon, Estela Mara, Alicia C. Dowd, and Keith Witham. 2016. "Five Principles for Enacting Equity by Design." *Diversity and Democracy* 19.1: 1–7.

Berlin, James. 1987. *Rhetoric and Reality: Writing Instruction in American Colleges, 1900–1985.* Carbondale: Southern Illinois University Press.

Berlin, James. 1988. "Rhetoric and Ideology in the Writing Class." *College English* 50.5: 477–494.

Bickerstaff, Susan, Elizabeth Kopko, Erika B. Lewy, Julia Raufman, and Elizabeth Zachry Rutschow. 2021. "Implementing and Scaling Multiple Measures Assessment in the Context of COVID-19." Center for the Analysis of Postsecondary Readiness. https://ccrc.tc.columbia.edu/media/k2/attachments/implementing-scaling-multiple-measures-covid.pdf.

Bishop-Clark, Cathy. 2012. *Engaging in the Scholarship of Teaching and Learning: A Guide to the Process, and How to Develop a Project from Start to Finish.* Sterling, VA: Stylus.

Blaauw-Hara, Mark. 2006. "Why Our Students Need Instruction in Grammar, and How We Should Go about It." *Teaching English in the Two-Year College* 34.2: 165–178.

Blaauw-Hara, Mark. 2015. "Transfer Theory, Threshold Concepts, and First-Year Composition: Connecting Writing Courses to the Rest of the College." *Teaching English in the Two-Year College* 41.4: 354–365.

Black Lives Matter. 2020. "Black Lives Matter: 2020 Impact Report." https://blacklivesmatter.com/wp-content/uploads/2021/02/blm-2020-impact-report.pdf.

Blum, Susan D., ed. 2020. *Ungrading: Why Rating Students Undermines Learning (and What to Do Instead).* Morgantown: West Virginia University Press.

Blythe, Stuart. 2016. "Attending to the Subject in Writing Transfer and Adaptation." In *Critical Transitions: Writing and the Question of Transfer*, edited by Chris Anson and Jessie Moore, 49–68. Fort Collins, CO: WAC Clearinghouse.

Borgman, Jessie, and Casey McArdle. 2019. *Personal, Accessible, Responsive, Strategic: Resources and Strategies for Online Writing Instructors.* Fort Collins and Boulder: WAC Clearinghouse and University Press of Colorado.

Boroch, Deborah J., Laura Hope, Bruce M. Smith, Robert S. Gabriner, Pamela M. Mery, Robert M. Johnstone, Rose Asera, and John Nixon. 2010. *Student Success in Community Colleges: A Practical Guide to Developmental Education.* San Francisco: Jossey-Bass.

Brandt, Deborah. 1995. "Accumulating Literacy: Writing and Learning to Write in the Twentieth Century." *College English* 57.6: 649–668.

Brandt, Deborah. 2009. *Literacy and Learning: Reflections on Writing, Reading, and Society.* San Francisco: Jossey-Bass.

Breedlove, Mari. 2021. "Community College Students: A Data-Driven Look at Enrollment." *Education Dynamics.* https://www.educationdynamics.com/community-college-students-enrollment-data/.

Brereton, John, ed. 1995. *The Origins of Composition Studies in the American College, 1875–1925: A Documentary History.* Pittsburgh: University of Pittsburgh Press.

Brewer, Meaghan. 2020. *Conceptions of Literacy: Graduate Instructors and the Teaching of First-Year Composition.* Boulder: University Press of Colorado.

Brewer, Meaghan, and Kristin diGennaro. 2022. "Naming What We Don't Know: Graduate Instructors and Declarative Knowledge about Language." *College Composition and Communication* 73: 410–436.

Britton, James. 1970. *Language and Learning.* London: Penguin.

Britton, James, Tony Burgess, Nancy Martin, Alex McLeod, and Harold Rosen. 1975. *The Development of Writing Abilities.* London: Macmillan.

Brooke, Collin, and Allison Carr. 2015. "Failure Can Be an Important Part of Writing Development." In *Naming What We Know: Threshold Concepts of Writing Studies*, edited by Linda Adler-Kassner and Elizabeth Wardle, 62–64. Logan: Utah State University Press.

Brookfield, Stephen. 1998. *Becoming a Critically Reflective Teacher.* San Francisco: Jossey-Bass.
Brookfield, Stephen. 2018. *Teaching Race: How to Help Students Unmask and Challenge Racism.* San Francisco: Jossey-Bass.
Burgstahler, Sheryl E., and Rebecca C. Cory, eds. 2008. *Universal Design in Higher Education: From Principles to Practice.* Cambridge, MA: Harvard Education Press.
Calhoon-Dillahunt, Carolyn. 2018. "Returning to Our Roots: Creating the Conditions and Capacity for Change." *College Composition and Communication* 70.2: 273–293.
California Acceleration Project. n.d. "Implementing Corequisite Models." https://accelerationproject.org/wp-content/uploads/documents/CAP%20Report%20v8.pdf.
Canagarajah, Suresh. 2006. "The Place of World English in College Composition: Pluralization Continued." *College Composition and Communication* 57.4: 586–619.
Canagarajah, Suresh. 2015. "Clarifying the Relationship between Translingual Practice and L2 Writing: Addressing Learner Identities." *Applied Linguistics Review* 6: 415–440.
Carillo, Ellen. 2015. *Securing a Place for Reading in Composition: The Importance of Teaching for Transfer.* Logan: Utah State University Press.
Carillo, Ellen. 2017. *A Writer's Guide to Mindful Reading.* Fort Collins: WAC Clearinghouse. https://wac.colostate.edu/docs/books/mindful/reading.pdf.
Carillo, Ellen. 2021. *The Hidden Inequities in Labor-Based Contract Grading.* Logan: Utah State University Press.
Carlo, Rosanne. 2020. *Transforming Ethos: Place and the Material in Rhetoric and Writing.* Logan: Utah State University Press.
Carnevale, Anthony P., and Jeff Stroh. 2013. *Separate and Unequal: How Higher Education Reinforces the Intergenerational Reproduction of White Racial Privilege.* Washington, DC: Georgetown Public Policy Institute.
Carr, Allison D., and Laura R. Micciche, eds. 2020. "Introduction: Failure's Sweat." In *Failure Pedagogies: Learning and Unlearning What It Means to Fail,* 1–10. New York: Peter Lang.
Carroll, Lee Ann. 2002. *Rehearsing New Roles: How College Students Develop as Writers.* Carbondale: Southern Illinois University Press.
Casazza, Martha E., and Sharon L. Silverman. 2013. *Meaningful Access and Support: The Path to College Completion.* Council of Learning Assistance and Developmental Associations. https://cladea.info/resources/white_paper_meaningful_access.pdf.
Castro, Erin L. 2015. "Addressing the Conceptual Challenges of Equity Work: A Blueprint for Getting Started." In *Understanding Equity in Community College Practice* (New Directions for Community Colleges 172), edited by Erin L. Castro, 5–12. San Francisco: Jossey-Bass.
Center for Urban Education. n.d. "Equity-Mindedness." University of Southern California. https://cue.usc.edu/about/equity/equity-mindedness/.
Center on Budget and Policy Priorities. 2022. "The COVID-19 Economy's Effects on Food, Housing, and Employment Hardships." Covid Hardship Watch. https://www.cbpp.org/sites/default/files/8-13-20pov.pdf.
Chardin, Mirko, and Katie Novak. 2021. *Equity by Design: Delivering on the Promise of UDL.* Thousand Oaks, CA: Corwin.
Charney, Davida. 2002. "Teaching Writing as a Process." In *Strategies for Teaching First-Year Composition,* edited by Duane Roen, Veronica Pantoja, Lauren Yena, Susan K. Miller, and Eric Waggoner, 92–96. Urbana, IL: National Council of Teachers of English.
Chávez, Alicia Fedelina, and Susan Diana Longerbeam. 2016. *Teaching across Cultural Strengths: A Guide to Balancing Integrated and Individualized Cultural Frameworks in College Teaching.* Sterling, VA: Stylus.
Cisco, Jonathan. 2020. "Exploring the Connection between Impostor Phenomenon and Postgraduate Students Feeling Academically Unprepared." *Higher Education Research and Development* 39.2: 200–214.
Clark, Burton. 1960. "The 'Cooling-Out' Function in Higher Education." *American Journal of Sociology* 65.6: 569–576.

Cohn, Jenae. 2021. *Skim, Dive, Surface: Teaching Digital Reading*. Morgantown: West Virginia University Press.

Cole, Kirsti, and Holly Hassel. 2021. "Introduction: Transformations in a Changing Landscape." In *Transformations: Change Work across Writing Programs, Pedagogies, and Practices*, edited by Kirsti Cole and Holly Hassel, 3–16. Logan: Utah State University Press.

Common Core State Standards Initiative. 2022. "Common Core State Standards for English Language Arts and Literacy in History/Social Studies, Science, and Technical Subjects." https://learning.ccsso.org/wp-content/uploads/2022/11/ELA_Standards1.pdf.

Community College Research Center. n.d. "Community College Facts." https://ccrc.tc.columbia.edu/community-college-faqs.html.

Conference on College Composition and Communication. 1974. "Students' Right to Their Own Language." National Council of Teachers of English. https://cccc.ncte.org/cccc/resources/positions/srtolsummary#:~:text=This%20statement%20provides%20the%20resolution,was%20first%20adopted%20in%201974.

Conference on College Composition and Communication. 1998. "CCCC Guideline on National Language Policy." Revised 2015. National Council of Teachers of English. https://cccc.ncte.org/cccc/resources/positions/nationallangpolicy.

Conference on College Composition and Communication. 2001. "CCCC Statement on Second Language Writing and Multilingual Writers." Revised 2009. National Council of Teachers of English. https://cccc.ncte.org/cccc/resources/positions/secondlangwriting.

Conference on College Composition and Communication. 2006. "Writing Assessment: A Position Statement." Revised 2009, reaffirmed 2014. National Council of Teachers of English. https://cccc.ncte.org/cccc/resources/positions/writingassessment.

Conference on College Composition and Communication. 2015. "Principles for the Postsecondary Teaching of Writing." National Council of Teachers of English. https://cccc.ncte.org/cccc/resources/positions/postsecondarywriting#principle2.

Conference on College Composition and Communication. 2020. "This Ain't Another Statement! This Is a Demand for Black Linguistic Justice." National Council of Teachers of English. https://cccc.ncte.org/cccc/demand-for-black-linguistic-justice.

Conference on College Composition and Communication. 2021a. "CCCC Position Statement on the Role of Reading in College Writing Classrooms." National Council of Teachers of English. https://cccc.ncte.org/cccc/the-role-of-reading.

Conference on College Composition and Communication. 2021b. "CCCC Statement on Ebonics." National Council of Teachers of English. https://cccc.ncte.org/cccc/resources/positions/ebonics.

Conference on College Composition and Communication. 2021c. "CCCC Statement on White Language Supremacy." https://cccc.ncte.org/cccc/white-language-supremacy.

Conference on College Composition and Communication, Two-Year College Association, Council of Writing Administrators, and National Council of Teachers of English. 2019. "Joint Position Statement on Dual Enrollment in Composition." National Council of Teachers of English. https://cccc.ncte.org/cccc/resources/positions/dualenrollment.

Corbett, Steven J., and Michelle LaFrance, eds. 2017. *Student Peer Review and Responses: A Critical Sourcebook*. Boston: Bedford/St. Martin's.

Council of Writing Program Administrators. 2014. "WPA Outcomes Statement for First-Year Composition." WPA Council. http://wpacouncil.org/files/WPA%20Outcomes%20Statement%20Adopted%20Revisions[1]_0.pdf.

Council of Writing Program Administrators, National Council of Teachers of English, and the National Writing Project. 2011. *Framework for Success in Postsecondary Writing*. http://wpacouncil.org/files/framework-for-success-postsecondary-writing.pdf.

Cousin, Glynis. 2006. "An Introduction to Threshold Concepts." *Planet* 17: 4–5.

Crenshaw, Kimberlé. 2015. "Why Intersectionality Can't Wait." *Washington Post*, September 24. https://www.washingtonpost.com/news/in-theory/wp/2015/09/24/why-intersectionality-cant-wait/.

Cullinan, Dan, and Dorota Biedzio. 2021. "Increasing Gatekeeper Course Completion: Three-Semester Findings from an Experimental Study of Multiple Measures Assessment and Placement." Community College Research Center. https://ccrc.tc.columbia.edu/media/k2/attachments/increasing-gatekeeper-course-completion.pdf.

Davila, Bethany. 2012. "Indexicality and 'Standard' Edited American English: Examining the Link between Conceptions of Standardness and Perceived Authorial Identity." *Written Communication* 29.2: 180–207.

Davis, Leslie, and Richard Fry. 2019. "College Faculty Have Become More Racially and Ethnically Diverse but Remain Far Less So than Students." Pew Research Center. https://www.pewresearch.org/fact-tank/2019/07/31/us-college-faculty-student-diversity/.

Devitt, Amy. 2015. "Genre." In *Keywords in Writing Studies*, edited by Paul Heilker and Peter Vandenberg, 82–87. Logan: Utah State University Press.

de Kleine, Christa, and Rachele Lawton. 2015. "Meeting the Needs of Linguistically Diverse Students at the College Level." *College Reading and Learning Association*. https://www.crla.net/images/whitepaper/CRLA_2015_WhitePaper_Ling-Diverse.pdf.

Del Principe, Annie, and Rachel Ihara. 2017. "A Long Look at Reading in the Community College: A Longitudinal Analysis of Student Reading Experiences." *Teaching English in the Two-Year College* 45.2: 183–206.

Dolmage, Jay Timothy. 2017. *Academic Ableism: Disability and Higher Education*. Ann Arbor: University of Michigan Press.

Doran, Erin E. 2019. "'What's Expected of Us as We Integrate the Two Disciplines?': Two-Year College Faculty Engage with Basic Writing Reform." *Teaching English in the Two-Year College* 47.2: 149–167.

Douglas, Wallace. 1976. "Rhetoric for the Meritocracy: The Creation of Composition at Harvard." In *English in America: A Radical View of the Profession*, edited by Richard Ohmann, 97–132. New York: Oxford University Press.

Downs, Douglas, and Elizabeth Wardle. 2007. "Teaching about Writing, Righting Misconceptions: (Re)Envisioning 'First-Year Composition' as 'Introduction to Writing Studies.'" *College Composition and Communication* 53.4: 552–585.

Doyle, Terry. 2011. *Learner-Centered Teaching: Putting the Research on Learning into Practice*. Sterling, VA: Stylus.

Driscoll, Dana Lynn, and Jennifer Wells. 2012. "Beyond Knowledge and Skills: Writing Transfer and the Role of Student Dispositions." *Composition Forum* 26: 1–15. http://compositionforum.com/issue/26/beyond-knowledge-skills.php.

Dryer, Dylan. 2012. "At a Mirror, Darkly: The Imagined Undergraduate Writers of Ten Novice Composition Instructors." *College Composition and Communication* 63.3: 420–452.

"Dual Credit Programs." 2020. Special issue of *Teaching English in the Two-Year College*. https://library.ncte.org/journals/tetyc/issues/v48-1/30875.

Dunlosky, John, Katherine A. Rawson, Elizabeth J. Marsh, Mitchell J. Nathan, and Daniel T. Willingham. 2013. "Improving Students' Learning with Effective Learning Techniques: Promising Directions from Cognitive and Educational Psychologists." *Psychological Science in the Public Interest* 14.1: 4–58.

Ede, Lisa, and Andrea Lunsford. 1984. "Audience Addressed/Audience Invoked: The Role of Audience in Composition Theory and Pedagogy." *College Composition and Communication* 35.2: 155–171.

Education Trust. 2021. "The State of Higher Education Equity." https://edtrust.org/the-state-of-higher-education-equity/.

Elbow, Peter. 1973. *Writing without Teachers*. New York: Oxford University Press.

Elon University Center for Engaged Learning. 2013. "Elon Statement on Writing Transfer: Working Draft." http://www.elon.edu/e-web/academics/teaching/ers/writing_transfer/statement.xhtml.

Emig, Janet. 1971. *The Composing Processes of 12th Graders.* Champaign, IL: National Council of Teachers of English.

Eyler, Josh. 2018. *How Humans Learn: The Science and Stories Behind Effective College Teaching.* Morgantown: West Virginia University Press.

Fain, Paul. 2019. "Race, Geography, and Degree Attainment." *InsideHigherEd.* www.insidehighered.com/news/2019/06/27/rural-areas-lag-degree-attainment-while-urban-areas-feature-big-racial-gaps.

Federal Communications Commission. 2019. "2019 Broadband Deployment Report." https://www.fcc.gov/reports-research/reports/broadband-progress-reports/2019-broadband-deployment-report.

Feldman, Joe. 2019. *Grading for Equity: What It Is, Why It Matters, and How It Can Transform Schools and Classrooms.* Thousand Oaks, CA: Corwin.

Felix, Eric R., Estela Mara Bensimon, Debbie Hanson, James Gray, and Libby Klingsmith. 2015. "Developing Agency for Equity Minded Change." In *Understanding Equity in Community College Practice* (New Directions for Community Colleges 172), edited by Erin L. Castro, 25–42. San Francisco: Jossey-Bass.

Fink, L. Dee. 2013. *Creating Significant Learning Experiences: An Integrated Approach to Designing College Courses.* San Francisco: Jossey-Bass.

Flippo, Rona, and Thomas W. Bean, eds. 2018. *Handbook of College Reading and Study Strategy Research*, 3rd ed. Oxfordshire, UK: Routledge.

Flower, Linda, and John R. Hayes. 1981. "A Cognitive Process Theory of Writing." *College Composition and Communication* 32.4: 365–387.

Garcia de Mueller, Gabrielle, and Iris Ruiz. 2017. "Race, Silence, and Writing Program Administration: A Qualitative Study of U.S. College Writing Programs." *WPA Journal* 40.1: 19–39.

Gay, Geneva. 2018. *Culturally Responsive Teaching: Theory, Research, and Practice.* New York: Teachers College Press.

Geller, Anne Ellen, and Harry Denny. 2013. "Of Ladybugs, Low Status, and Loving the Job: Writing Center Professionals Navigating Their Careers." *Writing Center Journal* 33.1: 96–129.

Giordano, Joanne Baird. 2020. "Second Chance Pedagogy: Integrating College-Level Skills and Strategies into a Developmental Writing Course." In *Sixteen Teachers Teaching: Two-Year College Perspectives*, edited by Patrick Sullivan, 219–240. Logan: Utah State University Press.

Giordano, Joanne Baird, and Holly Hassel. 2016. "Unpredictable Journeys: Academically At-Risk Students, Developmental Education Reform, and the Two-Year College." Special issue of *Teaching English in the Two-Year College* 43.4: 371–390.

Giordano, Joanne Baird, and Holly Hassel. 2019. "Intersections of Privilege and Access: Writing Programs, Disciplinary Knowledge, and the Shape of a Field." *WPA: Writing Program Administration* 43.1: 33–53.

Giordano, Joanne Baird, and Holly Hassel. 2021. "Developing Critical Readers in the Age of Literacy Acceleration." *Pedagogy: Critical Approaches to Teaching Literature, Language, Composition, and Culture* 21.2: 241–259.

Giordano, Joanne Baird, and Holly Hassel. 2023. "First-Year in the Two-Year: Preliminary Results from a Study of New Two-Year College Teacher Transitions." *Teaching English in the Two-Year College* 50.3: 255–277.

Giordano, Joanne Baird, Holly Hassel, Jennifer Heinert, and Cassandra Phillips. 2017. "Student Retention and Professional Development in Two-Year College English Departments." In *Overcoming Writer's Block: Retention, Persistence, and Writing Programs*, edited by Todd Ruecker, Dawn Shepherd, Heidi Estrem, and Beth Brunk Chavez, 74–92. Logan: Utah State University Press.

Giordano, Joanne Baird, Holly Hassel, Jeff Klausman, and Patrick Sullivan. 2021. "TYCA Working Paper #9: Contingent Labor and Workload in Two-Year College English." *Two-Year College English Association.* https://ncte.org/wp-content/uploads/2021/04/TYCA_Working_Paper_9.pdf.

Giordano, Joanne Baird, Holly Hassel, and McKenna Wegner. 2020. "TYCA Working Paper #2: Two-Year College English Faculty Teaching Adjustments Related to Workload." TYCA Workload Task Force. https://ncte.org/wp-content/uploads/2020/12/TYCA_Working_Paper_2.pdf.

Giordano, Joanne Baird, and Cassandra Phillips. 2021. "Designing an Open-Access Online Writing Program: Negotiating Tensions between Disciplinary Ideals and Institutional Realities." In *Transformations: Change Work across Writing Programs, Pedagogies, and Practices,* edited by Holly Hassel and Kirsti Cole, 240–258. Logan: Utah State University Press.

Giordano, Joanne Baird, and McKenna Wegner. 2020. "TYCA Working Paper #3: Workload Management Strategies for Teaching English at Two-Year Colleges." TYCA Workload Task Force. https://ncte.org/wp-content/uploads/2020/11/TYCA_Working_Paper_3.pdf.

Glau, Gregory R. 2007. "'Stretch' at 10: A Progress Report on Arizona State University's 'Stretch Program.'" *Journal of Basic Writing* 26.2: 30–48.

Gravely, Alexis. 2021. "Removing Barriers for Students with Disabilities." *InsideHigherEd* 26. https://www.insidehighered.com/news/2021/08/26/bill-would-improve-access-accommodations-disabled-students.

Grego, Rhonda C., and Nancy S. Thompson. 1996. "Repositioning Remediation: Renegotiating Composition's Work in the Academy." *College Composition and Communication* 47.1: 62–84.

Grego, Rhonda C., and Nancy S. Thompson. 2007. *Teaching/Writing in Third Spaces: The Studio Approach.* Carbondale: Southern Illinois University Press.

Griffin, Sarah. 2018. "English Transition Courses in Context: Preparing Students for College Success." Community College Research Center. https://ccrc.tc.columbia.edu/media/k2/attachments/english-transition-courses-preparing-students.pdf.

Griffiths, Brett, Lizbett Tinoco, Joanne Baird Giordano, Holly Hassel, Emily K. Suh, and Patrick Sullivan. 2021. "Community College English Faculty Pandemic Teaching: Adjustments in the Time of COVID-19." *Community College Journal of Research and Practice* 46.1–2: 60–73.

Gross, Daniel, and Jonathan Alexander. 2016. "Frameworks for Failure." *Pedagogy* 16.2: 273–295.

Hairston, Maxine. 1982. "The Winds of Change: Thomas Kuhn and the Revolution in the Teaching of Writing." *College Composition and Communication* 33.1: 76–88.

Hammond, Zaretta L. 2014. *Culturally Responsive Teaching and the Brain: Promoting Authentic Engagement and Rigor among Culturally and Linguistically Diverse Students.* Thousand Oaks, CA: Corwin.

Hansen, Kristine, and Christine R. Farris, eds. 2010. *College Credit for Writing in High School: The "Taking Care of" Business.* Urbana, IL: National Council of Teachers of English.

Hartwell, Patrick. 1985. "Grammar, Grammars, and the Teaching of Grammar." *College English* 47.2: 105–127.

Hassel, Holly, and Joanne Baird Giordano. 2009. "Transfer Institutions, Transfer of Knowledge: The Development of Rhetorical Adaptability and Underprepared Writers." *Teaching English in the Two-Year College* 37.1: 24–40.

Hassel, Holly, and Joanne Baird Giordano. 2011. "FYC Placement at Open-Admission, Two-Year Campuses: Changing Campus Culture, Institutional Practice, and Student Success." *Open Words: Access and English Studies* 5.2: 29–59.

Hassel, Holly, and Joanne Baird Giordano. 2013. "Occupy Writing Studies: Rethinking College Composition for the Needs of the Teaching Majority." *College Composition and Communication* 61.1: 117–139.

Hassel, Holly, and Joanne Baird Giordano. 2015. "The Blurry Borders of College Writing: Remediation and the Assessment of Student Readiness." *College English* 78.1: 656–680.

Hassel, Holly, and Joanne Baird Giordano. 2017. "Contingency, Access, and the Material Conditions of Teaching and Learning in the 'Statement of Principles.'" In *Labored: The State(ment) and Future of Work in Composition*, edited by Randall McClure, Dayna V. Goldstein, and Michael A. Pemberton, 147–166. Anderson, SC: Parlor Press.

Hassel, Holly, Joanne Baird Giordano, Jennifer Heinert, and Cassandra Phillips. 2017. "The Imperative of Pedagogical and Professional Development to Support the Retention of Underprepared Students at Open-Access Institutions." In *Retention, Persistence, and Writing Programs*, edited by Todd Ruecker, Dawn Shepherd, Heidi Estrem, and Beth Brunk-Chavez, 74–92. Logan: Utah State University Press.

Hassel, Holly, and Jeff Klausman. 2020. "Working Paper #6: Two-Year College English Faculty Workload, Making the Labor of Assessment Visible." TYCA Workload Task Force. https://ncte.org/wp-content/uploads/2020/11/TYCA_Working_Paper_6.pdf.

Hassel, Holly, Jeffrey Klausman, Joanne Baird Giordano, Margaret O'Rourke, Leslie Roberts, Patrick Sullivan, and Christie Toth. 2015. "TYCA White Paper on Developmental Education Reforms." *Teaching English in the Two Year College* 42.3: 227–243.

Hassel, Holly, and Christie Launius. 2017. "Crossing the Threshold in Introductory Women's and Gender Studies Courses: An Assessment of Student Learning." *Teaching and Learning Inquiry* 5.2: 30–46.

Hassel, Holly, and Cassandra Phillips. 2022. *Materiality and Writing Studies: Aligning Labor, Teaching, and Scholarship*. Urbana, IL: National Council of Teachers of English.

Hassel, Holly, Patrick Sullivan, and McKenna Wegner. 2020. "TYCA Working Paper #7: Making the Emotional Labor of Open-Access Teaching Visible." TYCA Workload Task Force. https://ncte.org/wp-content/uploads/2020/11/TYCA_Working_Paper_7.pdf.

Healey, Mick, Kelley E. Matthews, and Alison Cook-Sather. 2020. *Writing about Learning and Teaching in Higher Education: Creating and Contributing to Scholarly Conversations across a Range of Genres*. Elon University Center for Engaged Learning. https://doi.org/10.36284/celelon.oa3.

Hearn, Mark Chung. 2012. "Positionality, Intersectionality, and Power: Socially Locating the Higher Education Teacher in Multicultural Education." *Multicultural Education Review* 4.2: 38–59.

Heilker, Paul, and Peter Vandenberg. 2015. *Keywords in Writing Studies*. Logan: Utah State University Press.

Hewett, Beth L., and Kevin Eric DePew, eds. 2015. *Foundational Practices of Online Writing Instruction*. Fort Collins, CO, and Anderson, SC: WAC Clearinghouse and Parlor Press.

Hillocks, George. 1986. *Research on Written Composition: New Directions for Teaching*. National Conference on Research in English 83. http://muwriting.wdfiles.com/local-files/annotated-readings/rhetoricalreading.pdf.

Horner, Bruce, Min-Zhan Lu, Jacqueline Jones Royster, and John Trimbur. 2011. "Language Difference in Writing: Toward a Translingual Approach." *College English* 73.3: 303–321.

Horner, Winifred Bryan. 1990. "The Roots of Modern Writing Instruction: Eighteenth and Nineteenth Century Britain." *Rhetoric Review* 8.2: 322–345.

Horning, Alice, and Elizabeth W. Kraemer. 2013. *Reconnecting Reading and Writing*. Andersonville, SC: Parlor Press.

Horning, Alice, Deborah-Lee Gollnitz, and Cynthia R. Haller, eds. 2017. *What Is College Reading?* Fort Collins and Boulder: WAC Clearinghouse and University Press of Colorado. https://doi.org/10.37514/ATD-B.2017.0001.

Horrigan, John B. 2019. "Analysis: Digital Divide Isn't Just a Rural Problem." *Daily Yonder*, August 14. https://dailyyonder.com/analysis-digital-divide-isnt-just-a-rural-problem/2019/08/14/.

Hubler, Shawn. 2020. "Colleges Slash Budgets in the Pandemic, with 'Nothing Off-Limits.'" *New York Times*, October 26. https://www.nytimes.com/2020/10/26/us/colleges-coronavirus-budget-cuts.html.

Ihara, Rachel, and Annie Del Principe. 2016. "'I Bought the Book and I Didn't Need It': What Reading Looks Like at an Urban Community College." *Teaching English in the Two-Year College* 43.3: 229–244.

Inoue, Asao. 2015. *Antiracist Writing Assessment Ecologies: Teaching and Assessing Writing for a Socially Just Future*. Fort Collins, CO: WAC Clearinghouse. https://wac.colostate.edu/books/perspectives/inoue/.

Inoue, Asao. 2019. *Labor-Based Grading Contracts: Building Equity and Inclusion in the Compassionate Writing Classroom*. Fort Collins: Colorado State University Open Press.

Institute of Education Sciences. 2022. "Use of Supports among Students with Disabilities and Special Needs in College." National Center for Education Statistics. https://nces.ed.gov/pubs2022/2022071.pdf.

Institute of Education Sciences. n.d. "Fast Facts: Students with Disabilities." National Center for Education Statistics. https://nces.ed.gov/fastfacts/display.asp?id=60.

Isaacs, Emily. 2018. *Writing at the State U: Instruction and Administration at 106 Comprehensive Universities*. Logan: Utah State University Press.

Jenkins, David, Hana Lahr, and Amy Mazzariello. 2021. "How to Achieve More Equitable Community College Student Outcomes: Lessons from Six Years of CCRC Research on Guided Pathways." Community College Research Center. https://ccrc.tc.columbia.edu/media/k2/attachments/equitable-community-college-student-outcomes-guided-pathways.pdf.

Kahn, Seth. 2021. "Anyone Can Teach Writing." In *Bad Ideas about Writing*, edited by Cheryl Ball and Drew Loewe, 363–368. Morgantown: West Virginia University Press. https://human.libretexts.org/@go/page/60988.

Kahn, Seth, William B. Lalicker, and Amy Lynch-Biniek. 2017. *Contingency, Exploitation, and Solidarity: Labor and Action in English Composition*. Fort Collins: WAC Clearinghouse.

Kalish, Katie, Holly Hassel, Cassandra Phillips, Jennifer Heinert, and Joanne Baird Giordano. 2019. "Inequitable Austerity: Pedagogies of Resilience and Resistance in Composition." *Pedagogy: Critical Approaches to Teaching Literature, Language, Composition, and Culture* 19.2: 261–281.

Kareem, Jamila. 2019. "A Critical Race Analysis of Transition-Level Writing Curriculum to Support the Racially Diverse Two-Year College." *Teaching English in the Two-Year College* 46.4: 271–296.

Keller, Daniel. 2013. *Chasing Literacy: Reading and Writing in an Age of Acceleration*. Logan: Utah State University Press.

Kerschbaum, Stephanie. 2014. *Toward a New Rhetoric of Difference*. Urbana, IL: National Council of Teachers of English.

Kezar, Adrianna, Elizabeth Holcombe, Darsella Vigil, and Jude Paul Matias Dizon. 2021. *Shared Equity Leadership: Making Equity Everyone's Work*. American Council on Education. https://www.acenet.edu/Documents/Shared-Equity-Leadership-Work.pdf.

Kirwan Institute for the Study of Race and Ethnicity. 2012. "Understanding Implicit Bias." https://kirwaninstitute.osu.edu/article/understanding-implicit-bias.

Klausman, Jeffrey, Christie Toth, Wendy Swyt, Brett Griffiths, Patrick Sullivan, Anthony Warnke, Amy L. Williams, Joanne Giordano, and Leslie Roberts. 2016. "TYCA White Paper on Placement Reform." *Teaching English in the Two-Year College* 44: 135–175.

Kuh, George D., Daniel Chen, and Thomas F. Nelson Laird. 2007. "Why Teacher-Scholars Matter: Some Insights from FSSE and NSSE." *Liberal Education* 93.4. https://www.aacu

.org/publications-research/periodicals/why-teacher-scholars-matter-some-insights-fsse-and-nsse.

Kynard, Carmen. 2013. *Vernacular Insurrections: Race, Black Protest, and the New Century in Composition-Literacies Studies*. Albany: State University of New York Press.

Ladson-Billings, Gloria. 1995. "Toward a Theory of Culturally Relevant Pedagogy." *American Research Journal* 32.3: 465–491.

Ladson-Billings, Gloria. 2021. *Culturally Relevant Pedagogy: Asking a Different Question*. New York: Teachers College Press.

Laine, Michaelene E. 2003. "A Qualitative Study of College Developmental Students' Perceptions of the Reading and Writing Relationships in a Co-taught Paired Reading Course." In *College Reading Research and Practice: Articles from "The Journal of College Literacy and Learning,"* edited by Eric J. Paulson, Michaelene E. Laine, Shirley A. Biggs, and Terry L. Bullock, 88–101. Newark, DE: International Reading Association.

Laird, Thomas F., Rick Shoup, George D. Kuh, and Michael J. Schwarz. 2008. "The Effects of Discipline on Deep Approaches to Student Learning and College Outcomes." *Research in Higher Education* 49: 469–494.

Land, Ray, Glynis Cousin, Jan H. F. Meyer, and Peter Davies. 2006. "Conclusion: Implications of Threshold Concepts for Course Design and Evaluation." In *Overcoming Barriers to Student Understanding: Threshold Concepts and Troublesome Knowledge*, edited by Jan H. F. Meyer and Ray Land, 195–206. Oxfordshire, UK: Routledge.

Land, Ray, Jan H. F. Meyer, and Caroline Baillie. 2010. "Editors' Preface: Threshold Concepts and Transformational Learning." In *Threshold Concepts and Transformational Learning*, edited by Ray Land, Jan H. F. Meyer, and Caroline Baillie, ix–xlii. Rotterdam: Sense Publishers.

Lauer, Janice. 1984. "Composition Studies: Dappled Discipline" *Rhetoric Review* 3.1: 20–29.

Leary, Christopher. 2019. "Editing, Translation, and Recovery Work in Community College English Classes." *Teaching English in the Two-Year College* 46.3: 210–222.

Leonard, Rebecca Lorimer. 2021. "The Role of Writing in Critical Language Awareness." *College English* 84.2: 175–198.

Lippi-Green, Rosina. 2012. *English with an Accent: Language, Ideology, and Discrimination in the United States*. Oxfordshire, UK: Routledge.

Lipson, Sarah Ketchen, Emily G. Lattie, and Daniel Eisenberg. 2018. "Increased Mental Health Rates of Mental Health Service Utilization by U.S. College Students: 10 Year Population-Level Trends (2007–2017)." *Psychiatric Services*. https://ps.psychiatryonline.org/doi/10.1176/appi.ps.201800332.

Looker, Samantha. 2016. "Writing about Language: Studying Linguistic Diversity with First-Year Writers." *Teaching English in the Two-Year College* 44.2: 176–198.

Lovas, John C. 2002. "All Good Writing Develops at the Edge of Risk." *College Composition and Communication* 54.2: 264–288.

Lu, Min-Zhan, and Bruce Horner. 2013. "Translingual Literacy, Language Difference, and Matters of Agency." *College English* 75.6: 582–607. http://www.jstor.org/stable/24238127.

Lunsford, Andrea. 2015. "Writing Addresses, Invokes, and/or Creates Audiences." In *Naming What We Know: Threshold Concepts of Writing Studies*, edited by Linda Adler-Kassner and Elizabeth Wardle, 20–21. Logan: Utah State University Press.

Lunsford, Andrea A., and Karen Lunsford. 2008. "Mistakes Are a Fact of Life: A National Comparative Study." *College Composition and Communication* 59.4: 781–806.

Macrorie, Ken. 1968. *Writing to Be Read*. New York: Hayden Book Co.

Malenczyk, Rita, Susan Miller-Cochran, Elizabeth Wardle, and Kathleen Yancey, eds. 2018a. *Composition, Rhetoric, and Disciplinarity*. Logan: Utah State University Press.

Matsuda, Paul Kei. 2006. "The Myth of Linguistic Homogeneity in U.S. College Composition." *College English* 68.6: 637–651.

Matsuda, Paul Kei. 2014. "The Lure of Translingual Writing." *PMLA* 129.3: 478–483. http://www.jstor.org/stable/24769484.

McClure, Randall, Dayna Goldstein, and Michael Pemberton. 2017. *Labored: The State(ment) and Future of Work in Composition*. Anderson, SC: Parlor Press.

McNair, Tia Brown, Susan Albertine, Michelle Asha Cooper, Nicole McDonald, and Thomas Major Jr. 2016. *Becoming a Student-Ready College: A New Culture of Leadership for Student Success*. San Francisco: Jossey-Bass.

McNair, Tia Brown, Estela Mara Bensimon, and Lindsey Malcom-Piqueux. 2020. *From Equity Talk to Equity Walk: Expanding Practitioner Knowledge for Racial Justice in Higher Education*. San Francisco: Jossey-Bass.

Mehl, Gelsey, Joshua Wyner, Elisabeth A. Barnett, John Fink, and Davis Jenkins. 2020. "The Dual Enrollment Playbook: A Guide to Equitable Acceleration for Students." The Aspen Institute and the Community College Research Center. https://ccrc.tc.columbia.edu/media/k2/attachments/dual-enrollment-playbook-equitable-acceleration.pdf.

Melzer, Dan. 2014. *Assignments across the Curriculum: A National Study of College Writing*. Logan: Utah State University Press.

Meyer, Jan H. F., and Ray Land. 2003. "Threshold Concepts and Troublesome Knowledge: Linkages to Ways of Thinking and Practising within the Disciplines." *ETL Project*, Occasional Report 4. Edinburgh: University of Edinburgh.

Meyer, Jan H. F., and Ray Land. 2006. *Overcoming Barriers to Student Understanding: Threshold Concepts and Troublesome Knowledge*. Oxfordshire, UK: Routledge.

Micciche, Laura R. 2004. "Making a Case for Rhetorical Grammar." *College Composition and Communication* 55.4: 716–737.

Middendorf, Joan, and David Pace. 2004. "Decoding the Disciplines: A Model for Helping Students Learn Disciplinary Ways of Thinking." *New Directions for Teaching and Learning* 22.98: 1–12.

Middendorf, Joan, and Leah Shopkow. 2017. *Overcoming Student Learning Bottlenecks: Decode the Critical Thinking of Your Discipline*. Sterling, VA: Stylus.

Miller, Carolyn R. 1984. "Genre as Social Action." *Quarterly Journal of Speech* 70: 151–167.

Milu, Esther. 2021. "Diversity of Raciolinguistic Experiences in the Classroom: An Argument for a Transnational Black Language Pedagogy." *College English* 83.6: 415–441.

Mintz, Steven. 2021. "How to Stand up for Equity in Higher Education." *Inside Higher Ed*. https://www.insidehighered.com/blogs/higher-ed-gamma/how-stand-equity-higher-education.

Mitchell, Donald, Jr., Charlana Y. Simmons, and Lindsay A. Greyerbiehl, eds. 2014. *Intersectionality and Higher Education: Theory, Research, and Practice*. New York: Peter Lang.

Moe, Peter Wayne. 2018a. "Inhabiting Ordinary Sentences." *Composition Studies* 46.2: 287–295.

Moe, Peter Wayne. 2018b. "A Sequence for Teaching the Sentence." *Teaching English in the Two-Year College* 46.1: 70–83.

Moore, Jessie L. 2012. "Designing for Transfer: A Threshold Concept." *Journal of Faculty Development* 26.3: 19–24.

Moore, Jessie L., and Chris Anson. 2017. *Critical Transitions: Writing and the Question of Transfer*. Boulder: University Press of Colorado.

Mullin, Christopher M. 2010. "Doing More with Less: The Inequitable Funding of Community Colleges." American Association of Community Colleges. https://files.eric.ed.gov/fulltext/ED522916.pdf.

Murray, Donald M. 1968. *A Writer Teaches Writing: A Practical Method of Teaching Composition*. Boston: Houghton Mifflin.

National Center on Education and the Economy. 2013. "What Does It Really Mean to Be College and Work Ready? The English Literacy Required of First-Year Community College Students." http://ncee.org/wp-content/uploads/2013/05/NCEE_EnglishReport_May2013.pdf.

National Council for Online Education. 2022. "Emergency Remote Instruction Is Not Quality Online Learning." *InsideHighered.* https://www.insidehighered.com/views/2022/02/03/remote-instruction-and-online-learning-arent-same-thing-opinion.

National Council of Teachers of English. 1974. "Students' Right to Their Own Language." https://ncte.org/statement/nctes-definition-literacy-digital-age/adopted 1974, affirmed 2014.

National Council of Teachers of English. 1984. "Teaching Composition: A Position Statement." *College English* 46.6: 612–614.

National Council of Teachers of English. 2016. "Professional Knowledge for the Teaching of Writing: A Position Statement." http://www2.ncte.org/statement/teaching-writing/.

National Council of Teachers of English. 2018a. "Literacy Assessment: Definitions, Principles, and Practices." https://ncte.org/statement/assessmentframingst/.

National Council of Teachers of English. 2018b. "Understanding and Teaching Writing: Guiding Principles." http://www2.ncte.org/statement/teachingcomposition.

National Council of Teachers of English. 2019. "Definition of Literacy in a Digital Age." https://ncte.org/statement/nctes-definition-literacy-digital-age/.

National Council of Teachers of English. 2022. "Position Statement on Writing Instruction in School." https://ncte.org/statement/statement-on-writing-instruction-in-school/.

Nilson, Linda. 2015. *Specifications Grading: Restoring Rigor, Motivating Students, and Saving Faculty Time.* Sterling, VA: Stylus.

Nilson, Linda. 2016. *Teaching at Its Best: A Research-Based Resource for College Instructors.* Hoboken, NJ: John Wiley.

North, Stephen. 1987. *The Making of Knowledge in Composition: The Portrait of an Emerging Field.* Portsmouth, NH: Boynton/Cook.

NSC Research Center. 2017. "Two-Year Contributions to Four-Year Completions—2017." National Student Clearinghouse. https://nscresearchcenter.org/snapshotreport-twoyearcontributionfouryearcompletions26/.

Olson, Gary, ed. 2002. *Rhetoric and Composition as Intellectual Work.* Carbondale: Southern Illinois University Press.

Ong, Walter J. 1975. "The Writer's Audience Is Always a Fiction." *PMLA* 90.1: 9–21. DOI: 10.2307/461344.

Ortiz, Angelica Paz, Beth Tarasawa, Noelle Al-Musaifry, Anmarie Trimble, and Jack Straton. 2018. "Positionality in Teaching: Implications for Advancing Social Justice." *Journal of General Education* 67.1–2: 109–121.

Pace, David, and Joan Middendorf. 2004. "Decoding the Disciplines: A Model for Helping Students Learn Disciplinary Ways of Thinking." *New Directions for Teaching and Learning* 98: 1–22.

Page, Lindsay, and Judith Scott-Clayton. 2015. "Improving College Access in the United States: Barriers and Policy Responses." Working Paper 21781. Cambridge, MA: National Bureau of Economic Research. https://www.nber.org/system/files/working_papers/w21781/w21781.pdf.

Parrott, Jill. 2017. "Some People Are Just Born Good Writers." In *Bad Ideas about Writing*, edited by Cheryl Ball and Drew Loewe, 71–75. Morgantown: West Virginia University Press.

Paulson, Eric, and Jodi Patrick Holschuh. 2018. "College Reading." In *Handbook of College Reading and Study Strategy Research*, edited by Rona Flippo and Thomas W. Bean, 27–41. London: Lawrence Erlbaum Associates.

Perkins, D. N., and Gavriel Solomon. 1988. "Teaching for Transfer." *Educational Leadership* 46.1: 22–32.

Perl, Sondra. 1979. "The Composing Processes of Unskilled College Writers." *Research in the Teaching of English* 13.4: 317–336.

Perryman-Clark, Staci, David E. Kirkland, and Austin Jackson. 2014. *Students' Right to Their Own Language: A Critical Sourcebook.* Boston: Bedford/St. Martin's.

Phelps, Louise Wetherbee, and John Ackerman. 2010. "Making the Case for Disciplinarity in Rhetoric, Composition, and Writing Studies: The Visibility Project." *College Composition and Communication* 62.1: 180–215.

Phillips, Cassandra, and Greg Ahrenhoerster. 2009. "The Scholarship of Assessment: Increasing Agency and Collaboration through SoTL." In *Assessment in Writing: Assessment in the Disciplines Series*, edited by Marie C. Paretti and Katrina Powell, 85–106. Tallahassee: Association of Institutional Research.

Phillips, Cassandra, and Joanne Baird Giordano. 2016. "Developing a Cohesive Academic Literacy Program for Underprepared Students." *Teaching English in the Two-Year College* 44.1: 79–89.

Phillips, Cassandra, and Joanne Baird Giordano. 2020. "Messy Processes into and out of Failure: Professional Identities and Open-Access Writers." In *Failure Pedagogies: Systems, Risks, and Failures*, edited by Allison D. Carr and Laura R. Micciche, 153–162. New York: Peter Lang.

Phillips, Cassandra, Holly Hassel, Jennifer Heinert, Katie Kalish, and Joanne Baird Giordano. 2019. "Thinking Like a Writer: Threshold Concepts and First-Year Writers in Open-Admissions Classrooms." In *(Re)Considering What We Know: Learning Thresholds in Writing, Composition, Rhetoric, and Literacy*, edited by Linda Adler-Kassner and Elizabeth Wardle, 56–75. Logan: Utah State University Press.

Powell, Pegeen Reichert. 2009. "Retention and Writing Instruction: Implications for Access and Pedagogy." *College Composition and Communication* 60.4: 664–682.

Powell, Pegeen Reichert. 2014. *Retention and Resistance: Writing Instruction and Students Who Leave*. Logan: Utah State University Press.

Ran, Florence Xiaotao, Susan Bickerstaff, and Nikki Edgecombe. 2022. "Improving College Success for Students in Corequisite Reading." Community College Research Center, Teachers College, Columbia University. https://strongstart.org/resource/improving-college-success-for-students-in-corequisite-reading/?file_id=1051#full-content.

Ran, Florence Xiaotao, and Yuxin Lin. 2019. "The Effects of Corequisite Remediation: Evidence from a Statewide Reform in Tennessee." Community College Research Center, Teachers College, Columbia University. https://ccrc.tc.columbia.edu/media/k2/attachments/effects-corequisite-remediation-tennessee.pdf.

Reiff, Mary Jo, and Anis Bawarshi. 2011. "Tracing Discursive Resources: How Students Use Prior Genre Knowledge to Negotiate New Writing Contexts in First-Year Composition." *Written Communication* 28.3: 312–327.

Reynolds, Nedra, and Elizabeth Davis. 2013. *Portfolio Teaching: A Guide for Instructors*. Boston: Bedford/St. Martins.

Richardson, Elaine. 2003. *African American Literacies*. New York: Routledge.

Ritter, Kelly. 2009. *Before Shaughnessy: Basic Writing at Yale and Harvard, 1920–1960*. Carbondale: Southern Illinois University Press.

Roozen, Kevin. 2015. "Writing Is a Social and Rhetorical Activity." In *Naming What We Know: Threshold Concepts of Writing Studies*, edited by Linda Adler-Kassner and Elizabeth Wardle, 17–19. Logan: Utah State University Press.

Rose, Mike. 1981. "Sophisticated, Ineffective Books—the Dismantling of Process in Composition Texts." *College Composition and Communication* 32: 65–74.

Rosner, Mary, Beth Boehm, and Debra Journet. 1999. *History, Reflection, and Narrative: The Professionalization of Composition, 1963–1983*. Westport, CT: Greenwood.

Royster, Jackie Jones. 1996. "When the First Voice You Hear Is Not Your Own." *College Composition and Communication* 47.1: 29–40.

Ruecker, Todd, Dawn Shepherd, Heidi Estrem, and Beth Brunk-Chavez. 2017. *Retention, Persistence, and Writing Programs*. Logan: Utah State University Press.

Ruiz, Iris, and Raul Sanchez. 2016. *Decolonizing Rhetoric and Composition Studies: New Latinx Keywords for Theory and Pedagogy*. New York: Palgrave-McMillan.

Runyan, Anne Sisson. 2018. "What Is Intersectionality and Why Is It Important: Building Solidarity in the Fight for Social Justice." *Academe* 104.6. https://www.aaup.org/article/what-intersectionality-and-why-it-important#.

Rutschow, Elizabeth Zachry, and Emily Schneider. 2011. *Unlocking the Gate: What We Know about Improving Developmental Education.* New York: Manpower Demonstration Research Corporation.

Saxon, D. Patrick, Nara M. Martirosyan, and Nicholas T. Vick. 2016a. "Best Practices and Challenges in Integrated Reading and Writing: A Survey of Field Professionals, Part 1." *Journal of Developmental Education* 39.2: 32–34.

Saxon, D. Patrick, Nara M. Martirosyan, and Nicholas T. Vick. 2016b. "Best Practices and Challenges in Integrated Reading and Writing: A Survey of Field Professionals, Part 2." *Journal of Developmental Education* 39.2: 34–35.

Sealey-Ruiz, Yolanda. 2021. *Racial Literacy: A Policy Research Brief.* Urbana, IL: National Council of Teachers of English. https://ncte.org/wp-content/uploads/2021/04/SquireOfficePolicyBrief_RacialLiteracy_April2021.pdf.

Seas, Kristen, Jennifer Heinert, Cassandra Phillips, and Holly Hassel. 2016. "'Flexible' Learning, Disciplinarity, and First-Year Writing: Critically Engaging Competency-Based Education." *WPA: The Journal of the Council of Writing Program Administrators* 40.1: 10–32.

Shanahan, Timothy, and Cynthia Shanahan. 2012. "What Is Disciplinary Literacy and Why Does It Matter?" *Topics in Language Disorders* 32.1: 7–18.

Shapiro, Shawna. 2022. *Cultivating Critical Language Awareness in the Writing Classroom.* New York: Routledge.

Skinnell, Ryan. 2016. *Conceding Composition: A Crooked History of Composition's Institutional Fortunes.* Logan: Utah State University Press.

Slinkard, Jennifer, and Jeroen Gevers. 2020. "Confronting Internalized Language Ideologies in the Writing Classroom: Three Pedagogical Examples." *Composition Forum* 44. http://compositionforum.com/issue/44guage-ideologies.php.

Smilges, J. Logan. 2021. "Neuroqueer Literacies; or, against Able-Reading." *College Composition and Communication* 73.1: 103–125. https://library.ncte.org/journals/ccc/issues/v73-1/31589.

Smith, Kevin, Kristi Girdharry, and Chris W. Gallagher. 2021. "Writing Transfer, Integration, and the Need for the Long View." *College Composition and Communication* 73.1: 4–26.

Smitherman, Geneva. 1986. *Talkin and Testifyin: The Language of Black America.* Detroit: Wayne State University Press.

Sommers, Nancy. 1980. "Revision Strategies of Student Writers and Experienced Adult Writers." *College Composition and Communication* 31.4: 378–388.

Sommers, Nancy, and Laura Saltz. 2004. "The Novice as Expert: Writing the Freshman Year." *College Composition and Communication* 56.1: 124–149.

Staats, Cheryl, Kelly Capatosto, Lena Tenney, and Sarah Mamo. 2017. *State of the Science: Implicit Bias Review 2017 Edition.* Columbus, OH: Kirwan Institute.

Stallings, Lynne, and Dawn M. Formo. 2014. "'Where's the Writer?' Examining the Writer's Role as Solicitor of Feedback in Composition Textbooks." *Teaching English in the Two-Year College* 41.3: 259–277.

Stanford Study of Writing. n.d. Stanford University. https://ssw.stanford.edu/about.

Steele, Claude M. 1997. "A Threat in the Air: How Stereotypes Shape Intellectual Identity and Performance." *American Psychologist* 52.6: 613–629.

Steele, Claude M. 2010. *Whistling Vivaldi: How Stereotypes Affect Us and What We Can Do.* New York: Norton.

Sternglass, Marilyn. 1997. *Time to Know Them: A Longitudinal Study of Writing and Learning at the College Level.* Mahwah, NJ: Lawrence Erlbaum.

Sue, Derald Wing, and Lisa Beth Spanierman. 2020. *Microaggressions in Everyday Life,* 2nd ed. Hoboken, NJ: Wiley.

Suh, Emily, Joanne Baird Giordano, Brett Griffiths, Holly Hassel, and Jeffrey Klausman. 2021. "The Profession of Teaching English in the Two-Year College: Findings from the 2019 TYCA Workload Survey." *Teaching English in the Two-Year College* 38.2: 332–349.

Suh, Emily K., Sam Owens, Ekateryna O'Meara, and Leanna Hall. 2021. "Clarifying Terms and Reestablishing Ourselves within Justice: A Response to Critiques of Developmental Education as Anti-Equity." NOSS Equity, Access, and Inclusion Network White Paper. National Organization for Student Success. https://thenoss.org/resources/Documents/Clarifying%20Terms%20Final%20Revision%20July%202021.pdf.

Suh, Emily, Janine Williams, and Sam Owens. 2021. "Raciolinguistic Justice in College Literacy and Learning: A Call for Reflexive Practice." College Reading and Learning Association White Paper. https://www.crla.net/images/whitepaper/CRLA_2021_WhitePaper_Raciolinguistic_Justice_FA.pdf.

Sullivan, Patrick. 2015. "The Two-Year College Teacher-Scholar-Activist." *Teaching English in the Two-Year College* 42.4: 327–350. https://library.ncte.org/journals/tetyc/issues/v42-4/27228.

Sullivan, Patrick. 2019. "The World Confronts Us with Uncertainty: Deep Reading as Threshold Concept." In *(Re)Considering What We Know: Learning Thresholds in Writing, Composition, Rhetoric, and Literacy*, edited by Linda Adler-Kassner and Elizabeth Wardle, 113–134. Logan: Utah State University Press.

Sullivan, Patrick. 2021. "Composition in the Age of Neoliberalism: An Interview with Holly Hassel and Joanne Baird Giordano." *College Composition and Communication* 73.1: 126–155.

Sullivan, Patrick, Howard Tinberg, and Sheridan Blau, editors. 2017. *Deep Reading: Teaching Reading in the Writing Classroom*. Urbana, IL: National Council of Teachers of English.

Suskie, Linda. 2018. *Assessing Student Learning: A Common Sense Guide*. San Francisco: Jossey-Bass.

Tan, Amy. 2006. "Mother Tongue." *Read* 56.4: 20–23.

Tayles, Melissa. 2021. "Trauma-Informed Writing Pedagogy: Ways to Support Student Writers Affected by Trauma and Traumatic Stress." *Teaching English in the Two-Year College* 48.3: 296–313.

Tinberg, Howard. 2015a. "Metacognition Is Not Cognition." In *Naming What We Know: Threshold Concepts of Writing Studies*, edited by Linda Adler-Kassner and Elizabeth Wardle, 75–76. Logan: Utah State University Press.

Tinberg, Howard. 2015b. "Reconsidering Transfer Knowledge at the Community College: Challenges and Opportunities." *Teaching English in the Two-Year College* 42.1: 7–31.

Tinberg, Howard, and Jean-Paul Nadeau. 2010. *The Community College Writer: Exceeding Expectations*. Carbondale: National Council of Teachers of English/Conference on College Composition and Communication and Southern Illinois University Press.

Tinoco, Lizbett, Emily Suh, Joanne Baird Giordano, and Holly Hassel. 2022. "The COVID-19 Pandemic and Workload: Results from a National Survey." Two-Year College English Association. https://ncte.org/wp-content/uploads/2022/03/COVID-19-Pandemic-Workload-Results-from-a-National-TYCA-Survey.pdf.

Tobin, Thomas, and Kristen Behling. 2018. *Reach Everyone, Teach Everyone: Universal Design for Learning in Higher Education*. Morgantown: West Virginia University Press.

Toth, Christie, Jessica Nastal, Holly Hassel, and Joanne Giordano. 2019. "Introduction: Writing Assessment, Placement, and the Two-Year College." *Journal of Writing Assessment* 12.1. https://escholarship.org/uc/item/8393560s.

Tsao, Ting Man. 2005. "Open Admissions, Controversies, and CUNY: Digging into Social History through a First-Year Composition Course." *History Teacher* 38.24: 469–482. https://www.jstor.org/stable/30036716.

Two-Year College English Association Research Committee. 2015. "TYCA White Paper on Developmental Education Reforms." *Teaching English in the Two-Year College* 42.3: 227–243.

Two-Year College English Association Workload Committee. 2019. "2019 Workload Survey." Unpublished data. https://sites.google.com/view/tycaworkloadcommittee/survey-info-and-link?authuser=0&pli=1.
US Department of Justice. 2022. "Guide to Disability Rights Laws." ADA.gov.
US Surgeon General. 2021. "Protecting Youth Mental Health." December 7. https://www.hhs.gov/sites/default/files/surgeon-general-youth-mental-health-advisory.pdf.
Voss, Ralph. 1983. "Composing Processes: Assessments of Recent Research, New Research, Applications in the Classroom." *College Composition and Communication* 34.3: 278–283.
Walker, Guy. 2013. "A Cognitive Approach to Threshold Concepts." *Higher Education* 65.2: 247–263.
Wardle, Elizabeth. 2007. "Understanding 'Transfer' from FYC: Preliminary Results of a Longitudinal Study." *WPA: Writing Program Administration* 31.2: 65–86.
Wardle, Elizabeth. 2009. "'Mutt Genres' and the Goal of FYC: Can We Help Students Write the Genres of the University." *College Composition and Communication* 60.4: 765–789.
Wardle, Elizabeth, and Doug Downs. 2020. *Writing about Writing*, 4th ed. New York: Macmillan.
Weimer, Maryellen. 2013. *Learner-Centered Teaching: Five Key Changes to Practice*. San Francisco: Jossey-Bass.
Whinnery, Erin, and Sarah Pompelia. 2019. *Common Elements of Developmental Education Policies*. Education Commission of the States. https://www.ecs.org/common-elements-of-developmental-education-policies/.
Wiggins, Grant, and Jay McTighe. 1998. *Understanding by Design*. Alexandria, VA: Association for Supervision and Curriculum Development.
Williams, Joseph. 1981. "The Phenomenology of Error." *College Composition and Communication* 32.2: 152–168.
Wilner, Arlene Fish. 2020. *Rethinking Reading in College: An Across the Curriculum Approach*. Urbana, IL: National Council of Teachers of English.
Winkelmes, Mary-Ann, Allison Boye, and Suzanne Tapp, eds. 2019. *Transparent Design in Higher Education Teaching and Leadership*. Sterling, VA: Stylus.
Witham, Keith, Lindsey E. Malcom-Piqueux, Alicia C. Dowd, and Estela Mara Bensimon. 2015. *America's Unmet Promise: The Imperative for Equity in Higher Education*. Washington, DC: Association of American Colleges and Universities.
Yancey, Kathleen Blake. 1998. *Reflection in the Writing Classroom*. Logan: Utah State University Press.
Yancey, Kathleen Blake. 2019. *ePortfolio as Curriculum: Models and Practices for Developing Students' ePortfolio Literacy*. Sterling, VA: Stylus.
Yancey, Kathleen Blake, Matthew Davis, Liane Robertson, Kara Taczak, and Erin Workman. 2018. "Writing across College: Key Terms and Multiple Contexts as Factors Promoting Students' Transfer of Writing Knowledge and Practice." *WAC Journal* 29: 44–66.
Yancey, Kathleen Blake, Matthew Davis, Liane Robertson, Kara Taczak, and Erin Workman. 2019. "The Teaching for Transfer Curriculum: The Role of Concurrent Transfer and Inside-and-Outside School Contexts in Supporting Students' Writing Development." *College Composition and Communication* 71.2: 268–295.
Yancey, Kathleen Blake, Liane Robertson, and Kara Taczak. 2014. *Writing across Contexts: Transfer, Composition, and Sites of Writing*. Logan: Utah State University Press.
Young, Vershawn Ashanti. 2009. "Nah, We Straight: An Argument against Code-Switching." *JAC: Journal of Advanced Composition* 29.1: 49–76.
Young, Vershawn Ashanti, and Aja Y. Martinez, eds. 2011. *Code-Meshing as World English: Pedagogy, Policy, Performance*. Urbana, IL: National Council of Teachers of English.

INDEX

Locators with an *f* indicate a figure. Locators with a *t* indicate a table.

accessibility in teaching practices, 39–40
accommodations for students, 11–12
Adler-Kassner, Linda, 75, 76, 223
Ambrose, Susan A., 98
American Council on Education, 27
Andrus, Sonja, 72, 73
Angelo, Thomas A., 52*n*2
Anson, Chris, 85
antiracist pedagogy, 61
"Anyone Can Teach Writing" (Kahn), 19
Armstrong, Sonya L., 200
Aronson, Joshua, 60
assessment: course goals and, 213–14; deficit model and, 35–36; effective teaching and, 37; equity-minded course design and, 41, 42; focusing on purpose of, 98; formative, 40; grading and, 53, 213; instructor perspectives on, 101, 136; language choice and diversity in, 202; "Literacy Assessment" statement and, 52; monitoring literacy development through, 50–52; process-based, 52; rhetorical learning and, 130–32; short process activities and, 159–61; student learning and, 47, 48–49, 52–53, 68; student literacy experiences and, 118; summative, 40; writing process and, 142–43. *See also* feedback
asset approach to student learning, 36–37
assignments: annotated bibliography, 126; for connecting reading and writing, 179–83; critical reading, 128; independent research, 182–83; low-stakes activities and, 120, 128–29, 130*t*; principles for rhetorical analysis, 122–25; research activities for connecting reading and writing, 172–73; rhetorical analysis, 122–25; rhetorical awareness and adaptability through, 119–27; shared course texts, 180–81; source analysis, 126; student reflection, 183, 184*t*; teaching writing process through, 149, 150–51*t*; text analysis, 127, 181; text comparison, 127; website analysis, 126–27; writing about process work, 159*f*; writing development, 97*t*; writing process activities, 159–61, 162*t*. *See also* course design
Association of College and Research Libraries (ACRL), 173
"Audience Addressed/Audience Invoked: The Role of Audience in Composition Theory and Pedagogy" (Ede and Lunsford), 110
audiences. *See* "writers write for different purposes and audiences" (threshold concept)

backward design: assessment of student learning and, 48–53, 68; assignments and projects in, 49–50, 51*t*; evidence in, 48; identifying desired results in, 45–46; student learning goals and, 45–48, 53–55; transfer and understanding in, 45
Bad Ideas about Writing (Kahn), 19
Baker-Bell, April, 110, 203
Barkley, Elizabeth, 40
Bawarshi, Anis, 110–11, 112, 223
Bazerman, Charles, 111, 112, 147
Bean, Thomas, 173
Beaufort, Anne, 71–72, 111, 223
Bensimon, Estela Mara, 25, 30
best practices in teaching, 38
biases, 59–60. *See also* linguistic bias
Bias-Free Language, 207
big picture learning about writing, 93
Blaauw-Hara, Mark, 72
Blythe, Stuart, 72
bottlenecks, 70
Brandt, Deborah, 170
Brereton, John, 193
Brooke, Collin, 143
Brookfield, Stephen, 38–39

Canagarajah, Suresh, 194
Carlo, Rosanne, 223
Carr, Allison, 90, 143
Castro, Erin L., 30–31
Center for Urban Education, 27
Charney, Davida, 145

Chen, Daniel, 61
College Credit for Writing in High School (Hansen and Farris), 223
College Reading and Learning Association, 169, 197
College Writing and Beyond: A New Framework for University Writing Instruction (Beaufort), 71
Common Core State Standards, 64
Community College Research Center, 13*n*2
community colleges, 13*n*2, 14–15, 227. *See also* open-access teaching contexts; two-year colleges
Conference on College Composition and Communication (CCCC), 38, 169. *See also individual statements by name*
conferences with students. *See* course design
context and rhetorical knowledge, 114–16
contingent faculty, 28–29. *See also* instructors
co-requisite support courses, 17, 26, 171, 189, 218
correctness in writing. *See* error and correctness in writing
course design: adapting to different reading purposes and, 177–78*t*; analyzing a text project for, 181–82; approach to assignments in, 48–49; autonomy of instructor and, 44; components for learning about writing in, 95–96*t*; connecting reading and writing in, 176–87; course policies and, 96*t*; critical reading strategies for, 128–29; disciplinary principles for, 55–58; effective instruction and, 67–69; for equitable and inclusive education, 41–43; equity-mindedness and, 41–43, 62; feedback and, 100*t*, 132–34, 154*t*; grading *versus* learning assessments in, 213; group discussion activities for, 129*t*, 130*t*; guided learning for, 93–94; independent research and, 182–83; individualized learning about writing for, 94; instructor perspectives on, 91*t*, 136–38; language choices in, 207–12; learning about literacy for, 176, 178; learning outcomes and, 46; linguistic diversity in, 209–11, 214; low-stakes activities for reflecting on literacy in, 183–85, 186*t*; process activities for, 150–51*t*; process of, 50–51*t*; program constraints and, 138–40; purposeful, 41; resisting linguistic bias and discrimination for, 208–9; revision activities for, 95*t*; rhetorical analysis and, 122–27; rhetorical approach to grammar and style for, 208; rhetorical awareness and adaptability in, 119–22, 127–30; rhetorical choices and, 129*t*, 130*t*, 131*t*, 132; rhetorical features and, 129*t*; rhetorical knowledge and, 129*t*, 130–31, 130*t*, 131*t*; rhetorical strategies in, 131–32; scaffolding and sequencing assignments in, 54–55; skills for drawing from learning as readers in, 178–79; strategies for, 43–55; student-centered learning in, 93*t*; student conferences and, 153–54; student goals and assessing learning outcomes in, 211–14; student reading experience and, 185, 187; technology and changing literacies in, 118–19; threshold concepts for, 77*t*, 106–7, 214–15; workshop activities and, 153*t*; writing assignment design process, 50–51*t*; writing contexts and, 129–30; writing development and, 97*t*, 183, 184*t*; writing processes and, 146, 148–52, 152*t*. *See also* backward design; first-year writing; threshold concepts

COVID-19 pandemic: educational preparation and, 16; effect on writing programs of, 8; reform initiatives and, 18; student mental health challenges and, 11

Crenshaw, Kimberlé, 59
critical reflection, 38–39, 42, 53, 56*t*, 61
Cross, K. Patricia, 52*n*2
curriculum: effective course design and, 68; first-year writing, 6; perspectives on constraints in, 138–40. *See also* Writing about Writing

Decoding the Disciplines approach, 70
deficit model of student learning, 35–36; equity-minded course design and, 42–43; feedback and, 99; instructors' backgrounds and, 37
"Definition of Literacy in a Digital Age" (NCTE), 66, 169–70, 191–92
Del Principe, Annie, 171
demographic shifts, 227
development shell, 44
Devitt, Amy, 112
dialogic communities, 147–48
digital literacy, 12, 169–70, 222. *See also* information literacy
direct instruction for writing development, 97*t*
disabilities, students with, 39–40
disciplinarity and rhetorical awareness, 111

disciplinary knowledge: dispositions (habits of mind) and, 65–66; equity-minded course design and, 42; first-year writing and areas of proficiency in, 65; threshold concepts and, 69–70, 74
disciplinary principles, 55–58. *See also* threshold concepts
disciplinary statements, 9, 65–67, 219–20
"discourse community knowledge," 71–72
discrimination and linguistic bias, 206. *See also* linguistic bias
dispositions for student success, 65–66
diversity: in classroom community, 34; of course content, 34; deficit model and, 35–36; *versus* equity and inclusion, 34; rhetorical awareness and context, 110
Douglas, Wallace, 193
Dowd, Alicia C., 25
Downs, Douglas, 73, 111
Doyle, Terry, 39
Driscoll, Dana Lynn, 72, 223
Dryer, Dylan, 85–86
dual credit courses, 105–6, 223–24
Dunkerly-Bean, Judith, 173

Ede, Lisa, 110
education, developmental, 171
educational contexts, 14–15. *See also* open-access teaching contexts
effective teaching, concepts for, 37–40
Elbow, Peter, 144
"Elon Statement on Writing Transfer," 71
Emig, Janet, 144
"enabling conditions," and disciplinary principles, 57
English, Standard, 194, 195, 197, 201, 203–204
equitable and inclusive teaching: concepts for further study in, 58–62; instructor identification of, 29; positionality and, 58–59
equitable education: access to technology and, 12; assessments of student learning in, 52; barriers to, 25; centering, 16; compared to inclusive teaching, 32; course design for, 41–43; culturally-responsive teaching in, 60; description and definition of, 29–31; educational contexts and, 14; educational privilege and, 13; equitable teaching in, 29–31; equity talk/walk and, 30; first-year writing and, 14; inclusive teaching in, 31–34; institutional and pedagogical strategies for, 24–25; institutional responsibilities in, 27, 28; issues confronting, 26–27; material realities of instructors, 13; as ongoing, reflective, and challenging process, 32–33; open-admissions institutions and, 14, 26; pedagogical adaptability and, 10, 13; racial literacy development for, 32–33; reform initiatives and, 18; responsibility of state systems, institutions, and writing programs for, 29; role of instructors in, 30; shared leadership model for, 27; strategies for developing, 29–30; structural disadvantages in, 25–26; students with disabilities and, 11; students with mental health challenges and, 11–12; systemic inequities within institutions and, 27; teaching contexts and, 31; writing studies professionals and, 14
equity-mindedness, 25, 27
error and correctness in writing, 86, 204–6, 213. *See also* assessment

failure, 90, 143
"Failure Can Be an Important Part of Writing Development" (Brooke and Carr), 143
Failure Pedagogies: Learning and Unlearning What It Means to Fail (Carr and Micciche), 90
Farris, Christine R., 223
feedback: assessment practices and, 98–99, 100t, 101; conferences with students and, 153–54; in course design, 95t; instructor workloads and, 165–66; online teaching and strategies for, 155t; peer review and, 132–33; realistic expectation and, 133; on rhetorical awareness and adaptability, 132–43; strategies for in-person teaching and, 154t; structured opportunities for, 132; writing processes and, 146, 149, 151–52, 156–58, 161, 162t
Fink, L. Dee, 39
"First-Year in the Two-Year" (Giordano and Hassel), 104, 105, 166, 188, 217
first-year writing: assessment of, 14; disciplinary principles and, 55–57; disciplinary statements and, 65; dual credit students and, 105; equitable education and, 25; evidence of learning in, 48; evolution of writing studies and, 71; feedback strategies for, 100t; focus of, 76; genres and, 111; guided learning for, 93–94; instructor background and, 63; literacy development and, 96–97; open-admissions context and, 104; rhetorical awareness in, 113; rhetorical knowledge and, 16; as safe space for

250   INDEX

exploration, 102; student backgrounds and, 63–64; student learning goals and outcomes of, 47t; threshold concepts for, 77–78; writing about literacy approach to, 176, 178; writing studies and, 64. *See also* assignments; course design
flexible learning processes, 42, 43
Flower, Linda, 144
"Framework for Information Literacy for Higher Education" (ACRL), 173
Framework for Success in Postsecondary Writing (CWPA et al.), 64–66, 109, 112–13, 128, 147, 172
From Equity Talk to Equity Walk (McNair et al.), 30

gatekeeping devices, 35
Gay, Geneva, 60
gender, 11–12, 206–7
genre, 110–11, 116, 121, 131t
Genre: An Introduction to History, Theory, Research, Pedagogy (Bawarshi and Reiff), 110–11
Giordano, Joanne, 72, 104, 105, 110, 134, 136, 166, 215. *See also* "First-Year in the Two-Year" (Giordano and Hassel)
grading. *See* assessment
grammar, 91t, 202, 204–5, 207–8, 213. *See also* English, Standard; "writers make choices about language" (threshold concept)
Gregory, Kristen, 173
guided learning, 93–94

habits of mind for student success, 65–66
Hansen, Kristine, 223
Hassel, Holly, 72, 104, 105, 110, 134, 136, 166, 215. *See also* "First-Year in the Two-Year" (Giordano and Hassel)
Hayes, John R., 144
Healthy Minds study, 11
Holschuh, Jodi Patrick, 172
Horner, Winifred Bryan, 193–94
Horning, Alice, 173
How Learning Works (Ambrose et al.), 98

Ihara, Rachel, 171
impostor phenomenon, 60–61
"Improving College Success for Students in Corequisite Reading" (Ran et al.), 189
inclusive language, 206–7
inclusive teaching, 31–34, 41–43. *See also* equitable education
inequities in education, 10, 12, 27

information literacy, 173, 180t. *See also* digital literacy
Inoue, Asao, 198
instructors: acceptable evidence for assessment by, 48; active engagement of, 32–33; assessments of student learning and, 49–52; autonomy of, 44; awareness of how writing is learned and, 84–85; background of, 192–93; challenges of students and, 102–3; classroom literacies and, 222–23; concepts of equitable and inclusive teaching for, 58–62; constraints on, 28–29; as contingent faculty, 28–29; contrast of institutional needs for, 26; course components and, 91t; course revisions by, 53; disciplinary backgrounds of, 5–6; disciplinary principles framework for, 57; diverse student needs and, 20; dual credit courses and, 105, 223–24; educational context and, 22, 75; effective teaching and, 37–40, 62, 67–69; encouraging writing beyond the classroom and, 96–97; equitable education and, 10, 16, 29–31; equity-mindedness and, 27, 31, 41–45; error and "failure" and, 86, 90; expectations of, 43, 86–87, 88t; feedback and, 98–99, 151–52; final projects and, 52–53; first-year writing and, 104; graduate students as, 15–16, 28; helping students locate resources, 102; in-class conferences and, 153–54; inclusive teaching and, 31–34; learning outcomes and, 46–47, 47t; material realities for, 10, 13; new contexts and, 85–86; normalizing uncertainty of drafting and revision by, 156–58; ongoing learning for, 224–26; open-access education preparation and, 14; at open-admissions institutions, 26; organized resources for, 20; pedagogical adaptability and, 7–10, 12–13, 16, 22; pedagogical situations and, 9; privileging standardized language norms and, 88–89; process-based assessment activities and, 52; reform initiatives and, 16–19; reinforcing myth of writing as talent by, 89; responding, reading, and teaching with purpose and, 136–38; revisions to courses and, 45; rhetorical adaptability and, 136; rhetorical awareness and, 112–13; rhetorical strategies and, 133–34; role in equitable education, 25; self-assess for assessment approach questions for, 101; strategies for course design for, 43–55; student

backgrounds and, 196–202; students with disabilities and, 11; sustaining careers as, 226–28; systemic inequities facing, 28; teaching writing processes, 145–46; threshold concepts and, 22, 78, 92; unintentional creation of barriers by, 34–35; workloads of, 28, 165–66. *See also* assignments; backward design; course design
intersectionality, 59
Isaacs, Emily, 63*n1*, 65*n2*

Jackson, Austin, 195
"Joint Position," 105

Kahn, Seth, 19
Kareem, Jamila, 110
Keller, Daniel, 167, 170
Kirkland, David E., 195
Kirwan Institute for the Study of Race and Ethnicity, 60
Koshnick, Damian, 75
Kuh, George, 61

Ladson-Billings, Gloria, 60
Laird, Thomas F. Nelson, 61
Land, Ray, 69–70, 83–84
language. *See* "writers make choices about language" (threshold concept)
learner-centered teaching, 39, 42, 47
Learning Assessment Techniques (Barkley and Major), 40
learning environments and modalities, 43
learning management systems, 44
learning outcomes, 46–48, 67–68
learning support and student learning experience, 56*t*
Leary, Christopher, 209
linguistic bias, 203, 206–9
linguistic diversity: biased uses of language and, 206–7; definitions of, 193; misconceptions about language correctness and, 204–6; normalizing, 209; Standard English and, 203–4; United States and, 203
linguistic hegemony, 204
Lippi-Green, Rosina, 198, 204
literacy: academic, 7; access to technology and, 12; adapting to context and, 194–95; "culture of acceleration" and, 170; development of, 25, 144; disciplinary statements to support student choices in, 194; diverse classrooms and, 194; equitable access and, 16; expanding definition of, 192; history of, 193–94; as meaning-making practice, 222–23; multilingual and multicultural, 194; pedagogical adaptability and, 9; "right" kinds of skills for, 170; studies and assessments of, 6; threshold concepts and postsecondary, 21. *See also* digital literacy; information literacy
"Literacy Assessment" statement (NCTE), 48, 52
literacy landscapes, 118–19, 122
literacy program coordinators, 22–23
Lunsford, Andrea, 110, 204–5
Lunsford, Karen, 204–5

Macrorie, Ken, 144
Majewski, John, 75
Major, Claire Howell, 40
Malcom-Piqueux, Lindsey, 30
Maleczyk, Rita, 111
Martinez, Aja Y., 110
Matsuda, Paul Kei, 194, 204
McNair, Tia Brown, 30
McTighe, Jay, 45
"Meeting the Needs of Linguistically Diverse Students at the College Level" (CRLA), 209
mental health challenges for students, 11–12
meta-cognition and writing processes, 147
Meyer, Jan H. F., 69, 83–84
Micciche, Laura R., 90, 207–8
microaggressions, 61
Microaggressions in Everyday Life (Sue and Spanierman), 61
Middendorf, Joan, 69
Miller, Carolyn R., 112
Milu, Esther, 198–99
Mitchler, Sharon, 72, 73
Mueller, Gabriel Garcia de, 74
Murray, Donald M., 144

Naming What We Know: Threshold Concepts of Writing Studies (Adler-Kassner and Wardle), 64, 75–77, 84, 90, 92, 112
National Center on Education and the Economy, 171–72
National College Health Assessment, 11–12
National Council of Teachers of English (NCTE), 32, 38, 84, 168. *See also individual statements by name*

objectives *versus* student learning, 46*n1*
office hours. *See* course design
Ong, Walter, 110
online education, 155*t*, 186*t*, 222
open-access teaching contexts: adapting to, 5–8, 14–17; issues with equity in, 26, 28; workloads and, 227; writing studies

252 INDEX

professionals and, 14. *See also* community colleges; two-year colleges
"Outcomes Statement for First-Year Composition" (WPA), 201

Pace, David, 69
Parrott, Jill, 87–89
Paulson, Eric, 172
pedagogical adaptability: adjusting course material to context and, 22; career sustainability and, 226–28; characteristics of, 9; context and, 8–9; external factors to writing programs and, 17–18; first-year writing and, 14; focus of book and, 19; local teaching context and, 26–27; material conditions and, 10; ongoing learning and, 224–26; open-access teaching contexts and, 14–16; preparation of graduate students and, 15–16; questions for, 22; synthesizing and contextualizing foundational texts for, 66; technologies, modalities, and, 224–25
pedagogy: antiracist, 61, 198–99; constraints on, 138–40; development of, 68; diverse linguistic backgrounds and, 191; effective course design and, 68; evidence-based, 38; new areas of research in, 222; reform initiatives and, 17; writing studies and, 20n4. *See also* course design; curriculum
peer review, 132–33, 149, 151. *See also* dialogic communities
Perkins, D. N., 72
Perl, Sondra, 109, 144
Perryman-Clark, Staci, 195
positionality, 58–59
"Position Statement on the Role of Reading in College Writing Classrooms" (CCCC), 168, 169, 189
"Position Statement on Writing Instruction in School" (NCTE), 35
"Principles for the Postsecondary Teaching of Writing" (CCCC), 57, 113, 119, 146
privilege: educational, 13, 16, 25–26, 87; social, 59
"Professional Knowledge for the Teaching of Writing" (NCTE), 83, 85, 96, 98, 145, 167

race and language, 198–99. *See also* linguistic bias
Racial Literacy: A Policy Brief (NCTE), 32
racial literacy development, stage of, 32–33
reading: activities for reflecting on experience of, 185, 187; adapting to different purposes of, 177–78*t*; analyzing sources and, 175–76; assigning *versus* teaching, 167; assumptions about student literacy skills and, 169–70, 171; beyond the classroom, 170–71; CCCC Position Statement principles on, 189; college-level, 173–75, 177*t*; "culture of acceleration" and, 170; deep, 167–68; difficulty of texts and, 172; digital literacy and, 169–70; first-year writing course as foundational for, 172; importance of teaching, 168; information literacy and, 173; instructor text selections for, 181; prevalence of assignments of complex, 171–72; research on connection between writing and, 168–71. *See also* assignments
"reading and writing are interconnected activities" (threshold concept): college-level reading and, 174–75, 177*t*; college-level reading skills and, 173–74; curricular questions and, 188; drawing from learning as readers and, 179–83; importance of teaching, 168, 171–72, 176–87; information literacy and, 173; language choices and, 215; learning about literacy and, 176, 178; low-stakes activities for reflecting on literacy and, 183–85, 186*t*; questions for reflection on, 189–90; reading-aware curriculum and, 189; research activities and, 172–73; research on, 168–71; student perspectives on, 187–88; textual analysis and, 175–76; transfer of skills and, 171–72; writing about literacy approach and, 176, 178; writing courses and, 172, 187
(Re)Considering What We Know: Learning Thresholds in Writing, Composition, Rhetoric, and Literacy (Adler-Kassner and Wardle), 77, 84, 92, 167–68
reform initiatives, educational, 16–19, 170–71
Reiff, Mary Jo, 110–11, 112, 223
revision. *See* "writing processes are individualized" (threshold concept)
rhetorical analysis assignments, principles for, 122–25
rhetorical awareness and adaptability, 16; activities for teaching, 129*t*, 130*t*, 131*t*; assessment and, 118, 130–32; assignments for teaching, 128–29, 130*t*; course design and, 42, 119–22; definition of, 109; developing, 114–16, 122–27; disciplinary studies on, 109–12; diverse contexts and, 110; experienced *versus* novice writers and, 109–10; feedback

on, 132–34; meta-cognitive awareness and, 130; principles of, 113; questions for reflection on, 140–41; student perspectives on, 134–35; for students, 108; teaching, 127–30
rhetorical flexibility, 134
rhetorical grammar, 207–8
rhetorical knowledge, 109, 113–16
Richardson, Elaine, 194
Robertson, Liane, 72, 223
Roozen, Kevin, 112
Royster, Jackie Jones, 194
Ruiz, Iris, 74

Salomon, Gavriel, 72
Saltz, Laura, 109, 145
scaffolding. *See* course design
Scholarship of Teaching and Learning (SOTL), 69
Sealey-Ruiz, Yolanda, 32
sequencing. *See* course design
"significant learning experiences," 39
small picture learning about writing, 93–94
Smilges, J. Logan, 222–23
Smitherman, Geneva, 194
Sommers, Nancy, 109, 144, 145
"sound writing instruction" and disciplinary principles, 57
Spanierman, Lisa Beth, 61
Standard English, 194, 195, 197, 201, 203–4
standard language ideology, 204
Stanford Study of Writing, 145
"Statement on Second Language Writing and Multilingual Writers" (CCCC), 194, 199
Steele, Claude M., 60
stereotype threat, 60–61
student learning: asset approach to, 36–37; designing assessments of, 48–54; diverse needs and, 39; goals for, 45–48, 56*t*; at open-admissions and two-year college, 6; reflecting on experiences and assumptions about, 88*t*; scaffolding and sequencing for, 54–55; types of learning support for, 56*t*
students: accessing resources for, 102; backgrounds and circumstances of community college, 14–15; contexts for learning English by, 197; deficit model and, 35–36; disabilities and, 11; diverse learning needs of, 196–97; educational privilege and, 13; expectations about writing processes by, 143; "failure" and, 90; hearing that writing can be taught and learned, 92; inequities experience by, 87; influence of cultural and linguistic backgrounds of, 199–200; learning about self as writer for, 92–93; linguistic bias and identity of, 198–99; linguistic diversity of, 196–97; material challenges faced by, 10; mental health challenges and, 11–12; misconceptions of correctness by, 204–6; perception of prior literacy experiences of, 92; reflecting on perspectives of writing by, 103; reform initiatives and, 17; rhetorical awareness and adaptability for, 109–10, 113–14; transition to college reading and writing of, 6; types of guided learning for, 93–94; writing ability anxieties of, 86–87
"Students' Right to Their Own Language" statement (NCTE), 66, 201
students with disabilities, 11
Sue, Derald Wing, 61
Sullivan, Patrick, 167–68
summative assessments, 40

Taczak, Kara, 72, 223
teacher-centered education, 39
teacher-scholar, concept of, 61–62
"teacher-scholar-activism," 228
"Teaching Composition: A Position Statement" (NCTE), 66
teaching contexts and disciplinary principles, 57–58
Teaching for Transfer, 71–73, 145. *See also* transfer, concept of
thinking like a writer, 79, 84
"Thinking Like a Writer: Threshold Concepts and First-Year Writers in Open-Admissions Classrooms" (Phillips et al.), 77
"This Ain't Another Statement! this is a DEMAND for Black Linguistic Justice" (CCCC), 194, 219–20
threshold concepts: as aid to instructors, 21; applicability of, 20–21, 74; audience and, 110; definition and role of, 68–70; "discourse community knowledge" and, 71–72; first-year writing and, 64–65, 77–78; goals of, 78; identification of, 70; intersections of, 214–15; NTCE's "Guiding Principles" and, 66–67; practical questions and, 70–71; program design and, 23; rhetorical awareness and adaptability and, 112; students understanding of, 70; Writing about Writing and, 73; writing studies and, 73, 75–76. *See also* "reading and writing are interconnected activities"

254 INDEX

(threshold concept); "writers make choices about language" (threshold concept); "writers write for different purposes and audiences" (threshold concept); "writing can be taught and learned" (threshold concept)
Tinberg, Howard, 72, 73, 147
transfer, concept of: future research on, 223; literacy educators and, 7–8; student preparation and, 6–7; theory and, 6n1; understanding and, 45. *See also* Teaching for Transfer
Two-Year College English Association Workload Committee survey, 165
two-year colleges: student populations at, 15; student preparation at, 7; students of color and, 74; workloads at, 28. *See also* community colleges; "First-Year in the Two-Year" (Giordano and Hassel); open-access teaching contexts
TYCA national survey, 136

"Understanding and Teaching Writing: Guiding Principles" (NCTE), 66, 199–200, 201
Understanding by Design (Wiggins and McTighe), 45
Universal Design for Learning, 39

"Value of Troublesome Knowledge: Transfer and Threshold Concepts in Writing and History, the" (Adler-Kassner et al.), 75

Wardle, Elizabeth, 72, 73, 111
Weimer, Maryellen, 39
Wells, Jennifer, 72, 223
What Is College Reading? (Horning), 173
Wiggins, Grant, 45
Wiley, Terrence, 204
Williamson, S. J., 137–38
Witham, Keith, 25
Workload Issues Committee, 188, 227
workloads: career sustainability and, 227; instructor descriptions of, 165–66; program perspectives on, 166
WPA Outcomes Statement for First-Year Composition (CWPA), 65, 66–67, 74
"Writers' Audience Is Always a Fiction, the" (Ong), 110
"writers make choices about language" (threshold concept): aligning assessment and instruction about, 202; context and, 192–93; disciplinary perspectives on, 219–20; diverse learning needs and, 196–97; instructors and, 195–96, 200, 217–18; linguistic bias and, 198–99, 208–9; linguistic diversity and, 193, 209–11, 213; programs perspectives on, 218–19; questions for reflection on, 220; race and identity in, 198–99; research on, 193–95; resisting misconceptions about, 200–201; respecting others and, 199–200; rhetorical approach to teaching and, 207–8; student learning diversity and, 196–97; student linguistic backgrounds and, 196; student perspectives on, 216–17; teaching, 191–92, 211–14
"writers write for different purposes and audiences" (threshold concept): course design and, 119–22; first-year writing and, 108–9; language choices and, 214–15; purposes and, 117*t*; questions for reflection on, 140–41; rhetorical awareness and adaptability and, 109–12, 114–16; rhetorical choices and, 115*t*; student backgrounds and, 117–18
Writing about Writing, 71, 73, 176
Writing about Writing (Wardle and Downs), 73
Writing across Contexts: Transfer, Composition, and Sites of Writing (Yancey, Robertson, and Taczak), 72
"Writing Assessment," 98
writing as talent, 87–89, 96
Writing at the State U (Isaacs), 64n1
"writing can be taught and learned" (threshold concept): assessments and, 98; challenges of new contexts and, 85; educational inequality and, 101–2; "failure" and, 90; feedback and, 98–99; implications of, 84; importance for students to understand that, 83–84; instructor perspectives on, 104–5; language choices and, 214; program or disciplinary perspectives on, 105–6; questions for reflection on, 106–7; reinforcing, 156–58; student-centered concepts for learning about writing, 93*t*; student perspectives on, 103; writing as talent *versus*, 87–89
writing for transfer. *See* Teaching for Transfer; transfer, concept of
"Writing Is an Activity and a Subject of Study" (Adler-Kassner and Wardle), 75–76. *See also* threshold concepts
"writing processes are individualized" (threshold concept): assessment and, 158; communicating support by, 156; dialogic communities and, 147–48; disciplinary research on, 144–45; draft-

ing and revision and, 148, 156; error and correctness and, 205; feedback and, 146, 149; incomplete drafts and, 156, 157; individual in-class work and, 157; informal feedback on, 151–52; in-person teaching of, 154*t*; instructor workload limitations and, 165–66; language choices and, 215; learning flexibility in, 146; misconceptions and, 145–46; online teaching of, 155*t*; process challenges and, 157–58; program perspectives on, 165–66; questions for reflection on, 166; reflective writing and, 159*t*; rhetorical situations and, 147; sequenced process activities and, 149; structured activities and, 149, 158; student expectations of, 143; student learning and, 159–61; student reflection on, 146–47; student writing example and, 163–64*f*; teaching, 142–44, 148–52, 150–51*t*; traditional views on, 143–44; writing workshops and, 149, 151, 152*t*

Writing Program Administration Outcomes Statement for First-Year Composition (CWPA), 64

writing programs: administration and race, 74–75; course learning outcomes and, 46; discrimination and inequality in, 34–35; instructor autonomy and, 44–45; missions and placements in, 118; perspectives on constraints and flexibility in, 138–40; sequence preparation in, 47–48; student learning goals or outcomes of, 47*t*

writing studies: achieving equity in, 14; equity-minded course design in, 42; evolution and conceptual work of, 71; first-year writing and, 64; focus of, 10; as independent discipline, 19–20; pedagogical implications of future research in, 221–24; research on connections between reading and writing in, 168–71; research on rhetorical awareness in, 109–12; selective institutions and, 14–15; use of term, 20*n*4. *See also* threshold concepts

writing transfer, 71–72

Yancey, Kathleen Blake, 72, 223
Young, Vershawn Ashanti, 110, 199

ABOUT THE AUTHORS

Joanne Baird Giordano is associate professor of English, Linguistics, and Writing Studies at Salt Lake Community College where she coordinates the integrated reading and writing program. She teaches faculty development courses that support community college instructors in using equitable, inclusive, and culturally responsive teaching practices. Her scholarship focuses on students' transitions to college reading and writing, along with the working conditions and teaching experiences of two-year college literacy educators. She is Chair of the Two-Year College English Association.

Holly Hassel is director of composition and professor in the department of Humanities at Michigan Technological University. She was previously on the faculty at North Dakota State University and the University of Wisconsin-Marathon County, a two-year open-admissions campus. She earned her PhD from the University of Nebraska-Lincoln. She is the author of many books and articles on the topic of writing assessment, writing program administration, and writing pedagogy, as well as feminist pedagogy and shared governance. She has served in national elected and appointed roles in professional organizations including the Conference on College Composition and Communication and the Two-Year College English Association.

Jennifer Heinert is professor of English at University of Wisconsin Milwaukee where she currently serves as a Faculty Development and Assessment Coordinator. Jennifer earned her PhD at Marquette University. Like her coauthors, she was previously faculty at University of Wisconsin Colleges, where she served as a faculty development coordinator and chair of English. Her work with open-admissions students informs and inspires her research, which has focused on pedagogy, literacy, and student learning. Jennifer's work includes publication in journals and edited collections as well as a monograph.

Cassandra Phillips is a professor of English at the University of Wisconsin Milwaukee where she also serves as the Writing Program and Developmental English Coordinator for the College of General Studies. She earned her PhD at the University of Louisville. Her research focuses on writing programs, curriculum development, reading & writing pedagogy, assessment, online teaching, and literacy studies. Her work has appeared in books, edited collections, and journals.

www.ingramcontent.com/pod-product-compliance
Lightning Source LLC
Chambersburg PA
CBHW060554080526
44585CB00013B/563